Money and the Beast

The Entanglements of the Political-Monetary System

Steven Allen

Copyright – Money and the Beast© 2025
by Steven Allen
All Rights Reserved.

Niagara Falls, NY 2025

Contents

Money and the Beast

Dedication

Introduction: The Entanglements of the Political-Monetary System i

Chapter 1: Who Is Pulling the Strings? 1

    Vanguard: How Much Control Does the Company Have? 2
    BlackRock: The Fourth Branch of Government................... 9
    A Revolving Door of Interlocks 16
    Retirement Accounts: Your Money or Theirs? 17
    Corporate Socialists 34
    Conclusion 38

Chapter 2: The Influence of Elite Foundations and NGOs 41

    The Reece Committee 41
    The Bill and Melinda Gates Foundation 52
    Socialism versus the Constitution 57
    A Smoking Gun Witness 60
    Non-Governmental Organizations 62
    Movements Toward One World Government 68
    The Goals of the IPR Towards Globalism 72
    Secret Insurance Agents? 81
    Trilaterals and Other Related NGO's 82
    Is Democracy Effective Today? 88
    Global Public–Private Partnerships 91

Chapter 3: The Power of Central Banks and the Banking System 95

    The Federal Reserve Corporation 95
    The Formation of the Federal Reserve 101
    What Is Publicly Known about the Federal Reserve? 102

The Bank of International Settlements 104
The Digital Currency Monetary Authority 110
Insights into Banking 122
Money from Nothing 124
Comrade Commerce 129

Chapter 4: Technology Control Systems 133

Eugenics, Technocracy, and Transhumanism 135
John Ruskin and Elite Imperialism 139
"The Preservation of Favoured Races in the Struggle for Life"
.... 141
Cold Springs Harbor Laboratory 143
Population Control 148
A Planetary Regime? 154
Information versus Disinformation 158
Pandemic Advice from Bankers? 166
Technocracy at Columbia University 173
Modern Technocrats 176
The NSA and IBM: Working Behind the Scenes 179
Climate Change Technology 185

Chapter 5: What Can We Really Know about Secret Societies? 189

The Bilderberg Group 190
Quotes about Secret Societies from Famous Leaders 191
"Providence Has Favored Our Undertakings" 195
The Shadow Government 200
Cecil Rhodes and the Rise of the Modern Secret Societies
.... 202
The Rothschild Connection to the Secret Society 207
The Plans of Cecil Rhodes 210
The Roundtable Group 211

Communism or Capitalism? 214
The Rosicrucian Order 217

Chapter 6: The Influence of Science 221

The Connections of Francis Bacon 225
The Order of the Magi and Hermetic Tradition 227
Modern Science as Magic 232
The Center of the Universe 233
Multiverse or Parallel Universe? 238
The Science of Money 240
The Human Mind Has Yet to Understand Itself 245
Rocket-Man Science 246
Science Working Together with Religion, Philosophy, and Magic 247
Does Banking Promote Science? 248

Chapter 7: All Roads Lead to…? 253

The Founding of Rome's Power Center 254
The Influence of the Beast upon Western Culture 263
The Greatest Traders of History 267
The Babylonian Beast System 270
Imperial Rome Revisited 272
The Emperor's New Clothes 274
The Incorporation of the Beast 276
England as a Trade and Banking Power 279

Chapter 8: Life and Liberty, or Laziness? 286

Are Life, Liberty, and Happiness Guarantees? 287
The Rights of the People 293
The Founding Documents 297
The Big Lie 302
Know Your Rights 302
Conclusion 304

Who or What Is the Beast? 305
Chapter 9: Ideas for the Future 308
    Predetermined Free Will 308
    What Options Do We Have?..309
    Simple Steps..310
About the Author...315

Dedication

To my wonderful wife, whom I owe everything to. You refined my life to the highest degree possible through your unwavering love and support, for which I am forever grateful. I love you so much.

Steve

Introduction: The Entanglements of the Political-Monetary System

Gabrielle-Suzanne de Villeneuve's *Beauty and the Beast* – a tale that was probably penned with fairy dust that is no longer available – has a happy ending after the Beast undergoes a dramatic change. Can we expect that our own sad story, of *Money and the Beast*, will have a similarly happy ending, with us riding off into the sunset?

Since it has not yet concluded, our story is a work in progress. We will need to take notes by learning from the past, and then using this knowledge to complete our journey.

Let's compare *Beauty and the Beast* with our current condition. In the fairy tale, after she helps the Beast to improve himself, Belle learns a lesson to improve her own overall character. The Beast turns back into a prince, but only after changing himself on the inside.

Let's pretend we are Belle for a moment and we are attempting to change some of our core misconceptions, to avoid judging books by their covers. What are our thoughts about money? This book attempts to improve our understanding about how money is created and controlled.

We would be very fortunate to change the financial and governance systems that constrain us in debt. Are the chains tightening, keeping us in the galleys, rowing in the direction they want us to go? Or do we have any ability to change the non-fiction Beast we will examine in this book?

When we consider the current monetary system, we notice it is not designed to improve the lives of normal people, who end up deeper in fiscal depression. We must learn how to tame the Beast and combat the monetary system. Maybe the Beast is involved in areas in which we would tend to think we are independent.

Can we still rely on middle-men to do the work of change for us? Is there any hope that our governing bodies will straighten out this system if we simply yell louder or vote harder? If we allow the Beast to continue to control these bodies, we will be forever doomed to debt servitude.

Currently, we are witnessing the failure of monetary controls and entire nations not being able solve this issue. Money is becoming more of a problem; record debts are climbing and the Beast is at the helm, driving us into submission. Perhaps there are solutions we have not yet tried, or ways to get out of this mess that have been forgotten.

In order to find solutions to our problems, we need to learn more about how we got here. There are so many theories, so many people claiming to have the answers. Solving the puzzle laid before us feels overwhelming.

William Greider's book *Secrets of the Temple* (1987) offers insights into the nature of the US Federal Reserve, which is neither a federal agency nor a reserve of our assets. (In fact, its name was invented to lend the body legitimacy.) Instead, today the Federal Reserve acts as a private entity, to control inflation and the monetary system.

In a speech to Congress on December 22, 1913, Charles A. Lindbergh Sr. spoke about the "trust" acting as the Federal Reserve:

> This act establishes the most gigantic trust on earth... When the President signs this act the invisible government by the money power, proven to exist by the Money Trust investigation, will be legalized...
>
> The new law will create inflation whenever the trusts want inflation...[1]

---

[1] Charles A. Lindbergh, *The Economic Pinch* (Noontide Press, 1921), pp. 87–89.

We will unpack the formation of the Federal Reserve and other historic events as we embark on an important tour of landmarks and key dates. We will identify those who have lied and who have taken away our rights without us knowing that they were doing so. In many cases, while we might think we have the freedom to choose our own financial path, in reality we can only wiggle around a little in a box that has been designed to limit us. We mistakenly think we can take small steps toward a better life, but a freedom guide has led us down a path that is still inside the box.

In this book, we will look for the exit by answering the following questions.
- Can we identify who is pulling the strings?
- What is the role of non-governmental organizations, and what power do they have?
- How does monetary policy constrain society?
- How does technology help us, and how does it harm us?
- What about secret societies, and how can we find information about them?
- Can new scientific findings help us find what we are looking for?
- Can we revolt against the Beast, and if so, what have past revolutions taught us?
- If not all roads lead to Rome, where are they now leading us?
- What kinds of trade networks existed in the past, and how do they differ from the modern system?
- If a sovereign no longer has the right to rule over us, does that mean we are sovereign?
- What can we learn about the transition of power over the years, and can we spot trends so we can predict what may happen next?
- What actions can we take that differ from what we have tried before?

We will take an integrative approach, looking at a broad spectrum of issues to begin answering these questions. We will not find one smoking gun. We will find faint vapor trails. These trails will lead us to the source of the crimes committed against us. We will need to look into the mirror, far and wide, and everywhere in between.

We won't indict any Jewish or Jesuit conspiracies; there will be no families like the Rockefellers and Rothschilds, nor secret organizations like the Illuminati or Bilderberg Group, holding the gun. Instead, we will observe an intentional pattern of controls and schemes—which are themselves visible—to find the "invisible hand" behind our dilemma. Once we recognize the pattern, we can better see through the veil that has been placed over our minds.

Will the Beast change for the good so that we might have better monetary and governmental systems? Do self-corrections by the markets work? Or, having armed ourselves with the information needed to find the weakness and slay the dragon, are we supposed to change the system?

Money and the Beast is based on the study of various topics surrounding finance, governance, and the corporate world, in addition to areas of philosophy, science and history. This book attempts to explain the complex web of relationships between these intersections that we often think are unrelated.

We need to understand integrated systems and interlocks to guide us. C. Wright Mills provides an excellent summary for us in *The Power Elite* (1956). To support his point, he first quotes from another of his works, *Character and Social Structure* (1953).

> There is a political economy linked, in a thousand ways, with military institutions and decisions. On each side of the world-split running through central Europe and around the Asiatic rimlands, there is an ever increasing interlocking of economic, military, and political structures.[2]
>
> If there is government intervention in the corporate economy, so is there corporate intervention in the governmental process.

---

[2] Hans Gerth and C. Wright Mills, *Character and Social Structure* (Harcourt, Brace, 1953), pp. 457ff.

> In the structural sense, this triangle of power is the source of the interlocking directorate that is most important for the historical structure of the present.[3]

If we can find out where the Beast has a hold over governments, banks and corporations, then we can respond. We have two jobs:

- to investigate the **hidden** trail of the Beast once we know how to see it;
- to interpret our observations of the true **public** workings of the Beast.

The problem with public messages about the Beast is that they may be based upon false premises. Public leaders or spokespersons don't provide the complete story, either by knowingly lying to us or by being duped themselves. The problem with a hidden Beast is that it is difficult to find. We must look for open signs and concealed clues to uncover what is really going on.

A quote from JFK. will start to shine some much-needed light on the web of darkness that covers us today. We should heed this warning as we begin our journey.

> The very word "secrecy" is repugnant in a free and open society; and we are as a people inherently and historically opposed to secret societies, to secret oaths and to secret proceedings ... And there is very grave danger that an announced need for increased security will be seized upon by those anxious to expand its meaning to

---

[3] C. Wright Mills, *The Power Elite* (Oxford University Press, 1956), chapter 1.

the very limits of official censorship and concealment.[4]

Can we trace the activities of secret societies to find out if they are pulling the strings? Perhaps they are not so secret when we look from another perspective and see the obvious.

---

[4] John F. Kennedy, "The President and the Press," Address before the American Newspaper Publishers Association, April 27, 1961. www.jfklibrary.org/archives/other-resources/john-f-kennedy-speeches/american-newspaper-publishers-association-19610427. Archive - https://web.archive.org/web/20250105222621/www.jfklibrary.org/archives/other-resources/john-f-kennedy-speeches/american-newspaper-publishers-association-19610427

Chapter 1: Who Is Pulling the Strings?

Do corporations run the world? Do politicians have any genuine power to control them? Let's trace the root causes of **corporatocracy**.

In his novel *Coningsby* (1844), Benjamin Disraeli writes: "So you see, my dear Coningsby, that the world is governed by very different personages from what is imagined by those who are not behind the scenes." The translation: We need to look behind the scenes to find out what is really going on in the world.

How can we find out who is pulling the strings if we are not backstage?

Disraeli was prime minister of the United Kingdom in 1868 and again in 1874–1880. In a speech at Aylesbury on September 20, 1876, he said:

> In the attempt to conduct the government of this world, there are new elements to be considered which our predecessors had not to deal with ... the secret societies – an element which at the last moment may baffle all our arrangements, which have their agents everywhere, which have reckless agents which countenance assassination, and which, if necessary, could produce a massacre.[1]

Mysterious people like Rasputin or John Dee have on occasions worked behind the scenes to influence emperors, pharaohs, and kings. What about today's practices, in the form of lobbying and other crafts that wield power over the highest levels of

---

[1] Robert Norman William Blake, "Benjamin Disraeli," Britannica. www.britannica.com/biography/Benjamin-Disraeli.

government? It is our job to uncover these mechanisms, even if they occur in the shadows or off to the side.

Sometimes we can find statements that provide information about who is calling the shots. For example, we know who is driving some of the social issues of today, like diversity, equity and inclusion (DEI) and the "greentech" movement. One would assume it is the government. After the following section, we might want to think again.

Vanguard: How Much Control Does the Company Have?

The first company we will investigate is Vanguard. Perhaps it is already in your portfolio; it is one of the largest fund managers in the world, with over $7.5 trillion in assets. Vanguard is the biggest issuer of mutual funds worldwide and the second-biggest issuer of exchange-traded funds (ETFs).[2]

The first question is: Who owns Vanguard? It states that it has an ownership structure whereby the member funds, ultimately the fund-holders, own Vanguard. "**Vanguard isn't owned by shareholders. It's owned by the people who invest in our funds … Vanguard is investor-owned, meaning the fund shareholders own the funds, which in turn own Vanguard.**"[3]

It has set up a nice loophole. However, the next question is: Who controls Vanguard? It will tell you that the member funds are in control through the shareholdings, making it sound like you get a voice by letting your investment desires be heard on an individual level.[4]

---

[2] "World's Top Asset Management Firms," Adv Ratings. www.advratings.com/top-asset-management-firms; "All ETF Issuers: ETF Issuer League Tables," VettaFi. www.etfdb.com/etfs/issuers/.
[3] Vanguard, "Our History: Serving Investors for Nearly Five Decades." https://corporate.vanguard.com/content/corporatesite/us/en/corp/who-we-are/sets-us-apart/our-history.html.
[4] Vanguard, "Vanguard At a Glance: Facts and Figures." https://corporate.vanguard.com/content/corporatesite/us/en/corp/who-we-are/sets-us-apart/facts-and-figures.html.

We know little else about Vanguard, since it is a private company. The shareholders are unknown to the public, while the company claims that "people" own it. Something doesn't seem right.

Vanguard and BlackRock are the biggest fund management firms globally. What's interesting is that Vanguard owns around 9 percent of BlackRock. Why is there a need to own another competitor's shares? Isn't this circular reasoning – and does it accomplish anything? Perhaps it is just a Ponzi scheme. We'll see.[5]

The management of companies like Vanguard is determined by the controlling shareholders, who are mostly institutional investors that invest in each other. They do not represent the voice of ordinary shareholders. They don't disclose much. Do they have our best interests at heart if they are not transparent about if they are not transparent about simple things like basic disclosures?[6]

The management of Vanguard can direct companies that their funds own large chunks of. Their proposals compel companies with agendas of diversity in the workplace or green technology. Why are these managers trying to compel oil companies to be carbon-neutral? This has nothing to do with making money for investors.

---

[5] "BlackRock, Inc.," yahoo! finance. https://finance.yahoo.com/quote/BLK/holders/?p=BLK.
[6] Bloomberg, "Vanguard Keeps Its Own Management Pay under Wraps," Investment News, January 24, 2017. https://www.investmentnews.com/industry-news/vanguard-keeps-its-own-management-pay-under-wraps/70402; Oisin Breen, "Vanguard May be Shorting Much Vaunted 'Owners' of Its Low-Cost Index Funds as It Upshifts to More Wall Street-Style Exec-Comp to Thwart Competitors and Chase High-Net-Worth Investors," RIABiz, May 15, 2022. https://riabiz.com/a/2022/5/15/vanguard-may-be-shorting-much-vaunted-owners-of-its-low-cost-index-funds-as-it-upshifts-to-more-wall-street-style-exec-comp-to-thwart-competitors-and-chase-high-net-worth-investors.

The red flag is that governments are supposed to enforce policies and laws, leaving us wondering why groups like Vanguard are doing the job of a government. Since when did greedy corporations become all nice and philanthropic?[7]

In 2022, Vanguard directed investment bank Goldman Sachs to divest from fossil-fuel funding. This is like a rhino beating up on an 800-pound gorilla, since Goldman manages about $2 trillion in total assets, putting it on the top-ten list worldwide (yet it is not as big as Vanguard or BlackRock). Interestingly, Vanguard is the largest shareholder of Goldman, so we know the incest continues down the line.[8]

> At the annual meeting for Goldman Sachs, the U.S.-based financial services company, the Vanguard funds did not support a shareholder proposal to adopt a policy that would proactively ensure that Goldman Sachs' underwriting and lending did not contribute to new fossil fuel development.[9]

"Vanguard funds" refers to the fact that it was not the "people" who own shares but the management and institutional investors who made this recommendation. We can look at more examples of Vanguard beating up on other major players, like Google, by "encouraging" them to adjust their share structure. We can guess who is the largest shareholder of Google (Alphabet).[10]

---

[7] Vanguard, "Investment Stewardship." https://corporate.vanguard.com/content/corporatesite/us/en/corp/how-we-advocate/investment-stewardship/index.html.
[8] "The Goldman Sachs Group, Inc.," yahoo! finance. https://finance.yahoo.com/quote/GS/holders/?p=GS.
[9] "Vanguard Investment Stewardship Insights", May 2022. https://corporate.vanguard.com/content/dam/corp/advocate/investment-stewardship/pdf/perspectives-and-commentary/Voting-Insights-Goldman-Sachs-06152022.pdf
[10] "Alphabet Inc.," yahoo! finance. https://finance.yahoo.com/quote/GOOG/holders/?p=GOOG.

Recapitalization plan for outstanding stock. Alphabet utilizes a multi-class voting structure, where Class B shares have 10 times the voting rights as Class A shares. As a result, Alphabet's co-founders control over 51% of the voting power while owning less than 12% of the company. While we appreciate the intention of the company's co-founders to promote long-term stability with Alphabet's voting structure, **our** research determined that there was a misalignment of voting and economic interests. The Vanguard funds supported the proposal to recapitalize the company's voting structure.

What we look for from companies on this matter: We encourage companies to adopt governance structures that ensure that boards and management serve in the best interest of the shareholders they represent. We believe that such governance structures can serve as a safety net to safeguard and support foundational rights for shareholders.[11]

Here, we notice the largest shareholder attempting to take more control of Google. Companies like Google are becoming more submissive to large fund managers, but it's not always clear who controls them. It looks like there is an inner circle, in which large fund-management companies own most of the largest companies on earth.

One would think it is the government's responsibility to handle issues like the climate, yet here we notice that Vanguard is all

---

[11] "Vanguard Investment Stewardship Insights", July 2022. https://corporate.vanguard.com/content/dam/corp/advocate/investment-stewardship/pdf/perspectives-and-commentary/voting_insights_alphabet_07272022.pdf

over this topic, with the involvement of non-governmental organizations (NGOs). Again, this has little to do with investing for profit.

> Climate change was a prominent topic of discussion and analysis in the first half of 2021; we analyzed proposals that sought enhanced disclosures of companies' energy transition plans and how those plans aligned with the Paris Agreement goals on climate change. We also saw the emergence of Say on Climate proposals.

> We saw a 70% increase in climate proposals in 2021 compared with 2020. The increase was due, in part, to the emergence of Say on Climate proposals that allow shareholders to cast annual votes on a company's climate plan or report. Proposals also focused on emissions reduction targets, scenario analysis, climate-related lobbying, and increased reporting and disclosure requests.[12]

Now for the scary stuff. A Bloomberg article from 2017 is now becoming true as the two biggest assets managers almost obtained $20 trillion under management at the end of 2024. The article outlined a vision of these fund managers and large institutional shareholders literally taking over the earth.

> Imagine a world in which two asset managers call the shots, in which their wealth exceeds current U.S. GDP and

---

[12] "Vanguard Investment Stewardship Insights", May 2022. https://corporate.vanguard.com/content/dam/corp/advocate/investment-stewardship/pdf/perspectives-and-commentary/Voting-Insights-Santos-06132022.pdf

where almost every hedge fund, government and retiree is a customer.

It's closer than you think. BlackRock Inc. and Vanguard Group—already the world's largest money managers—are less than a decade from managing a total of $20 trillion, according to Bloomberg News calculations. Amassing that sum will likely upend the asset management industry, intensify their ownership of the largest U.S. companies and test the twin pillars of market efficiency and corporate governance.

None other than Vanguard founder Jack Bogle, widely regarded as the father of the index fund, is raising the prospect that too much money is in too few hands, with BlackRock, Vanguard and State Street Corp. together owning significant stakes in the biggest U.S. companies.

"That's about 20 percent owned by this oligopoly of three," Bogle said at a Nov. 28 appearance at the Council on Foreign Relations in New York. "It is too bad that there aren't more people in the index-fund business."[13]

It is too bad that there aren't more people who have a say in their investment portfolio. At least Vanguard has recently reported on the weakness of their investors' voting power and finally admitted the vast voting control that their fund managers have.

---

[13] Rachel Evans, Sabrina Willmer, Nick Baker, and Brandon Kochkodin, "BlackRock and Vanguard Are Less Than a Decade Away from Managing $20 Trillion," Bloomberg, December 4, 2017. www.bloomberg.com/news/features/2017-12-04/blackrock-and-vanguard-s-20-trillion-future-is-closer-than-you-think.

A recent Vanguard survey of more than 1,000 investors shows a strong interest among investors in having a voice in the proxy voting process.

Asset managers have begun offering proxy voting choice programs that enable investors to help direct how their equity index funds vote at company shareholder meetings. The survey delved into investors' perspectives on these programs, and its results provided key insights about investors' interest in participating, along with the topics they consider important to weigh in on and their general awareness of proxy voting.

Key findings from the survey include:

- Most investors (83%) believe it is important that asset managers consider investors' preference when casting votes for their funds, with more than half (57%) interested in participating in voting programs.
- Two-thirds (66%) of investors say they would participate in a proxy voting choice program offered through their employer retirement plan.
- Fifty-eight percent of investors would be more likely to invest in a fund if they could influence the fund's proxy voting decisions, while a third (33%) would be willing to change firms if another firm offered them the ability to influence proxy voting.
- Less than half of investors (47%) are aware that fund managers cast proxy votes at shareholder meetings.[14]

---

[14] Vanguard, "Investors report strong interest in proxy voting choice",

BlackRock: The Fourth Branch of Government

Now, let's investigate a different aspect concerning BlackRock. The company structure is very similar to Vanguard's, so we do not need to repeat any similarities. However, its power is already immense in terms of influencing governments and banks.

> It's impossible to think of BlackRock without thinking of them as a fourth branch of government.
>
> William Birdthistle, Professor at the Chicago-Kent College of Law[15]

> They are so intertwined in the market and government that it's a really interesting tangle of conflicts.
>
> Graham Steele, Director of the Corporations and Society Initiative at the Stanford Graduate School of Business[16]

You can check out Charlie Munger's statements for more information about Blackrock in *The Wall Street Journal*.[17] He and

---

April 24, 2025. https://corporate.vanguard.com/content/corporatesite/us/en/corp/articles/investors-report-strong-interest-proxy-voting-choice.html

[15] Annie Massa and Caleb Melby, "In BlackRock We Trust: Larry Fink's Key Role in US Rescue Package," *Financial Review*, May 29, 2020. www.afr.com/policy/economy/in-blackrock-we-trust-larry-fink-s-key-role-in-us-rescue-package-20200522-p54vnn. Quote also published in *The Wealth Advisor*, May 22, 2020.

[16] "BlackRock: Unofficial Fourth Arm Of Government" *The Wealth Advisor*, May 22, 2020. www.thewealthadvisor.com/article/blackrock-unofficial-fourth-arm-government

[17] Orla McCaffrey, "Charlie Munger Expects Index Funds to Change the World—and Not in a Good Way," *The Wall Street Journal*, February 16, 2022. www.wsj.com/articles/charlie-munger-expects-index-funds-to-change-the-worldand-not-in-a-good-way-11645055334.

others reveal the extreme power that Blackrock and index funds have in voting and control.

Renowned investor and Berkshire Hathaway vice president Charlie Munger has joined the chorus warning against the growing power of index funds and the large stakes they control in the majority of companies across the US.

Speaking at the annual meeting of Daily Journal Corp, a publishing company he has chaired for almost five decades, Warren Buffett's business partner cautioned: "We have a new bunch of emperors, and they are the people who vote the shares in the index funds."

In 1980, common ownership of US companies by asset managers stood at 10%. By 2017 this stood at 80%. The 'Big Three' alone comprised 5% of ownership of all US-listed, large companies in 1998, up to around 20% in 2019, with the potential for this to grow to 33% within the next decade, according to Harvard Law School's Lucian Bebchuk and Boston University's Scott Hirst.

As Robin Wigglesworth, author of *Trillions: How a Band of Wall Street Renegades Invented the Index Fund and Changed Finance Forever*, told *ETF Stream*: "The scale nature of the index industry means the big will naturally get bigger and barring any unforeseen regulatory intervention, BlackRock and Vanguard are going to become even more titanic than they are today.

"At some point, they will control the majority of votes of every major company in the US and globally. This will be one of the defining battlegrounds for index funds and ETFs in the coming decade given the trend shaping the market today."[18]

We also notice something about BlackRock's relationship to the banking establishment:

> BlackRock's software platform, Aladdin, appealed to the Fed. The program evaluates risk for clients that include governments, insurers, and rival wealth managers, monitoring more than $US20 trillion in assets.[19]

Not surprisingly, BlackRock is entangled with central banks. It made a deal with the Federal Reserve to license its computer resources and management. BlackRock's supercomputer Aladdin is of great interest to the Fed, as mentioned in section 8.5 of BlackRock's Investment Management Agreement:

> *8.5 Model Validation.* The Manager [of BlackRock] shall cooperate with the Company and the FRBNY [the Federal Reserve Bank of New York] in the manner set forth below to validate the conceptual soundness and implementation of models used by the Manager in its performance of services under this Agreement if such model is used in such a way that an error related to the model's formulation or implementation is likely to have a material adverse effect on the Company ... For purposes of this Section 8.5, as of the Effective Date, the

---

[18] ETF Stream, *Charlie Munger blasts index funds and the 'emperors' behind them*, February 22, 2022.
https://www.etfstream.com/articles/charlie-munger-blasts-index-funds-and-the-emperors-behind-them
[19] Massa and Melby, "In BlackRock We Trust."

> Manager has identified as "Material Models" those models used in the performance of services that are based on BlackRock Solutions Aladdin interest rate modeling and yield curve construction techniques utilized for the generation of cash flows, projection of floating rate coupons, and discounting, in support of the regular reporting and analytics to be delivered pursuant to Section 9.1, as agreed upon with FRBNY.[20]

Appendix A of the original March 25, 2020 Investment Agreement shows the objective; here, we see BlackRock agreeing to help the Fed "smooth market functioning" and transmit "monetary policy" to the economy. Does the Federal Reserve need help to do this? I thought they were experts.

> I. Policy Objective
>
> The policy objective is to purchase agency commercial mortgage-backed securities in the amount needed to support smooth market functioning and effective transmission of monetary policy to broader financial conditions and the economy.[21]

Before we jump to conclusions, let's consider what experts have said about this. The following summary was written for the *Financial Times* by Richard Henderson and Owen Walker.

---

[20] Federal Reserve Bank of New York, email to BlackRock Financial Management, Inc., "Re: Investment Management Agreement," January 6, 2021.
www.newyorkfed.org/medialibrary/media/markets/pmccf/PMCCF-Investment-Management-Agreement.
[21] Federal Reserve Bank of New York, Amendment to Investment Management Agreement.
www.newyorkfed.org/medialibrary/media/markets/special_facilities/ima-blackrock-fma.

As toxic mortgage-backed securities tore through the financial system more than a decade ago, the U.S. government turned to Larry Fink, one of their earliest pioneers, for help. Mr Fink made a fortune packaging mortgages together and selling off slices of the combined pools in the 1980s before founding BlackRock, which today stands as the world's largest asset manager. As the crisis deepened, Mr Fink spoke to Hank Paulson, U.S. Treasury secretary, more often than some chief executives of the big Wall Street banks, in brief, urgent calls. He offered the Treasury and Federal Reserve a powerful tool to gauge risk in the assets at the centre of the havoc. The arrangement would net BlackRock tens of millions of dollars in government contracts, awarded largely without a tender process, put it at the forefront of the fintech revolution and cement Mr Fink's standing at the intersection of politics and finance. At the heart of this exchange was Aladdin, BlackRock's vast technology platform. The system links investors to the markets, ensures portfolios hold the right assets and measures risk in the world's stocks, bonds and derivatives, currencies and private equity.

Aladdin's influence has surged since the financial crisis. Today, it acts as the central nervous system for many of the largest players in the investment management industry — and, as the Financial Times has discovered, for several huge non-financial companies.

Vanguard and State Street Global Advisors, the largest fund managers after BlackRock, are users, as are half the top 10 insurers by assets, as well as Japan's $1.5tn government pension fund, the world's largest. Apple, Microsoft and Google's parent firm, Alphabet — the three biggest U.S. public companies — all rely on the system to steward hundreds of billions of dollars in their corporate treasury investment portfolios.[22]

Are you thinking what I'm thinking? A computer can control world markets. BlackRock's Aladdin system uses artificial intelligence (AI); perhaps fund managers now abide by the advice of a computer programmed to gobble up the earth's resources. The biggest players are using the software, so it must be fantastic or terrible. Perhaps it is both bad for us and good for them.

This is an area of great concern. BlackRock's collaboration with the Fed extends beyond computer programming, making it a suspect of collusion, as suggested in the following extract from banking expert Richard Werner for *The Conversation* and *Fortune* magazine.

> In May 2020, as I conducted my latest monthly analysis of the quantity of credit creation across 40 countries, I was startled to find that something extraordinary had been happening since March that year. The major central banks across the globe were boosting the money supply dramatically through a coordinated programme of QE [quantitative easing].
>
> The reasons for this coordinated policy are not immediately apparent, although there is some evidence that it was sparked by a proposal presented to central bankers by

---

[22] Richard Henderson and Owen Walker, "BlackRock's Black Box: The Technology Hub of Modern Finance," *Financial Times*, February 24, 2024. www.ft.com/content/5ba6f40e-4e4d-11ea-95a0-43d18ec715f5.

the multinational investment company Blackrock at the annual meeting of central bankers and other financial decision-makers in Jackson Hole, Wyoming in August 2019. Soon after this, difficulties in the Fed's repurchase agreement ("repo") market in September 2019, triggered by private banking giant JP Morgan, may have made up their minds.

Apparently agreeing with my critique that pure fiscal policy does not result in economic growth unless it is backed by credit creation, Blackrock had argued at Jackson Hole that the "next downturn" would require central banks to create new money and find "ways to get central bank money directly in the hands of public and private sector spenders" – what they called "going direct", bypassing the retail banks. The Fed knew this would create inflation, as Blackrock later confirmed in a paper which stated that "the Fed is now committing to push inflation above target for some time".

This is precisely what was implemented in March 2020. We know this both from available data and because the Fed, largely without precedent, hired a private-sector firm to help it buy assets – none other than Blackrock.[23]

---

[23] Richard Werner and *The Conversation*, "The Expert Who Pioneered 'Quantitative Easing' Has Seen Enough: Central Banks are Too Powerful and They're to Blame for Inflation," *Fortune*, March 20, 2023. https://fortune.com/2023/03/20/is-federal-reserve-too-powerful-inflation-quantitative-easing-richard-werner/; see also Louise Ashley, "Class and the City of London: My Decade of Research Shows Why Elitism is Endemic and Top Firms Don't Really Care," *The Conversation*, February 23, 2023. https://theconversation.com/class-and-the-city-of-london-my-decade-of-research-shows-why-elitism-is-endemic-and-top-firms-dont-really-care-199474.

A Revolving Door of Interlocks

We need to search for more links between companies, governments and banks, since their collaborations may be world-changing, as with BlackRock and the central bank of the USA. Let's put on our private investigator hat.

Brian Deese was the director of the National Economic Council, and President Biden's senior advisor for economic policy.[24] Deese came from BlackRock, where he was global head of sustainable investing, and played a key role in negotiating the Paris Accords. We are getting warmer, coming closer to finding answers. We should take notice of these powerful connections between government agencies and the private sector.

Another former BlackRock employee who advised economic policy in the White House was Michael Pyle, senior economic adviser to Vice President Kamala Harris,[25] and formerly the global chief investment strategist at BlackRock, where he managed trillions of dollars. Pyle also was also a senior advisor to the undersecretary of the Treasury's Office for International Affairs in the Obama administration.[26]

These connections run deeper. Adewale Adeyemo was the deputy treasury secretary under Secretary Janet Yellen. Not so coincidentally, Adeyemo came from BlackRock, where he was a senior adviser and chief of staff to the CEO after leaving

---

[24] Matthew Johnston, "Brian Deese: Education, Achievements, National Economic Council," Investopedia, March 6, 2024. www.investopedia.com/who-is-brian-deese-5095167.
[25] Annie Massa, "BlackRock Exec Picked as Kamala Harris's Top Economic Advisor," Bloomberg, January 8, 2021. https://www.fa-mag.com/news/blackrock-exec-picked-as-kamala-harris-s-top-economic-advisor-59684.html. Original: www.bloomberg.com/news/articles/2021-01-08/blackrock-s-pyle-picked-as-kamala-harris-s-top-economic-adviser.
[26] Theodore Meyer, "Meet the New Jared Bernstein," Politico, March 22, 2021. www.politico.com/newsletters/transition-playbook/2021/03/22/meet-the-new-jared-bernstein-492200.

the Obama administration. Obama appointed Adeyemo president of the Obama Foundation in 2019.[27]

The connections between BlackRock and the White House under Obama and Biden are clear. However, the Trump administration is also well connected to Blackrock[28] such as with the Panama Canel project[29], so party lines do not matter. There is a revolving door. We do not have a smoking gun yet, but the evidence for a case is piling up.

Retirement Accounts: Your Money or Theirs?

First, let's consider the strong possibility that mega-corporations are somehow intertwined with government and banks to help solve today's social issues or problems like climate change. This concept of collaboration between entities turns out to be a common thread that we need to spend more time unraveling.

Think about your investment account. Are you in control of it? Do you understand how government pension fund managers or investment companies manage what you worked so hard to build up?

Retirement funds are the largest sector of investments in the markets by people living in the USA. Besides foreign investors pumping up our economy, investments from US citizens have the most impact on the markets, with the bulk of investments handled through retirement accounts such as IRAs, 401ks and pensions. Can we guess who are the largest managers of these funds? It is neither the government nor large companies like Apple or Walmart.

---

[27] US Department of the Treasury, "Wally Adeyemo: Deputy Secretary of the Treasury." https://home.treasury.gov/about/general-information/officials/Wally-Adeyemo.
[28] Jai Hamid, "BlackRock's Larry Fink abruptly becomes a part of Trump's inner circle. How'd he get there?" *Cryptopolitan*, April 6 2025. www.cryptopolitan.com/blackrocks-larry-fink-in-trumps-inner-circle/
[29] Silla Brush, Dinesh Nair, "Larry Fink phoned Trump directly to pitch BlackRock's Panama deal," *Fortune*, March 5, 2025. https://fortune.com/2025/03/05/larry-fink-phoned-trump-directly-to-pitch-blackrocks-panama-deal/

Investment funds are primarily managed by some of the largest state pension funds, and institutions like BlackRock and Vanguard. The latter receive management fees for handling the affairs of state pensions and corporate retirement funds. Some states and companies manage their own investment accounts, but they outsource the majority, for which they pay management fees.[30] According to the financial advisory firm Kroll, "the [NY pension] Fund utilizes several well-regarded firms as investment managers to execute specific mandates for which the Fund does not have the appropriate resources in-house."[31]

> When public pension funds do receive complete fee data from asset managers, there is no standard way to verify their accuracy, and neither the asset managers nor the pension funds are under any obligation to make these data available to the public…
>
> In 2015, the New York City Bureau of Asset Management (BAM) released a comprehensive study of the City's pension funds and found that high fees and underperformance cost the City's pension funds USD 2.5 billion over a decade.[32]

---

[30] For more information on management fees, see New York State and Local Retirement System, "Comprehensive Annual Financial Report, For Fiscal Year Ended March 31, 2021," pp. 105–134. www.osc.ny.gov/files/retirement/resources/pdf/comprehensive-annual-financial-report-2021.pdf.

[31] Kroll, "Fiduciary and Conflict of Interest Review of the New York State Common Retirement Fund," February 7, 2022. www.osc.ny.gov/files/common-retirement-fund/resources/pdf/nyscrf-fiduciary-and-conflict-of-interest-review-2022.pdf.

[32] CWC, "Pension Fund Cost Transparency," *Unison*, August 2018. www.workerscapital.org/IMG/pdf/cwc_pension_fund_cost_transparency.pdf

The lack of an obligation to report to the public sounds fishy. There are many examples of mismanaged fees and practices mentioned in the study referenced above like the one from NYC.

Of all retirement fund management, 55 percent or more is now outsourced.[33] Outsourcing has doubled since 2006. Does this mean the Beast is getting bigger?

Clearly, governments such as those of New York and California can indirectly influence the markets through massive retirement funds. By looking at their publications, we realize that these large state shareholders have a proxy voice in the retirement investment accounts that own most US corporations.

Let's take New York State's focus on environmental social governance (ESG) as an example.[34] NYS fund managers vote on ESG issues. This is a large voting block that uses the power of money to affect social reform, instead of significantly influencing corporations directly through laws and regulations. The retirement fund managers vote by proxy or committee regarding the corporate issues that governments do not control. You and I have minimal input since the managers seem to have all the power.

> According to the CRF's [Common Retirement Fund's] 2020 Corporate Governance Stewardship Report, in 2020, the Fund conducted 1,774 engagements with portfolio companies. Current issues being focused on by the CRF as outlined in the 2020 Stewardship Report, among many others, include:

---

[33] Jean-Pierre Aubry and Kevin Wandrei, "Internal vs. External Management for State and Local Pension Plans," *State and Local Pension Plans* 75, November 2020. https://crr.bc.edu/wp-content/uploads/2020/11/SLP75_.pdf.

[34] New York State Common Retirement Fund, *Environmental, Social and Governance Report*, March 2017. www.osc.ny.gov/files/reports/special-topics/pdf/esg-report-mar2017.pdf.

- Climate Change and Sustainable Investing
- Cyber Security and Technology Infrastructure Protections
- Pandemics and other Human Capital Management Issues
- Lobbying and Political Influence of Portfolio Companies
- Diversity, Equality, and Inclusion

In 2018, the Comptroller, on behalf of the Fund, joined over 315 organizations in expressing support for the Task Force on Climate-related Financial Disclosures ("TCFD"), which has developed recommendations for voluntary climate-related financial disclosures. In 2018, for the first time, the Fund implemented TCFD's recommendations to report on its climate change initiatives in the System's ACFR. In March 2018, the Comptroller announced his work with the New York State Governor to appoint and convene the Decarbonization Advisory Panel, a distinguished group of six experts, to develop recommendations for the CRF's climate-related work over the next decade. This group of investment, financial, environmental, energy and legal experts worked for nearly a year to deliver recommendations to the Comptroller that focused on climate-change-related investment opportunities and risk mitigation. In April of 2019, the Panel released a report recommending that the Fund transition its investments to 100% sustainable assets by the year 2030.[35]

---

[35] Office of the New York State Comptroller, "Governor Cuomo and Comptroller DiNapoli Appoint First-Ever Decarbonization Advisory

It seems like a lot of power is granted to a small group of people. Whether a governor selects this panel from altruistic motives or not, there is no involvement of any legislature when it comes to making laws regarding these matters. There is virtually no accountability if the pension fund is outsourced.

Do fund managers or committee members invest based on financial reasoning or social importance? Morgan Stanley provides a summary that gets to the heart of the matter.

> ...despite acknowledging the importance of incorporating diversity into their investment decisions, a majority of asset owners (56%) say that doing so comes at the expense of returns.[36]

Certain fiduciary responsibilities need to be followed, for example, state laws about hiring practices in the workplace. However, investment fund managers regularly exceed their responsibilities by introducing additional social concerns that have nothing to do with making returns on investments.

When you invest, do you care about ESG, how honest index fund management is, or do you want fund managers to simply follow the rules and laws to make a return for your retirement? It may sound nice to align moral interests with investment interests, yet there is a huge disconnect between them right now.

The simple example of a coffee shop company can illustrate the extent of influence. If this company becomes political, it risks disenfranchising some customers, leading them to boycott its

---

Panel," March 6, 2018.
www.osc.ny.gov/press/releases/2018/03/governor-cuomo-and-comptroller-dinapoli-appoint-first-ever-decarbonization-advisory-panel?redirect=legacy.

[36] Morgan Stanley, "Pension Funds Lead the Way in Prioritizing Diversity in Investing," October 20, 2021.
www.morganstanley.com/articles/pension-fund-investment-prioritize-diversity.

stores, while perhaps rallying other customers to be more loyal. The point is that we, the customers, get to choose if we want to buy our coffee here or somewhere else. On the other hand, we often have no option to pull our investments out of retirement accounts in order to boycott funds whose managers promote political agendas we may not like.

The Federal government has a very large retirement fund of about $800 billion. Of course, Blackrock manages it with State Street. The back-door agreements about the management fee amounts and other details we would like more transparency about are not disclosed in audits.[37]

> The five core funds offered in the Thrift Savings Plan loosely cover the basic range of publicly traded debt and equity securities. All five funds are managed by Blackrock Capital Advisers and State Street Global Advisors. They're only available to TSP participants. None of them trade on any public exchange although Blackrock does offer publicly traded equivalents of some TSP funds through iShares, its subsidiary company. [38]

The concept of our loss of control over our investment accounts is not limited to public funds. Private equity is also getting gobbled up by the Beast. In the words of economists William L. Megginson, Diego Lopez, and Asif I. Malik:

> State-owned investors (SOIs), including sovereign wealth funds and public pension

---

[37] KPMG, "Performance Audit of State Street Global Advisors Trust Company's Thrift Savings Plan Investment Management Operations," September 15, 2023. www.dol.gov/sites/dolgov/files/EBSA/about-ebsa/our-activities/resource-center/reports/thrift-savings-plan-audit/state-street-global-advisors-trust-company-tsp-investment-management-operations-2023.pdf

[38] Mark P. Cussen, "Breaking Down the TSP Investment Funds," Investopedia, April 08, 2025. www.investopedia.com/articles/investing/061113/breaking-down-tsp-investment-funds.asp

funds, have $27 trillion in assets under management in 2020, making these funds the third largest group of asset owners globally.[39]

Journalist Christine Idzells summarizes their paper as follows.

> University of Oklahoma finance professor William Megginson, Global SWF managing director Diego Lopez, and OU business school student Asif Malik wrote in a paper last month ... "The largest proportionate changes were observed for private equity, which more than tripled between 2008 and 2020" for public pension and sovereign wealth funds ...
>
> These funds, with $27 trillion of assets under management globally, have become "the largest and most important private equity investors" ...
>
> Almost half of public pension assets globally are controlled by 87 funds in the U.S., the researchers said.[40]

A report on stock ownership addresses the same topic.

> In a white paper, Steven Rosenthal and Lydia Austin of the Tax Policy Center have broken out exactly which kind of investors own the stock market. They found that a majority of corporate stock is owned by

---

[39] William L. Megginson, Diego Lopez, and Asif I. Malik, "The Rise of State-Owned Investors: Sovereign Wealth Funds and Public Pension Funds," *Annual Review of Financial Economics*, 13, 247–270. www.annualreviews.org/content/journals/10.1146/annurev-financial-110420-090352.

[40] Christine Idzells, "The World's Dominant Investors in Private Equity," Institutional Investor, November 6, 2020. www.institutionalinvestor.com/article/2bsx62pj43ssiqp84lhj4/portfolio/the-worlds-dominant-investors-in-private-equity.

different types of retirement plans, the largest being IRAs and defined-benefit plans.

Of the $22.8 trillion in stock outstanding (not including U.S. ownership of foreign stock and stock owned by "pass-through entities" such as exchange-traded funds), retirement accounts owned roughly 37%, the most of any type of holder.[41]

There is entanglement of corporations and government officials in the public and private sectors, and we are caught in the web that has been spun. They need us to feed their system. Our weekly paychecks go into these accounts, over which we have little or no control, leaving us to hope that our funds are being invested wisely so we can retire comfortably.

Most government pension funds and corporate retirement accounts are now at the mercy of market management firms. They have become part of the overall scheme of the Beast, and the markets are at the mercy of continual cash injections by ordinary citizens to sustain the charade. We are feeding the Beast, but is it worth what we get in return? Is there a way to stop the Beast from getting too big?

A retirement account does not function in the same way as a savings account, with simple transactions like deposits and withdrawals by the account holder. Nobody votes on how to use the money in your savings account, and it does not go toward social programs or private agendas. With a retirement account like a pension plan or a 401k, other people are using your funds to influence companies toward social reform, such as

---

[41] Bob Bryan, "Here's who actually owns the stock market," *Yahoo! Finance*. May 25, 2016. https://finance.yahoo.com/news/heres-actually-owns-stock-market-152537996.html. More information about this from the Tax Policy Center:
https://taxpolicycenter.org/taxvox/who-owns-us-stock-foreigners-and-rich-americans

redistributed equity programs that are unequitable in reality. The rich get richer, as they say.

In their 1994 book *The Earth Brokers*, Pratap Chatterjee and Matthias Finger summarize what is more likely occurring before our eyes, even though today's governmental and media spin might have us believe otherwise.

> UNCED [the United Nations Conference on Environment and Development] has promoted business and industry, rehabilitated nation-states as relevant agents, and eroded the Green movement. We argue that UNCED has boosted precisely the type of industrial development that is destructive for the environment, the planet, and its inhabitants. We see how, as a result of UNCED, the rich will get richer, the poor poorer, while more and more of the planet is destroyed in the process.[42]

Let's consider what one of the Big Four auditing and accounting firms says to back this up. KPMG (who audited State Street's management of the TSP fund in 2023 and found zero errors[43]) makes this bold statement:

> By 2030, poor performers have been weeded out and consistent non-compliance will be met with severe consequences including penalties, public naming, a prohibition to operate and even

---

[42] Pratap Chatterjee and Matthias Finger, *The Earth Brokers* (London: Routledge, 1994), p. 3.

[43] KPMG, "Performance Audit of State Street Global Advisors Trust Company's Thrift Savings Plan Investment Management Operations," September 15, 2023. www.dol.gov/sites/dolgov/files/EBSA/about-ebsa/our-activities/resource-center/reports/thrift-savings-plan-audit/state-street-global-advisors-trust-company-tsp-investment-management-operations-2023.pdf

imprisonment. The C-Suite and Directors will now be personally liable for ESG breaches.[44]

How do you feel about a state comptroller forcing a climate change agenda to promote not-very-green electric vehicles, all while using your pension money, without your voice? Money is the inflammatory disease spreading through the Beast network. It needs money to function. The Beast is growing larger every day by consuming money to accomplish its goals.

In one example of a state having caught on to the workings of the Beast, the Missouri State Treasurer's Office identified political—not financial—causes driving decisions by firms like BlackRock.

> At the MOSERS Board of Trustees meeting in June, the board directed staff to require BlackRock to abstain from voting proxies on behalf of the plan, due to concerns with their public statements and record of prioritizing ESG initiatives over shareholder return. BlackRock refused the Board's demand to abstain from voting the plan's proxies.
>
> Treasurer Fitzpatrick said ... "MOSERS has an obligation to manage its assets in a way that prioritizes providing maximum possible returns for retirees and taxpayers. We should not allow asset managers such as BlackRock, who have demonstrated that they will prioritize advancing a woke political agenda above the financial interests of their customers, to continue speaking on behalf of the state of Missouri."

---

[44] KPMG, *Looking Ahead: ESG 2030 Predictions*. https://assets.kpmg.com/content/dam/kpmg/au/pdf/2022/esg-predictions-2030.pdf.

> ... over the past several years, large asset managers such as BlackRock have begun to exercise the immense power they have amassed, even bragging about it publicly, to advance political causes which sacrifice return on investment for their customers.[45]

Several other states are acting similarly to Missouri. Formed in 1929, Consumers' Research is the oldest consumer advocacy group. It issued warnings to the top ten state governors whose pension funds are managed in part by BlackRock, as well as to retail and corporate managers who invest in BlackRock's funds. Consumers' Research focused on BlackRock's ties to the Chinese Communist Party (CCP).

> BlackRock's connections to China are outlined in our Consumer Warning. These ties date back to the early 2000s and create concerning conflicts that consumers should be aware of. These ties start from the top. BlackRock's CEO, Larry Fink, has become a trusted partner with China's communist leadership. So much so that he has been summoned to consult with them multiple times: during economic downturns and even when China was involved in trade negotiations with the United States, choosing China over America.[46]

---

[45] Missouri State Treasurer's Office, "Treasurer Fitzpatrick Announces MOSERS Has Pulled $500 Million in State Pension Funds from BlackRock," October 18, 2022. https://treasurer.mo.gov/newsroom/news-and-events-item?pr=80669a5f-5c6b-491f-a0f0-6abe4c012604.

[46] Consumers' Research, Letter to state governors, December 2, 2021. https://consumersresearch.org/wp-content/uploads/2021/12/CR-Letter-to-Governors-on-BlackRock-Consumer-Warning.pdf.

The following is an extract from the advocacy group's consumer warning.

> In 2008, BlackRock opened an office in Beijing in an attempt to "expand its business into China," saying the office would "help establish local contacts." Since then, BlackRock expanded investments into companies like Baidu, Pinduoduo, Xiaomi, and China National Offshore Oil Corporation (CNOOC) which reportedly have ties to the CCP. BlackRock has poured money into Chinese tech and telecommunication companies like Baidu and Xiaomi that have displayed their CCP allegiance by launching internal Communist Party committees within their companies to gain favor. Pinduoduo has contributed hundreds of millions to Chinese Communist Party initiatives within the country. BlackRock investments in CNOOC have helped aid the CCP's efforts to expand its influence across the globe.
>
> Retail investors with exposure to BlackRock should consider the risks associated with BlackRock's services, especially any holdings of passive investment funds that include Chinese companies.
>
> Employees should consider contacting their human resources department to determine if BlackRock manages their company's 401(k) accounts or pension fund. If so, inquire as to what safeguards the company has in place to protect their funds from CCP related risks.
>
> Individuals with state or municipal pensions should contact state officials to find out if any portion of their pension fund is managed by BlackRock. If so, encourage officials to safeguard your retirement

against the risks posed by BlackRock's investments in Chinese companies.

Chinese firms are not held to the same transparency standards as their western counterparts, so foreign investors are often hard pressed to appreciate the true risk profile of what they're investing in. Further, according to Chinese law those investments are not in the actual firms themselves but in a mechanism called a Variable Interest Entity (VIE). You could lose your shirt when a Chinese company's performance falls and have no legal recourse. And, perhaps riskiest of all, the central government exercises complete control over even ostensibly private firms, meaning foreign investments can rise and fall at the mercy of the CCP.[47]

In an interview with Bloomberg several years ago, Larry Fink of BlackRock stated that "markets like totalitarian governments" because "democracies are messy."[48] This explains a lot about the worldview of the leader of BlackRock regarding the company's strategy.

This cuts to the core issue of investors influencing behavior regarding ESG. At the 2017 DealBook Conference, Fink stated that "behaviors are going to have to change, and this is one thing that we are asking companies. You have to force behaviors, and here at Blackrock we are forcing behaviors."[49]

---

[47] Consumers' Research, "BlackRock: Taking Your Money, Betting on China," consumer warning. https://consumersresearch.org/wp-content/uploads/2021/12/Consumer-Warning-BlackRock.pdf.
[48] "BlackRock CEO Larry Fink: 'Markets Like Totalitarian Governments' (2011)," YouTube, user Eduardo Corrochio, uploaded August 8, 2022. https://www.youtube.com/watch?v=RmY4AvoPI0A
[49] "DealBook 2017: The Economy, Consumers and Redefining the Long Term," YouTube, user New York Times Events, November 9, 2017. www.youtube.com/watch?v=-cCs9Kh2Q08&ab_channel=NewYorkTimesEvents.

In the context of these comments, are we free to pull out of funds if we disagree with their managers' political positions? Some states, like New York, might agree with BlackRock's management practices on ESG, whereas others, like Missouri, do not. It is hard to tell whether a fund advisor from New York would influence BlackRock's management decisions, or if the state would instead agree with management.

Word is catching on more broadly, with the *Financial Times* addressing the pulling of funds from BlackRock.

> State treasurers in Louisiana, South Carolina, Arkansas, and Utah will divest a total of $1 billion from BlackRock by the end of 2022, according to The Financial Times.
>
> 19 Republican attorneys general signed a joint letter to BlackRock claiming the illegal nature of divesting out of the fossil fuel industry.[50]

A group of state attorneys general wrote the following to the BlackRock CEO on August 4, 2022.

> Based on the facts currently available to us, BlackRock appears to use the hard-earned money of our states' citizens to circumvent the best possible return on investment, as well as their vote. BlackRock's past public commitments indicate that it has used citizens' assets to pressure companies to comply with international agreements such as the Paris Agreement that force the phase-out of fossil fuels, increase energy prices, drive inflation, and weaken the national security of the United States. These agreements

---

[50] Patrick Temple-West, "US Republicans Pull $1bn from BlackRock over ESG Investing Concerns," *Financial Times*, October 9, 2022. www.ft.com/content/41de28af-a487-473e-bc17-5e8cb71f4ced.

have never been ratified by the United States Senate. The Senators elected by the citizens of this country determine which international agreements have the force of law, not BlackRock.

BlackRock's public commitments which indicate that BlackRock has already committed to accelerate net zero emissions across all of its assets, regardless of client wishes ...

BlackRock's commitment to the financial return of state pensions should be undivided. Many of our laws state that a fiduciary must "discharge [their] duties solely in the interest of the participants and beneficiaries ... for the exclusive purposes of ... providing benefits to participants and their beneficiaries; and ... defraying reasonable expenses of administering the system."

... state pensions must be invested only to earn a financial return.

BlackRock's coordinated conduct with other financial institutions to impose net-zero also raises antitrust concerns. Group boycotts, restraining trade, or concerted refusals to deal, "clearly run afoul of" Section 1 of the Sherman Act. Section 1 prohibits "[e]very ... combination ..., or conspiracy, in restraint of trade or commerce." Regarding the definition of a "combination," the Supreme Court has held that this language prohibits "concerted action." BlackRock's actions appear to intentionally restrain and harm the competitiveness of the energy markets. Disturbingly, a survey last year from the Federal Reserve Bank of Dallas asked: "Which of the following is the primary reason that publicly traded oil producers are restraining growth despite high oil prices?" Sixty percent of respondents referenced a form of "investor pressure."

Blanket statements regarding investing in particular asset classes without referencing price is not consistent with fiduciary and legal obligations. Nor are blanket commitments to vote for directors based upon protected characteristics, such as gender. Rather, BlackRock appears to be acting for a social purpose that may have a financial benefit if certain improbable assumptions occur.[51]

How should we interpret this evidence that retirement funds are not as straightforward as we might have thought? Are public and private retirement funds part of a scheme by corporations to meet ulterior motives? It looks like it.

Since 1978, Business Roundtable has periodically issued Principles of Corporate Governance. Each version of the document issued since 1997 has endorsed principles of shareholder primacy – that corporations exist principally to serve shareholders. With today's announcement, the new Statement supersedes previous statements and outlines a modern standard for corporate responsibility ...

"This is tremendous news because it is more critical than ever that businesses in the 21st century are focused on generating long-term value for all stakeholders and

---

[51] Mark Brnovich, Arizona Attorney General, et al., Letter to Laurence D. Fink, August 4, 2022. www.texasattorneygeneral.gov/sites/default/files/images/executive-management/BlackRock%20Letter.pdf.

> addressing the challenges we face, which will result in *shared prosperity and sustainability for both business and society*," said Darren Walker, President of the Ford Foundation.[52]

This may sound great at first; everyone wins according to the new Business Roundtable statement. Who gets to define "corporate responsibility"? It is the corporation in this case, not us. In reality, it is a type of corporate control by the few and not benefiting the many. We know this because of the record debts and inflation currently eroding the middle class. Buying power is declining and the wage gap is widening. Wall Street and billionaires' wealth are achieving record growth. Harvard law and economics professor John C. Coates writes the following.

> [T]he "Problem of Twelve": control of most public companies—that is, the wealthiest organizations in the world, with more revenue than most states— will soon be concentrated in the hands of a dozen or fewer people.
>
> Index funds increasingly possess the "median vote" in corporate contests. That gives them an ability, even if contingent, to make crucial decisions across most public companies. Unless law changes, the effect of indexation will be to turn the concept of "passive" investing on its head and produce the greatest concentration of economic control in our lifetimes.
>
> More fundamentally, the rise of indexing presents a sharp, general, political challenge to corporate law. The prospect of twelve people even potentially controlling most of the economy poses a

---

[52] Business Roundtable, "Business Roundtable Redefines the Purpose of a Corporation to Promote 'An Economy That Serves All Americans'," August 19, 2019, (emphasis added).

legitimacy and accountability issue of the first order—one might even call it a small "c" constitutional challenge.[53]

We must examine the stomach of the Beast to determine what it had for breakfast, in order to discover why it is growing this way. The workings of the Beast are not a recent phenomenon. We can learn from its earlier practices.

Corporate Socialists

Economist Antony C. Sutton, one of the most brilliant researchers in this area, was spat out from inside the belly of the Beast. His writing about corporate socialism identified a strange marriage of what we would think are unrelated concepts within a capitalistic economy. We can only summarize a few concepts from his thorough research here. Two pertinent books within our discussion are *Wall Street and F.D.R.* (1975) and *Wall Street and the Bolshevik Revolution* (1974).

Sutton's work at the Hoover Institute at Stanford University allowed him access to documents that were not easily accessible in the 1960s and 1970s. Some of his key findings came from the State Department Decimal File system. The following are prime examples of Sutton's research based on these sources.

> We find there was a link between some New York international bankers and many revolutionaries, including Bolsheviks. These banking gentlemen -- who are here identified -- had a financial stake in, and were rooting for, the success of the Bolshevik Revolution.[54]

---

[53] John C. Coates, *The Future of Corporate Governance Part I: The Problem of Twelve*, Discussion Paper No. 1001, Harvard Law School. www.law.harvard.edu/programs/olin_center/papers/pdf/Coates_1001.pdf.
[54] Antony C. Sutton, *Wall Street and the Bolshevik Revolution* (New York: Arlington House, 1974), p. 11.

While monopoly control of industries was once the objective of J.P. Morgan and J.D. Rockefeller, by the late nineteenth century the inner sanctums of Wall Street understood that the most efficient way to gain an unchallenged monopoly was to "go political" and make society go to work for the monopolists -- under the name of the public good and the public interest. This strategy was detailed in 1906 by Frederick C. Howe in his Confessions of a Monopolist.[55]

These are the rules of big business. They have superseded the teachings of our parents and are reducible to a simple maxim: Get a monopoly; let Society work for you: and remember that the best of all business is politics, for a legislative grant, franchise, subsidy or tax exemption is worth more than a Kimberly or Comstock lode, since it does not require any labor, either mental or physical, for its exploitation. [56]

Documents in the State Department files demonstrate that the National City Bank, controlled
by Stillman and Rockefeller interests, and the Guaranty Trust, controlled by Morgan interests, jointly raised substantial loans for the belligerent Russia before U.S. entry into the war, and that these loans were raised after the State Department pointed out to these firms that they were contrary to international law. Further, negotiations for the loans were undertaken through official U.S. government communications facilities

---

[55] Antony C. Sutton, *Wall Street and the Bolshevik Revolution*, p. 16.
[56] Frederick C. Howe, *Confessions of a Monopolist* (Chicago: Public Publishing, 1906), p. 157.

under cover of the top-level "Green Cipher" of the State Department.[57]

According to Sutton, there are financial motives for using political methods to widen monopolies. While we would not normally think like criminals, unfortunately we need to learn criminal tricks to understand the illusion they are performing. Perhaps we can then comprehend how today's social issues are being funded by extra-governmental actors.

Sutton also notes the following.

> A State Dept. report from Stockholm, dated October 9, 1922 (861.516/137), states in regard to Aschberg, "I met Mr. Aschberg some weeks ago and in the conversation with him he substantially stated all that appeared in this report. He also asked me to inquire whether he could visit the United States and gave as references some of the prominent banks. In connection with this, however, I desire to call the department's attention to Document 54 of the Sisson Documents, and also to many other dispatches which this legation wrote concerning this man during the war, whose reputation and standing is not good. He is undoubtedly working closely in connection with the Soviets, and during the entire war he was in close cooperation with the Germans" (U.S. State Dept. Decimal File, 861.516/137, Stockholm, October 9, 1922. The report was signed by Ira N. Morris).[58]

Sutton highlights seemingly counterintuitive corporate-socialist statements made by Max May of Guaranty Trust, whom he quotes as stating:

---

[57] Antony C. Sutton, *Wall Street and the Bolshevik Revolution*, p. 53.
[58] Antony C. Sutton, *Wall Street and the Bolshevik Revolution*, p. 61.

The United States, being a rich country with well developed industries, does not need to import anything from foreign countries, but ... it is greatly interested in exporting its products to other countries and considers Russia the most suitable market for that purpose, taking into consideration the vast requirements of Russia in all lines of its economic life.[59]

We also see the classic banker move to fund both sides, "What is really important is not so much that financial assistance was given to Germany, which was only illegal, as that directors of Guaranty Trust were financially assisting the Allies at the same time. In other words, Guaranty Trust was financing both sides of the conflict. This raises the question of morality."[60]

Sutton's work is worth quoting in more detail:

> [T]he police power of the state was a means of maintaining a private monopoly. This was exactly as Frederick C. Howe had proposed. The idea of a centrally planned socialist Russia must have appealed to Peabody. Think of it -- one gigantic state monopoly! And Thompson, his friend and fellow director, had the inside track with the boys running the operation![61]
>
> The British Home Office Directorate of Intelligence "Special Report No. 5 (Secret)," issued from Scotland Yard, London, July 14, 1919, and written by Basil H. Thompson, was based on this seized material; the report noted:

---

[59] U.S. State Dept. Decimal File, 861.516/144, November 18, 1922, quoted by Antony C. Sutton, *Wall Street and the Bolshevik Revolution*, p. 63.
[60] Antony C. Sutton, *Wall Street and the Bolshevik Revolution*, p. 67.
[61] Antony C. Sutton, *Wall Street and the Bolshevik Revolution*, p. 100.

"... Every effort was made from the first by Martens and his associates to arouse the interest of American capitalists and there are grounds for believing that the Bureau has received financial support from some Russian export firms, as well as from the Guarantee [sic] Trust Company, although this firm has denied the allegation that it is financing Martens' organisation."[62]

Meanwhile, inside Russia the economic situation had become critical and the inevitability of an embrace with capitalism dawned on the Communist Party and its planners. Lenin crystallized this awareness before the Tenth Congress of the Russian Communist Party:

"Without the assistance of capital it will be impossible for us to retain proletarian power in an incredibly ruined country in which the peasantry, also ruined, constitutes the overwhelming majority—and, of course, for this assistance capital will squeeze hundreds per cent out of us. This is what we have to understand. Hence, either this type of economic relations or nothing..."[63]

Conclusion

Having looked at Sutton's many examples of the duplicitous nature of corporate socialism, we can consider some pertinent questions:

- Did US banks and corporations fund the Bolsheviks for financial reward, or for the love of communism? Whatever the answer, it is certain that they invested in a major control scheme. Remember, today's top fund manager seems to prefer totalitarian systems of

---

[62] Antony C. Sutton, *Wall Street and the Bolshevik Revolution*, p. 115.
[63] Antony C. Sutton, *Wall Street and the Bolshevik Revolution*, p. 157..

government, which are easier to control, over democracies.
- What is to be gained by following DEI or ESG programs today? Will there be future financial rewards? Most likely, but perhaps something more; the ability to control the populus might be identified as the key driver, as pointed out by Lenin in the quote above. Similar to the goals of the DEI and ESG movements, his statement was clearly not about sharing wealth and prosperity.
- Why would anyone finance a losing proposition? Why would social concerns drive investments, and why are we still seeing bankers and corporations involved with governmental concerns?

We can conclude this chapter with a quote from Edward Bellamy, whose work *Looking Backward* (1888) predicts a world government run by corporate interest. He describes large corporations being taken over by even larger corporations until finally all commerce is merged into "The Great Trust."

> The nation ... organized as the one great business corporation in which all other corporations were absorbed; it became the one capitalist in the place of all other capitalists, the sole employer, the final monopoly in which all previous and lesser monopolies were swallowed up, a monopoly in the profits and economies of which all citizens shared. The epoch of trusts had ended in The Great Trust.[64]

Bellamy's vision hit the nail on the head; governments, banks, and corporations are achieving a broader distribution and becoming more intertwined at the same time. A large net of power stretches over the earth. The Beast has become a global threat, as can be seen in multinational corporations' collaboration with interlocked institutions and governments.

---

[64] Edward Bellamy, *Looking Backward* (New York: Dover Publications Inc., 1888 (republished 1996)), p. 15.

Changing this situation seems hopeless at this point; however, there are some issues we have not yet considered.

Chapter 2: The Influence of Elite Foundations and NGOs

In parallel with the actions of corporations and banks, foundations and NGOs have a somewhat less obvious, yet still great, influence over society. Are they in collusion with for-profit corporations, or governments, or both?

When people hear that an organization is a not-for-profit or a foundation, they generally think about charity and philanthropy. However, this is not the entire story regarding the biggest NGOs and foundations. Capital-F foundations are the big names like Ford, Carnegie, and Rockefeller. Public records and congressional reports have proven they consistently follow hidden agendas that the public is generally not aware of. Legal tax avoidance is an obvious reason to start a foundation, yet we will look at more nefarious aspects outside of tax shelters for the rich.

Surprisingly, there has only ever been one significant audit period of foundations approved by the US Congress. Otherwise, foundations have enjoyed free rein. If more people were aware of their motives, we would scream louder at Congress to require that foundations follow the rules.

Congressman Wright Patman's cry from the mountaintop, in the form of the *Chairman's Report to the Select Committee on Small Business* (House of Representatives, 87th Congress) of December 31, 1962, called for an immediate moratorium on Foundations. His scream was not heard.

The Reece Committee

The only audits of tax-exempt foundations by Congress were headed by the Cox and Reece Committees. Their findings are unbelievable when we consider that the audited foundations were based in America. These committees addressed the affairs of large, elite foundations, not small foundations with little influence. It would seem that these organizations were sent by foreign countries to destroy the USA; indeed, their mission becomes clear from the results of the Reece Committee.[1]

US Representative Carroll Reece continued to audit the affairs of foundations after he believed that the Cox Committee had previously failed to report all its findings to Congress (Cox only submitted a dozen pages out of several hundred). There are some important takeaways from the Reece Committee findings, in which alternative funding methods of foundations were identified as being used for the purpose of achieving subversive social agendas.

Foundations not only swayed domestic policy in the 1950s and earlier; they also influenced foreign policy. We can learn from the work of the Reece Committee that elite foundations desired the USA to transform into a global system as we shall see. In his book *Foundations: Their Power and Influence* (1958), Reece Committee General Counsel René Wormser makes the following statements.

> In his column in the *New York Daily News* of December 21, 1954, John O'Donnell said that the Reece Committee had the "almost impossible task" of telling "the taxpayers that the incredible was, in fact, the truth." "The incredible fact," he continued "was that the huge fortunes piled up by such industrial giants as John D. Rockefeller, Andrew Carnegie, and Henry Ford were today being used to destroy or discredit the free-enterprise system which gave them birth."[2]

---

[1] Special Committee to Investigate Tax-Exempt Foundations and Comparable Organizations, *Hearings of the House of Representatives, 83rd Congress, 2nd Session, H. Res 217* (Washington, DC: Government Printing Office, 1954). This audit is incredibly long, so it is useful to start with the relevant findings summarized in this chapter.
[2] René Wormser, *Foundations: Their Power and Influence* (New York: Devin-Adair: 1958), p. vii.

> An "elite" has truly emerged, in control of gigantic financial resources operating outside of our democratic processes, which is willing and able to shape the future of this nation and of mankind in the image of its own value concepts. An unparalleled amount of power is concentrated increasingly in the hands of an interlocking and self-perpetuating group. Unlike the power of corporate management, it is unchecked by stockholders; unlike the power of government, it is unchecked by the people ...[3]

The following extract from Wormser highlights how the elite can benefit from setting up foundations. This is an obvious motivation, as many of the wealthiest individuals look for tax shelters.

> Perhaps the best example of the use of foundations in estate and business planning is offered by the largest, The Ford Foundation. This foundation received about 90 percent of the stock of the Ford Motor Company, all nonvoting stock. Had not the Ford family created this foundation, it would have had to dispose of a large part of its ownership in the Ford Company to the public, for it is hardly possible that the family had enough liquid capital to pay the hundreds of millions of estate taxes which would have been due upon the deaths of two proprietors, Henry Ford and his son Edsel. It might have been difficult to make such a public sale without endangering their control of the company.[4]

---

[3] Wormser, *Foundations*, p. viii.
[4] Wormser, *Foundations*, p. xi.

A few pages later, Wormser makes an amazing prediction.

> It is possible that, in fifty or a hundred years, a great part of American industry will be controlled by pension and profit sharing trusts and foundations and a large part of the balance by insurance companies and labor unions. What eventual repercussions may come from such a development, one can only guess. It may be that we will in this manner reach some form of society similar to socialism, without consciously intending it.[5]

It is quite remarkable that Wormser hit the nail so firmly on the head more than sixty-five years ago, with his statement about pension funds controlling American industry towards socialist goals reflects exactly what we looked at in the previous chapter.

Our society has certainly become more socialistic since the 1950s. Is this a good or a bad thing? It looks bad to me; in the 1950s, only one parent needed to work to support a family. Now both parents need to work to have the same standard of living—or worse.[6]

Not only do many foundations exist to support their directors' elitist friends and families, rather than the apparent purpose of supporting the public good; foundations also leverage each other through sharing directors and trustees. These shared leaderships can implement their political agenda across larger initiatives in powerful efforts of collusion.

> That interlocks among foundation boards existed was clear enough. F. Emerson Andrews, in his Philanthropic Foundations, mentions two complex cases as evidence

---

[5] Wormser, *Foundations*, p. xiii.
[6] See Govind Bhutada, "Datastream Purchasing Power of the U.S. Dollar Over Time," Visual Capitalist, April 6, 2021. www.visualcapitalist.com/purchasing-power-of-the-u-s-dollar-over-time/.

of the national prominence of many foundation trustees. In one case, the foundation had 20 trustees who held a total of 113 positions as trustees or officers of other philanthropic organizations, or an average of 5.6 each ... The Board of the other foundation which Mr. Andrews cited was composed of 14 trustees, holding a total of 85 outside philanthropic positions, or an average of 6 per trustee.[7]

The effective interlock which exists in the foundation world finds expression in many ways, among them: 1. Trustees serving on more than one tax-exempt organization, often both granting and receiving organizations; 2. Joint support and/or control by several foundations of fund-receiving institutions, particularly "clearing-house organizations" and scientific, educational, and public affairs councils or associations; 3, Issuance of matched grants, or promises of grants with the proviso that funds are to be supplied only if and when others support the same project or cause;... 5. Service of foundation officials (trustees or managers) on government advisory boards, in control of government policy or spending in fields identified with foundation philanthropy.[8]

It is like everyone forgot the original intent of establishing foundations. Wormser summarizes: "Society does not grant tax exemption for the privilege of undermining itself."[9]

Many people have directly testified about the connections between foundations and international schemes, of which

---

[7] Wormser, *Foundations*, pp. 57–58.
[8] Wormser, *Foundations*, p. 59.
[9] Wormser, *Foundations*, p. 185.

somehow the public has never become fully aware. Even major newspapers have been involved in depicting foundations as a positive influence on America. The Reece Committee also predicted what would happen in the future. US Representative Carroll Reece made the following remark after the conclusion of his Committee's work.

> In my years of service in the Congress, I have never observed a better organized smear campaign against a congressional committee nor such wanton distortion of the facts by the public press. The editorials and articles appearing concurrently in the Daily Worker, the New York Times and Herald Tribune attacking the committee and its work would appear to be more than a coincidence.
>
> What I did not realize was that this influence would reach even into the conservative press.
>
> And from what has happened in the last month, it is obvious that the large foundations are trying to make certain that never again will a mere committee of the Congress have the temerity to look into their social and political science activities and into their financial power.[10]

In a speech at a National Press Club luncheon, Reece went further.

> The evidence that had been gathered by the staff pointed to one simple underlying situation, namely, that the major foundations by subsidizing collectivist-minded educators, had financed a socialist trend in American Government.

---

[10] Speech by B. Carroll Reece in the House of Representatives, August 20, 1954.

We informed the foundations in advance that our findings suggested that the foundations had for a long time been exercising powerful, although sometimes indirect political influence in both domestic and foreign policy, predominantly toward the left – to say nothing of the support by the foundations of the Institute of Pacific Relations which led the movement to turn China over to the Communists and which was admittedly Communist dominated.

The incredible fact was that the huge fortunes piled up by such industrial giants as John D. Rockefeller, Andrew Carnegie, Henry Ford, etc., were today being used to discredit the free enterprise system which gave them birth.

They cannot disprove the existence of the intellectual cartel which we so clearly disclosed – a cartel which, using public money, has so effectively influenced academic and public opinion both in the domestic and international fields.

One of the documents which frankly disclose their plans is the Conclusions and Recommendations of the American Historical Association's Commission on Social Studies, a call to American educators to teach collectivism to our youth.

... president, Charles Dollard, sought to deny the socialist nature of this report which became an important influence in education.

He stated: "The worst that can be said is that the authors (of this report) not only reported this trend but appeared to accept it cheerfully. What they were accepting was not socialism—it was the New Deal."

But gentlemen, this was not the New Deal.

My Authority is none other than Prof. Howard J. Laski, the top philosopher of the British Socialist Party, who said of these conclusions and recommendations: "At bottom and stripped of its carefully neutral phrases, the report is an educational program for a socialist America."

Yet, after the Conclusions and Recommendations was published, the president of the Carnegie Corp. stated that the public owed its authors a vote of thanks.

What are these foundation funds which this intellectual elite presumes to use for their own political purposes?

They are public funds, dedicated to the public and necessarily so because they are the product of tax exemption.[11]

Georgetown University historian and author Carroll Quigley explained why the Reece Committee was shut down.

> A congressional committee, following backward to their source the threads which led from admitted Communists like Whittaker Chambers, through Alger Hiss, and the Carnegie Endowment to Thomas Lamont and the Morgan Bank, fell into the whole complicated network of the interlocking tax-exempt foundations. The Eighty-third Congress in July 1953 set up a Special Committee to Investigate Tax-Exempt Foundations with Representative

---

[11] B. Carroll Reece, speech, National Press Club luncheon, February 23, 1955.

> B. Carroll Reece, of Tennessee, as chairman. It soon became clear that people of immense wealth would be unhappy if the investigation went too far and that the "most respected" newspapers in the country, closely allied with these men of wealth, would not get excited enough about any [revelations] to make the publicity worth while, in terms of votes or campaign contributions. An interesting report showing the Left-wing associations of the interlocking nexus of tax-exempt foundations was issued in 1954 rather quietly. Four years later, the Reece committee's general counsel, Rene A. Wormser, wrote a shocked, but not shocking, book on the subject called *Foundations: Their Power and Influence*.[12]

People had been made to forget that foundations should exist for the public benefit, not to its detriment. It is time we took some lessons from these speeches by Reece, which are just summaries of the vast amount of non-public information his committee gathered.

> In a report (H Kept. 2681) dated Dec. 16, the special Committee said that "With several tragically outstanding exceptions, such as The Institute of Pacific Relations, foundations have not directly supported organizations which, in turn, operated to support Communism. However, some of the larger foundations have directly supported 'subversion' in the true meaning of that term, namely, the process of undermining some of our vitally protective concepts and principles. They have actively supported attacks upon our social

---

[12] Carroll Quigley, *Tragedy and Hope: A History of the World in Our Time* (New York: MacMillan, 1966), p. 791.

and governmental system and financed the promotion of socialism and collectivist ideas."[13]

Yet the Reece Committee lost, while the foundations won handily. Despite the foundations' hand in forming communist China, the Committee failed to convince Congress to take any action against them. There has been no audit of these high-powered foundations since then. We are overdue for another look behind the curtain.

The Rockefeller Foundation disagreed with the Reece Committee's findings. While material has been removed from the foundation's website concerning this subject, a summary of then-Rockefeller Foundation CEO Dean Rusk's work has been archived. Apparently, the most sublime communication made under his tenure was the claim that the foundation was not subverting American values. Presented with more evidence, perhaps the American people would think otherwise.

> The highlight of this collection is the rough text of a statement that Rusk made to RF staff in December 1954, in which he addressed the subject of the Reece Committee investigation of foundations. Rusk welcomed the expected statement in the Reece Committee report that no new legislation would be sought to change the law affecting foundations. He took note of principal objections to the work of the philanthropic community, including the Rockefeller Foundation: that philanthropy supported something of a left-wing influence in American society, and that the Foundation's support of empirical research constituted a potential

---

[13] "Foundations Investigation," in *CQ Almanac 1954*, 10th ed. 04-238-04-241 (Washington, DC: Congressional Quarterly, 1955).

or actual subversion of established American values.[14]

Norman Dodd, who headed the Reece Committee investigation, gives a summary of major foundations in the 1950s. Dodd had a chip on his shoulder because he left a Morgan bank and he was on a mission against anything anti-American, so we should take this with a grain of salt; however, we should pay attention to his findings if they fit with other evidence. He was concerned about the subversive aspects of foundations.

> In summary, our study of these entities and their relationship to each other seems to warrant the inference that they constitute a highly efficient, functioning whole. Its product is apparently an educational curriculum designed to indoctrinate the American student from matriculation to the consummation of his education. It contrasts sharply with the freedom of the individual as the cornerstone of our social structure. For this freedom, it seems to substitute the group, the will of the majority, and a centralized power to enforce this will, presumably in the interest of all. Its development and production seems to have been largely the work of those organizations engaged in research, such as the Social Science Research Council and the National Research Council.[15]

---

[14] Rockefeller Foundation, Dean Rusk Papers, 1952–1962, archived at https://web.archive.org/web/20000709202358/http://www.rockefeller.edu/archive.ctr/rf_dr.html.

[15] Norman Dodd, *Dodd Report to the Reece Committee on Foundations* (New York: The Long House Inc., 1954). P.11. https://illinoisfamily.org/wp-content/uploads/2020/04/Dodd-Report-to-the-Reece-Committee-on-Foundations-1954.pdf.

What is the purpose of foundations' involvement in education? Don't we already have government funding for that? Shouldn't they focus on poverty, food or medicine, rather than on using education for social engineering? Dodd thought it was to indoctrinate the youth to be socialists.

I am no fan of Bertrand Russell, but I will quote him here as he states that education is a big part of globalists' plans.

> The society of experts will control propaganda and education. It will teach loyalty to the world government, and make nationalism high treason. The government, being an oligarchy, will instill submissiveness into the great bulk of the population, confining initiative and the habit of command to its own members. It is possible that it may invent ingenious ways of concealing its own power, leaving the forms of democracy intact, and allowing the plutocrats or politicians to imagine that they are cleverly controlling these forms … whatever the outward forms may be, all real power will come to be concentrated in the hands of those who understand the art of scientific manipulation.[16]

The Bill and Melinda Gates Foundation

The Bill and Melinda Gates Foundation has a focus on medicine and health, yet there seems to be an ulterior motive. Based upon Bill Gates' own comments, we can deduce that he found new ways to invest in his tax avoidance schemes and still accomplish his goals.

---

[16] Bertrand Russell, *The Scientific Outlook* (London: Allen and Unwin, 1919), pp. 243–244.
https://archive.org/details/in.ernet.dli.2015.126728/page/n241/mode/2up.

Are the foundation's goals for the public good, in the form of a philanthropic organization that invests in the distribution of vaccines to poor countries? What about the profits of NGOs and the companies Gates founded? Is there a conflict of interest? While the foundation is not-for-profit, profits are being realized by the drug companies and their shareholders.

> Wednesday, Gates revealed the best investment he has ever made in an essay in The Wall Street Journal. It's the $10 billion he's invested, through the Bill & Melinda Gates Foundation, into three particular organizations that increase access to vaccines and medicines for people who need them around the world.
>
> Gates says investing $10 billion in Gavi, the Vaccine Alliance; the Global Fund; and the Global Polio Eradication Initiative, which help deliver drugs to developing countries, has been a rewarding experience because unlike other kinds of investments, they are consistently successful.
>
> Gates says the $10 billion his foundation has put into the three organizations has created an estimated $200 billion in social and economic benefits. (The estimate is from the Copenhagen Consensus Center, a think tank that estimates cost analysis to global problems.)[17]
>
> Investing in global health organizations aimed at increasing access to vaccines creates a 20-to-1 return, the Microsoft co-founder and philanthropist says.

---

[17] Catherine Clifford, "Billionaire Bill Gates Says This Is the Best Investment He's Ever Made," NBC make it, January 17, 2019. www.cnbc.com/2019/01/17/bill-gates-says-this-is-the-best-investment-he-has-ever-made.html.

"We feel there's been over a 20-to-1 return," yielding $200 billion over those 20 or so years, Gates told CNBC's Becky Quick on "Squawk Box" from the World Economic Forum in Davos, Switzerland.[18]

A couple things jump out from Gates' statements. First, in his interview from Davos, he makes it seem like he personally made these investments. Is it a foundation or a dictatorship? While receiving one of the biggest public benefits on the planet in the form of the largest tax savings of all time, the Gates Foundation appears to be his own playground, without oversight or public scrutiny. We can't take his comments out of context; but while he may not be directly making profit from the sales of vaccines, is he doing so indirectly?[19]

Second, who purchases the vaccines that the Foundation's investments go toward supplying? It appears to be an interlocking scheme, whereby NGOs that Gates helped set up (for example, Gavi) receive funding from government agencies. This is taxpayer money, so these endeavors are not like business deals with market investors and private sales. Smells like collusion between NGOs, governments, and his foundation.

The BBC and India's *Economic Times* reported on Gates' investment in the private vaccine producer the Serum Institute of India, which made profits from taxpayer-subsidized distribution of vaccines during the pandemic, and how the company positioned itself for profit.

> [The Serum Institute of India] is privately owned, which enabled fast decision-making between Mr Poonawalla and his scientists.

---

[18] Matthew J. Belvedere, "Bill Gates: My 'Best Investment' Turned $10 Billion into $200 Billion Worth of Economic Benefit," CNBC, January 23, 2019. www.cnbc.com/2019/01/23/bill-gates-turns-10-billion-into-200-billion-worth-of-economic-benefit.html.

[19] See Gavi: The Vaccine Alliance, "Donor Contributions: 2021–2025." www.gavi.org/investing-gavi/funding/current-period-2021-2025.

> But funding proved a challenge. The firm invested around $260m (£186.7m) and raised the rest from philanthropists, such as Bill Gates, and advances from other countries.[20]
>
> Pune's Serum Institute of India, the world's largest vaccine manufacturer, is expected to generate $4 billion in revenues through its Covid vaccine deals by 2022, as a year after the pandemic the company starts to see its R&D risks pay off. Going by the listed price of the vaccine and the approval timelines, Serum Institute could rake in at least $1 billion by end of 2021 and overall revenue of $4 billion through the Covid vaccine deals.[21]

We can tie together what we learned about foundations from the Reece Committee's work with a great summary Tim Schwab wrote for *The Nation*, in which he shows the incredible conflict of interest in Gates' projects, which governments do not seem to be aware of or doing anything about.

> According to Tim Schwab in The Nation article "Bill Gates's Charity Paradox", the Gates Foundation uses "all the tools of capitalism" to "connect the promise of philanthropy with the power of private enterprise."
>
> ... a $250 million donation [was] given to media companies and groups to influence the news with a clear ideological agenda.

---

[20] Chiyo Robertson, "Covid: How This Indian Firm Is Vaccinating the World," BBC, February 28, 2021. www.bbc.com/news/business-56218058.
[21] Divya Rajagopal, "Serum Institute Could Earn $4 Billion From Vaccine Sales in 2 Years," *Economic Times*, March 25, 2021. https://economictimes.indiatimes.com/industry/healthcare/biotech/pharmaceuticals/serum-institute-could-earn-4-billion-from-vaccine-sales-in-2-years/articleshow/81680955.cms.

... close to $250 million was identified in charitable grants made to private companies where the Gates foundation holds corporate stocks and bonds, raising the underlying question as to whether these donations are providing the Gates Foundation with financial gains.

Gates is suspected of avoiding more taxes than anyone else, amounting in billions of dollars that otherwise could be a public subsidy.

The Gates Foundation has made notable donations to groups that push for industry-friendly governmental policy and regulations, and often "Gates' ideological interests overlap with his financial interests."

In the case of Gates' influence on the pharmaceutical industry, the foundation is known for pushing a pro-patent agenda, making life-saving drugs unaffordable in low resource countries.

The foundation's "strategic investment fund" is another area of concern, where "the Gates Foundation explicitly marries its investing and charitable activities."

Schwab describes Gate's charitable giving as creating a "blinding halo effect around his philanthropic work, as many of the institutions best placed to scrutinize his foundation are now funded by Gates."

The increased lack of scrutiny has made the Gates Foundation a major player in informing public policy, proving that "philanthropy can buy political influence."[22]

---

[22] Community Alliance for Global Justice, "The Nation: Bill Gates's Charity Paradox," April 10, 2020. https://cagj.org/2020/04/the-nation-

Socialism versus the Constitution

Since it is difficult to change laws or convince the public of globalist practices, foundations use loopholes to achieve their mission, operating outside of normal channels that include government oversight. We can see examples in the area of education, where it is possible that foundations attempt to bypass the Tenth Amendment of the US Constitution.

Let's refresh our understanding of state power. The Tenth Amendment is as follows.

> The powers not delegated to the United States by the Constitution, nor prohibited by it to the States, are reserved to the States respectively, or to the people.

Here, we find that the states have the right to control education, since there is no federally prescribed education system in the Constitution. The Fourteenth Amendment also helps to clarify this.[23]

> While education may not be a "fundamental right" under the Constitution, the equal protection clause of the 14th Amendment requires that when a state establishes a public school system (as in Texas), no child living in that

---

bill-gatess-charity-paradox/. This article refers to Tim Schwab, "Bill Gates's Charity Paradox," *The Nation*, March 17, 2020. www.thenation.com/article/society/bill-gates-foundation-philanthropy/.
[23] You can find the text of the Fourteenth Amendment at the Constitution Annotated website.
https://constitution.congress.gov/browse/amendment-14/#:~:text=No%20State%20shall%20make%20or,equal%20protection%20of%20the%20laws.

state may be denied equal access to schooling.[24]

Many people assume the right to public education is national, but it is the responsibility of the states to govern education. Further, each state is responsible for treating every student equally, as ensured by the Fourteenth Amendment.

Why is education so important that foundations want to influence it on a national level? Instead of working at the state level, they focus on relationships with agencies and NGOs working at the federal level to bypass the systems in place. Let's return to Norman Dodd's report on foundations for the Reece Committee.

> From our studies, it appears that the overall administration of this functioning whole and the careful selection of its personnel seem to have been the peculiar interest of the American Council of Learned Societies. It is interesting to note that, by legislative action recently, another entity has been brought into being known as the National Science Foundation, whose purpose is to develop a national policy with respect to science. Its additional purpose is to serve our Government in an advisory capacity in connection with the huge appropriations now being made for research in the interest of **effective controls**. Evidence exists of close cooperation between privately endowed Foundations, the agencies through which they have operated and the educational institutions through which they have been accustomed to make grants for research. This process may contribute to an

---

[24] Teach Democracy, "Education and the 14th Amendment," *Bill of Rights in Action* 7(4) (1991). https://teachdemocracy.org/online-lessons/bill-of-rights-in-action/bria-7-4-c.

undesirable degree of **concentrated power.**[25]

Now we can surmise that the possible motive is "concentrated power." It is easier to control influential groups than normal government channels, which must consider the will of the people. It is also more difficult to manage an agenda through each individual state. Instead, efforts are made to consolidate control through national agencies that operate outside of Congress to influence the education system nationally. Dodd adds:

> [E]ducation [is] under the tight control of organizations and persons, little known to the American public. Its operations and ideas are so complex as to be beyond public understanding or control.
>
> For these reasons, it has been difficult for us to dismiss the suspicion that, latent in the minds of many of the social scientists has lain the belief that, given sufficient authority and enough funds, human behavior can be controlled and that this control can be exercised without risk to either ethical principles or spiritual values and that therefore, the solution to all social problems should be entrusted to them.[26]

Susceptibility to indoctrination is not something people usually think can happen to them. We like to believe we are smart, free-thinking individuals. While our behavior may have been different in primary school, we decide to follow our own choices as adults. Maybe all our indoctrination to serve the Beast system happened when we were young. An important question is: Are we being manipulated, especially from a young age through the school system, in a way that is carried on into our adult lives

---

[25] Dodd, *Dodd Report to the Reece Committee on Foundations*, p. 11; (emphasis added).
[26] Dodd, *Dodd Report to the Reece Committee on Foundations*, p. 12.

as we consume media with programming geared towards control schemes? Is this system making us more critical of opposing beliefs to separate us, since unity of the masses seems detrimental to the elite?

Dodd cites an example of the Carnegie Foundation granting funds to publish books critical of the Constitution.

> "This study was made possible by funds granted by Carnegie Corporation of New York." While this refers to but one project out of many, it becomes significant when it is realized that the project to which these books relate involves some $250,000, and led to the publication of statements which were most critical of our Constitution.[27]

A Smoking Gun Witness

Dodd continues with references to the activities of the Ford Foundation.

> Ford appears to be capitalizing on developments which took place long before it was founded, and which have enabled it to take advantage of ... the wholesale dedication of education to a social purpose[;] the need to defend this dedication against criticism[;] the need to indoctrinate adults along these lines[;] the acceptance by the Executive branch of the Federal Government of responsibility for planning on a national and international scale[;] the diminishing importance of the Congress and the states and the growing power of the Executive branch of the Federal government[;] and

---

[27] Dodd, *Dodd Report to the Reece Committee on Foundations*, p. 13.

> the seeming indispensability of control over human behavior.[28]

The above quote is in the official record; more interesting is an alleged statement by the president of the Ford Foundation about the real motives of its work. Unfortunately, the following testimony was never published by the Reece Committee; in fact, a lot of evidence never made it to the public, as the Committee was shut down amid opposing political pressure. Decades after the investigation, Dodd disclosed a private conversation with Ford Foundation President Rowan Gaither.

> "Mr. Dodd, we have asked you to come up here today, because we thought that, possibly, off the record, you would tell us why the Congress is interested in the activities of foundations such as ourselves."
>
> And, before I could think of how I would reply to that statement, Mr. Gaither then went on, and voluntarily stated, "Mr. Dodd, all of us who have a hand in the making of policies here, have had experience either with the OSS during the war, or with European economic administration after the war. We have had experience operating under directives. The directives emanate, and did emanate, from the White House. Now, we still operate under just such directives. Would you like to know what the substance of these directives is?"
>
> I said, "Yes, Mr. Gaither, I would like very much to know." Whereupon, he made this statement to me, "Mr. Dodd, we are here to operate in response to similar directives, the substance of which is that we shall use our grant-making power so to alter life in the United States, that it can be

---

[28] Dodd, *Dodd Report to the Reece Committee on Foundations*, p. 14.

comfortably merged with the Soviet Union."[29]

Did Gaither mean to make a private confession because of a guilty conscience, or did he spill the beans because he felt pressure to account for his actions? If his admission is true, we can better understand he coordination between institutions and agencies to accomplish the spread of a control system. Even though the Soviet Union no longer exists, the goal of globalization is the same as in the past: control by an elite class. "Communism" seems to be a weaker word now, without carrying the meaning it once had. Is today's democracy becoming more like yesterday's communism?

Non-Governmental Organizations

Next, we will examine NGOs to find out if there are similar threads to compare. NGOs have vast influence in their cooperation with government agencies. Are some NGOs established to bypass bureaucracies so they can accomplish their goals more effectively? What are those goals?

On November 25, 1959, the Council on Foreign Relations (CFR) think tank published *Study No. 7*, in which we find the statement: "The U. S. must strive to: A. BUILD A NEW INTERNATIONAL ORDER—building a new international order must be responsive to world aspirations for peace, [and] for social and economic change ... including states labeling themselves as 'Socialist'."[30]

The Reece Committee reported the following about a similar mission of the CFR and major foundations.

---

[29] A transcript of this interview is available at www.supremelaw.org. "Transcript of Norman Dodd Interview, 1982, with G. Edward Griffin." www.supremelaw.org/authors/dodd/interview.htm.
[30] Council on Foreign Relations, *Basic Aims of United States Foreign Policy. Study Prepared at the Request of the Committee on Foreign Relations, United States Senate* [*Study No. 7*].
https://archive.org/details/basic-aims-of-united-states-foreign-policy.-study-prepared-at-the-request-of-the/.

> Globalists may be correct in believing we should ignore the national interest in the wider interest of creating a world collectivism; but we feel confident we are right in our conclusion that a public foundation has no right to promote globalism to the exclusion of support for a fair presentation of the opposite theory of foreign policy. The Council on Foreign Relations came to be in essence an agency of the United States government, no doubt carrying its internationalist bias with it.[31]

Thomas Dye reports this important quote to consider.

> Political scientist Lester Milbrath notes that "The Council on Foreign Relations, while not financed by government, works so closely with it that it is difficult to distinguish Council actions stimulated by government from autonomous actions."[32]

Admiral Chester Ward, a former high-level CFR member, seemed to blow the whistle about the organization's true intentions.

> [The CFR has as a goal of] submergence of U.S. sovereignty and national independence into an all-powerful one-world government ... this lust to surrender the sovereignty and independence of the United States is pervasive throughout most of the membership ... In the entire CFR lexicon, there is no term of revulsion

---

[31] Special Committee to Investigate Tax-Exempt Foundations and Comparable Organizations, *Hearings of the House of Representatives*, p. 177.

[32] Thomas R. Dye, Oligarchic Tendencies in National Policy-Making: the Role of the Private Policy-Planning Organizations. *The Journal of Politics*, 1978, Volume 40 Number 2, p.316.

carrying a meaning so deep as "America First."³³

Once the ruling members of the CFR have decided that the U.S. Government should adopt a particular policy, the very substantial research facilities of CFR are put to work to develop arguments, intellectual and emotional, to support the new policy, and to confound and discredit, intellectually and politically, any opposition.³⁴

Now let's hear something that should make us wonder about the future. CFR President Richard Haass stated on February 21, 2006, in an article titled, "State Sovereignty Must be Altered In a Globalized Era":

[S]tates must be prepared to cede some sovereignty to world bodies if the international system is to function. This is already taking place in the trade realm. Governments agree to accept the rulings of the WTO because on balance they benefit from an international trading order even if a particular decision requires that they alter a practice that is their sovereign right to carry out.

Some governments are prepared to give up elements of sovereignty to address the threat of global climate change. Under one such arrangement, the Kyoto Protocol, which runs through 2012, signatories agree to cap specific emissions. What is needed now is a successor arrangement in which a larger

---

³³ Admiral Chester Ward, quoted by Phyllis Schlafly, *Kissinger on the Couch* (Westport, CT: Arlington House, 1975), pp. 144–150.
³⁴ Ward, quoted by Schlafly, *Kissinger on the Couch*, p. 151.

number of governments, including the U.S., China, and India, accept emissions limits or adopt common standards because they recognize that they would be worse off if no country did.

All of this suggests that sovereignty must be redefined if states are to cope with globalization. At its core, globalization entails the increasing volume, velocity, and importance of flows—within and across borders—of people, ideas, greenhouse gases, goods, dollars, drugs, viruses, e-mails, weapons and a good deal else, challenging one of sovereignty's fundamental principles: the ability to control what crosses borders in either direction. Sovereign states increasingly measure their vulnerability not to one another, but to forces beyond their control.

Globalization thus implies that sovereignty is not only becoming weaker in reality, but that it needs to become weaker. States would be wise to weaken sovereignty in order to protect themselves, because they cannot insulate themselves from what goes on elsewhere. Sovereignty is no longer a sanctuary.

The goal should be to redefine sovereignty for the era of globalization, to find a balance between a world of fully sovereign states and an international system of either world government or anarchy.[35]

---

[35] Richard Haass, "State Sovereignty Must Be Altered In a Globalized Era," *Tapei Times*, February 21, 2006. www.taipeitimes.com/News/editorials/archives/2006/02/21/2003294021.

A summary by Carroll Quigley mentions how the CFR came into existence along with presenting other names we will research later.

> At the end of the war of 1914, it became clear that the organization of this system had to be greatly extended. Once again the task was entrusted to Lionel Curtis who established, in England and each dominion, a front organization to the existing Round Table Group. This front organization, called the Royal Institute of International Affairs, had as its nucleus in each area the existing submerged Round Table Group. In New York it was known as the Council on Foreign Relations, and was a front for J. P. Morgan and Company in association with the very small American Round Table Group. The American organizers were dominated by the large number of Morgan "experts," ... who had gone to the Paris Peace Conference and there became close friends with the similar group of English "experts" which had been recruited by the Milner group. In fact, the original plans for the Royal Institute of International Affairs and the Council on Foreign Relations were drawn up in Paris.[36]

Joseph Kraft wrote in *Harper's* in July 1958 that one of the key American agents in the founding of the Council on Foreign Relations was Colonel Edward M. House, who worked closely with Woodrow Wilson on the founding of the Federal Reserve and other initiatives. Kraft also described the extensive influence of the CFR.

> [The CFR] has been the seat of some basic government decisions, has set the context for many more, and has repeatedly served

---

[36] Quigley, *Tragedy and Hope*, pp. 951–952.

as a recruiting ground for ranking officials.[37]

Study No. 7, published on November 25, 1959, states the "basic aims" of the CFR.[38] The main goal the CFR presented to the US Senate was to establish an international order. It openly promoted granting more power to the United Nations and bringing communism into the fold. We have heard of the merger of East and West before.

This brings us to an important consideration. If the CFR and other organizations like it are so interested in reforming the world, and with their high-placed officials within the US government, why have they not accomplished their goals yet? Richard N. Gardner, former deputy assistant secretary of state at the Bureau of International Organization Affairs, wrote an article in 1974 that stated what was required to achieve the organization's goals. It is work in progress:

> [A]n end run around national sovereignty, eroding it piece by piece, will accomplish much more than the old fashioned assault.[39]

In order to research further, we need only check out the long list of present and former members of the CFR who hold or have held high-level positions in government. (The John Birch Society goes as far as wanting to eliminate all CFR members from being able to hold office because of their shady past work.[40])

CFR member and then-National Security Advisor James L. Jones made a speech at the 45th Munich Conference on Security

---

[37] Joseph Kraft, "School for Statesmen," *Harper's*, July 1958. https://archive.org/details/sim_harpers-magazine_1958-07_217_1298/page/64/mode/2up?view=theater.
[38] CFR, *Basic Aims of United States Foreign Policy*, pp. 9–17.
[39] Richard N. Gardner, "The Hard Road to World Order," *Foreign Affairs*, April 1, 1974. www.foreignaffairs.com/world/hard-road-world-order.
[40] The John Birch Society, "Eliminate CFR Members from Appointments." https://jbs.org/alert/eliminate-cfr-members-from-appointments/

Policy at the Hotel Bayerischer Hof on February 8, 2009, in which he made an unbelievable statement about the chain of command in a major government agency taking orders from the CFR. How can a non-elected person have this much power?

> Thank you for that wonderful tribute to Henry Kissinger yesterday. Congratulations. As the most recent National Security Advisor of the United States, I take my daily orders from Dr. Kissinger, filtered down through Generaal [sic] Brent Scowcroft and Sandy Berger, who is also here. We have a chain of command in the National Security Council that exists today.[41]

The above quotes are specific to the CFR and its members, but there are many other NGOs that exercise their influence through the United Nations and other organizations.

Movements Toward One World Government

We should explore how democratic and communistic ideologies could be merged, since the Beast appears to be interested in this, as highlighted in the previous sections.

In *The Socialist Democrat* (No. 40), Lenin proposed a "United States of the World." One world government would be easier to obtain out of socialism than a democratic system. Are democratic countries becoming more socialist? I think so.

The April 1945 issue of *Political Affairs*, the Communist Party's official journal, stated:

---

[41] The Obama White House, "Remarks by National Security Advisor Jones at 45th Munich Conference on Security Policy," Office of the Press Secretary, February 9, 2009.
https://obamawhitehouse.archives.gov/the-press-office/remarks-national-security-adviser-jones-45th-munich-conference-security-policy.

> Great popular support and enthusiasm for the United Nations policies should be built up, well organized and fully articulate. But it is also necessary to do more than that. The opposition must be rendered so impotent that it will be unable to gather any significant support in the Senate against the United Nations Charter and the treaties which will follow.[42]

It is evident how someone like Harry Dexter White, a confirmed communist spy, could have operated at the highest levels of government in the USA. He was clearly part of the plans to merge countries like the USA and the Soviet Union into a world government and to undermine the USA.

> [White was a] senior U.S. Department of Treasury official. He was the first head of the International Monetary Fund, played an important role in formation of the World Bank. He was also a Soviet secret agent—"the most highly-placed asset the Soviets possessed in the American government."[43]

We should take notice of White's involvement with the formation of the International Monetary Fund (IMF). Descriptions of his other high-level positions and duties are given below.

> On and after this date, Mr. Harry D. White, Assistant to the Secretary (of the Treasury), will assume full responsibility for all matters with which the Treasury Department has to deal having a bearing on foreign relations. Mr. White will act as liaison between the Treasury Department and the State

---

[42] Quoted in Forbes, www.forbes.com/sites/nathanlewis/2017/01/20/the-problems-of-free-trade-more-than-you-bargained-for/?sh=4eaa79056660

[43] John Earl Haynes, Harvey Klehr, and Alexander Vassiliev, *Spies: The Rise and Fall of the KGB in America* (New Haven, CT: Yale University Press, 2009), p. 258.

> Department, will serve in the capacity of adviser to the Secretary on all Treasury foreign affairs matters, and will assume responsibility for the management and operation of the Stabilization Fund without change in existing procedures. Mr. White will report directly to the Secretary.[44]

> [White] was a senior American official at the 1944 Bretton Woods conference that established the postwar economic order. He dominated the conference, and his vision of post-war financial institutions mostly prevailed over those of John Maynard Keynes, the British representative who was the other main founder. Through Bretton Woods, White was a major architect of the International Monetary Fund and World Bank.[45]

White was also involved with the delay of financial support to the Chinese nationalists that eventually led to the takeover of China by the communists. This was in conjunction with the Institute of Pacific Relations and the efforts of foundations to provide massive amounts of funding to the Soviets.

> The accusations against White revolved around four incidents with which White was involved. First, he was the real architect of the Morgenthau plan to pastorialize Germany to punish her for

---

[44] Secretary of the Treasury, *Interlocking Subversion in Government Departments*, Report of the Subcommittee to Investigate the Administration of the Internal Security Act and Other Internal Security Laws to the Committee on the Judiciary, United States Senate, 83rd Congress, 1st Session, July 30, 1953, p. 29.
[45] Wikipedia, "Harry Dexter White." https://en.wikipedia.org/wiki/Harry_Dexter_White. See also James M. Boughton, *Harry White and the American Creed: How a Federal Bureaucrat Created the Modern Global Economy (and Failed to Get the Credit)* (New Haven, CT: Yale University Press, 2021).

starting two World Wars in thirty years. Second, he used his position in the Treasury Department to develop a hostile U.S. policy toward prewar Japan. The reason was to distract Japan from their plans to attack the Soviet Union and draw the U.S. into the war as an ally with the Soviet Union. Next, White delayed financial support to Generalissimo Chiang Kai-shek's Nationalist Chinese government causing the triumph of Mao Tse-Tung's Communist Chinese government. Finally, he was instrumental in handing over the Allied Military mark printing plates to the Soviets. This caused a $250,000,000 deficit in the occupational government budget paid out by the U.S. Treasury. His accusers claim all this was done at the behest of the Russians to the detriment of U.S. policy and national security.[46]

These plans by White toward the formation of a new global structure fit the candid discussion that Rowan Gaither had with Norman Dodd, the CFR statements, and the other information we have looked at. The dots connect when we see people like White as architects of the IMF and World Bank, along with having worked on some of the same efforts to increase socialism globally as have been carried out by foundations and NGOs.

Alongside the obvious groups we can dive into is the not-so-famous Institute of Pacific Relations (IPR), an organization that has worked behind the scenes to accomplish the goal of merging nations in collaboration with foundations, as referenced in the Reece Committee's report.

---

[46] Tom Adams, "The Trial of Harry Dexter White: Soviet Agent of Influence," dissertation, University of New Orleans, 2004, pp. 2–3.

The Goals of the IPR Towards Globalism

While it may be hard to believe, communism was a public threat to the American way in the middle of the twentieth century. We have all heard about McCarthyism as a time of "persecution" against communists in government, Hollywood, and academia. Senators like Joseph McCarthy and Pat McCarran worked hard to root out those holding a red badge. The issue we seem to face today is not an open threat, but a subversive blending of global governance by an elite cabal. We need to understand the linked agendas of a powerful few, like those efforts identified in the Reece Committee's report.

Let's examine the findings of the Senate Internal Security Subcommittee (SISS) about the role of the IPR, foundations and Dexter White in the formation of the communist Chinese state.

> **13.71** Among the largest subcommittee holdings are the records of the Special Subcommittee to Investigate the Administration of the Internal Security Act and Other Internal Security Laws, 1951-77 (547 ft.). More commonly known as the Senate Internal Security Subcommittee (SISS), it was authorized under S. Res. 366, 81st Cong., approved December 21, 1950, to study and investigate (1) the administration, operation, and enforcement of the Internal Security Act of 1950 (Public Law 81-831, also known as the McCarran Act) and other laws relating to espionage, sabotage, and the protection of the internal security of the United States and (2) the extent, nature, and effects of subversive activities in the United States "including, but not limited to, espionage, sabotage, and infiltration of persons who are or may be under the domination of the foreign government or organization controlling the world Communist movement or any movement seeking to

overthrow the Government of the United States by force and violence."

13.76 The investigation of the Institute of Pacific Relations was the first major investigation initiated by the subcommittee. The IPR was established in 1925 to provide a forum for discussion of Asian problems and relations between Asia and the West. To promote greater knowledge of the Far East, the IPR established a large research program, which was supported financially by grants from the Rockefeller Foundation, the Carnegie Corporation, and other major corporations. While the IPR leadership maintained it was a nonpartisan body, others, including some former members, accused it of supporting the Communist line with respect to its analysis of political developments in the Far East. Some people accused the IPR leadership of spying for the Soviet Union. Owen Lattimore, editor of the IPR journal Pacific Affairs, was especially singled out for criticism.

13.84 Another special collection that focuses on China is the subcommittee's collection of files relating to the so-called diaries of Henry Morgenthau, Jr., Franklin D. Roosevelt's Secretary of the Treasury, 1934-45. The records of the Morgenthau Diary Study, 1953-65 (12 ft.), consist largely of copies of portions of memorandums, correspondence, transcripts of meetings, and other records preserved by Secretary Morgenthau in order to document his tenure. The original records are in the custody of the Franklin D. Roosevelt Library in Hyde Park, NY. In 1965, the SISS issued a two volume committee print entitled

> Morgenthau Diary (China), containing entries from the records at the Franklin D. Roosevelt Library selected to illustrate the implementation of Roosevelt administration policy in China. According to the editor of the publication, the subcommittee wanted to produce a documentary history on the subject and "also indicate the serious problem of unauthorized, uncontrolled and often dangerous power exercised by nonelected officials," specifically Harry Dexter White. White was a major figure in Senator William Jenner's investigation of interlocking subversion in Government departments in 1953. The records also include subject files accumulated by the editors of the volume and copies of subcommittee publications produced as a result of or accumulated during the study.[47]

Also remarkable is that we have access to Morgenthau's diary, mentioned by the SISS. There are written records of White's purposeful avoidance of providing assistance to nationalist China, which led to the rise of a communist state. What would have happened if the USA had maintained its support of nationalist China? Would this have saved tens of millions of lives? Here are some estimates that were researched by Ian Johnson and others.

> The first reliable scholarly estimates derived from the pioneering work of the demographer Judith Banister, who in 1987 used Chinese demographic statistics to come up with the remarkably durable estimate of 30 million, and the journalist

---

[47] US Senate, Guide to Senate Records: Chapter 13, Records of the Committee on the Judiciary and Related Committees, section "Senate Internal Security Committee."
www.archives.gov/legislative/guide/senate/chapter-13.html#SISS.

Jasper Becker, who in his 1996 work *Hungry Ghosts* gave these numbers a human dimension and offered a clear, historical analysis of the events. At the most basic level, the early works took the net decline in China's population during this period and added to that the decline in the birth rate—a classic effect of famine. Later scholars refined this methodology by looking at local histories compiled by government offices that gave very detailed accounts of famine conditions. Triangulating these two sources of information results in estimates that start in the mid-20 millions and go up to 45 million.

Two more recent accounts give what are widely regarded as the most credible numbers. One, in 2008, is by the Chinese journalist Yang Jisheng, who estimates that 35 million died. Hong Kong University's Frank Dikötter has a higher but equally plausible estimate of 45 million. Besides adjusting the numbers upward, Dikötter and others have made another important point: many deaths were violent. Communist Party officials beat to death anyone suspected of hoarding grain, or people who tried to escape the death farms by traveling to cities.

Regardless of how one views these revisions, the Great Leap Famine was by far the largest famine in history. It was also man-made—and not because of war or disease, but by government policies that were flawed and recognized as such at the time by reasonable people in the Chinese government.[48]

Getting back to White, we find details about his subterfuge that enabled these horrific deaths.

> Harry Dexter White in the Treasury Department played a key role in sabotaging U.S. economic aid to the Nationalists, as even his friendly biographer admits. In a December 9, 1944 memo to Treasury Secretary Morgenthau, White wrote, "We have stalled as much as we have dared and have succeeded in limiting gold shipments to $26 million during the past year. We think it would be a serious mistake to permit further large shipments at this time." The U.S. government had made a commitment to Chiang in writing to supply $200 million in gold to curb inflation in Nationalist China. White's policy prevented the shipment until it was too late to be effective in stemming the inflation, a contributing factor to loss of American confidence in Chiang and thus to Chiang's defeat. White also supported the propaganda line favorable to the Communists. Reporting to Morgenthau on the Dixie Mission on October 16, 1944, White wrote that the interests of the Chinese Communist Party.
>
> With White, unlike the China Hands, there is evidence that he was involved in Communist groups. Both Elizabeth Bentley and Whittaker Chambers named White as a member of Communist cells, the

---

[48] Ian Johnson, Who Killed More: Hitler, Stalin, or Mao? *The NY Review of Books*, February 5, 2018.
www.nybooks.com/online/2018/02/05/who-killed-more-hitler-stalin-or-mao

> Silvermaster and Ware groups respectively, though both testified that they did not know if White was actually a Communist. Investigations were never completed because White died of a heart attack in August 1948.[49]

Here are two more testimonies by former members of the IPR from the Reece Committee hearings.

> June 4. Professor David N. Rowe of Yale University, a trustee of the Institute of Pacific Relations from 1947–1950, said foundation grants to the IPR had helped "people who did not have the best interests of this country at heart." Rowe said several foundations had continued to contribute to the IPR after disclosures of pro-Communist influences in the organization (CQ Almanac, Vol. VIII, 1952, p. 255).

> June 8. Criticism of foundation grants to the IPR came from another ex-member, retired Northwestern Professor Kenneth W. Colegrove, then teaching at Queens College, N.Y. He said the Rockefeller Foundation should have investigated the IPR in 1945, "when the situation was brought energetically to its attention by Alfred Kohlberg," head of the American China Policy Association.[50]

There are a lot of debates about "who lost China," and there are a lot of complex reasons for the rise of the CCP. An extensive

---

[49] Anne W. Carroll, "Who Lost China," EWTN. www.ewtn.com/catholicism/library/who-lost-china-10801.
[50] Foundations Investigation, *CQ Almanac 1954*, 10th ed., 04-238-04-241. (Washington, DC: Congressional Quarterly, 1955). https://library.cqpress.com/cqalmanac/document.php?id=cqal54-1358084

debate is not necessary here, except to add some fuel to our fire that foundations supported the IPR and communist initiatives, while the US Treasury Department failed to support nationalist China like it said it would. Coincidence?

If foundations had not provided support for communism through the IPR, and if the US Treasury had given more financial support to Chiang Kai-Shek, the post-World War II era would have had a much different outlook. It's intriguing to ponder that US support for communist China came from subversive groups, despite the US government openly stating that nationalist China was an ally. All bases were covered.

The past provides examples of famous divide-and-conquer success stories, or of banks financing both sides of a war to come out the winner in the end. In the case of China, action on both sides of the communist takeover can be traced back to unexpected organizations. Did the Beast want conflict? What about more recent news?

> A representative from America's Frontier Fund said that a "kinetic event" in the Pacific would be very good for its bottom line.
>
> A war between China and Taiwan will be extremely good for business at America's Frontier Fund, a tech investment outfit whose co-founder and CEO sits on both the State Department Foreign Affairs Policy Board and President Joe Biden's Intelligence Advisory Board, according to audio from a February 1 event.
>
> AFF is surely not the only venture fund that would see stratospheric returns throughout their portfolio in the case of a destabilizing global crisis, like a "kinetic event in the Pacific"—that is to say, war. Unlike most other investment firms, though, AFF is closely tied to the upper echelons of American power, the very people who would craft any response to such a war.

Gilman Louie, AFF's co-founder and current CEO, serves as chair of the National Intelligence University, advises Biden through his Intelligence Advisory Board, and was tapped for the State Department's Foreign Affairs Policy Board by Secretary of State Antony Blinken in 2022. Louie previously ran In-Q-Tel, the CIA's venture capital arm.

AFF was founded in 2021, according to its website, "to build the companies, platforms, and capabilities that will generate once-in-a-generation returns for investors, while ensuring long-term economic competitiveness for the U.S. and its allies." Last year, the New York Times reported the techno-nationalist fund had met with U.S. lawmakers to request a $1 billion injection. AFF currently leads the Quad Investor Network, a White House-sponsored alliance of investors from the so-called Quad: a geopolitical bloc aimed at countering Chinese hegemony constituted by the U.S., Australia, India, and Japan.

AFF was founded last year with support from former Google CEO Eric Schmidt, whose closeness to Biden's government is attracting growing scrutiny and skepticism and investor Peter Thiel. Thiel and Schmidt, whose business interests in national security and defense both stand to profit immensely from war in the Pacific, have both advocated for a more hostile national stance toward China.

Schmidt is particularly dedicated to China alarmism, having spent much of his post-Google career thus far drumming up anti-China tensions; first at the National Security Commission on Artificial Intelligence, which he chaired, and today through his new think tank, the Special Competitive Studies Project, which regularly depicts China as a direct threat to the United States.[51]

There is too much information in the above article to digest properly—for example, why does the CIA own a venture capital arm? We can simply take away that there are grand chess games at the highest levels of agencies, foundations and NGOs in coordination with government offices.

To achieve their desired outcome, Beast-lovers seem to plan schemes that create problems on purpose, then implement pre-determined solutions (i.e., win a war by starting a war). Big events like wars may begin with seemingly minor events aligning coincidentally, but they may be designed to look that way in a plan to control outcomes on a grand scale.

In his 2016 book *The Iron Curtain Over America*, John Beaty writes:

> Thus President Truman, Ambassador Marshall, and the State Department prepared the way for the fall of China to Soviet control. They sacrificed Chiang, who represented the Westernized and Christian element in China, and they destroyed a friendly government, which was potentially our strongest ally in the world ...[52]

He continues:

> Lieutenant General Albert C. Wedemeyer who had served as Commander-in-Chief

---

[51] Sam Biddle, "White House-Linked Venture Capital Fund Boasts China War Would Be Great for Business," The Intercept, February 23, 2023. https://theintercept.com/2023/02/03/china-americas-frontier-fund/.
[52] John Beaty, *The Iron Curtain Over America* (Paul Bondarovsky and Deuteronomy Books, 2016), p. 114.

of American forces in the Asian Theater and Special Representative of the President of the United States, transmitted his report, United States Relations with China, to the President. In the section entitled, "Implications of 'No Assitance' to China or Continuation of 'Wait and See' Policy," General Wedemeyer wrote:

"To advise at this time a policy of 'no assistance' to China would suggest the withdrawal of the United States Military and Naval Advisory Groups from China and it would be equivalent to cutting the ground from under the feet of the Chinese Government (that of Chiang Kai-shek). Removal of American assistance, without removal of Soviet assistance, would certainly lay the country open to eventual Communist domination. It would have repercussions in other parts of Asia, would lower American prestige in the Far East and would make easier the spread of Soviet influence and Soviet expansion not only in Asia but in other parts of the world."[53]

Secret Insurance Agents?

What do the CIA, the insurance firm AIG and China have in common? The Office of Strategic Services (OSS) of World War II was the precursor to the CIA, and AIG was founded in 1919 in Shanghai. Both had deep connections in China. Secret agents were sometimes insurance agents at that time.

> The men behind the insurance unit were OSS [today known as the CIA] head William "Wild Bill" Donovan and California-born insurance magnate Cornelius V. Starr.

---

[53] Beaty, *The Iron Curtain Over America*, p. 117.

Starr had started out selling insurance to Chinese in Shanghai in 1919 and, over the next 50 years, would build what is now American International Group, one of the biggest insurance companies in the world. He was forced to move his operation to New York in 1939, when Japan invaded China.

Starr sent insurance agents into Asia and Europe even before the bombs stopped falling and built what eventually became AIG, which today has its world headquarters in the same downtown New York building where the tiny OSS unit toiled in the deepest secrecy.

Starr died in 1968, but his empire endures. AIG is the biggest foreign insurance company in Japan. More than a third of its $40 billion in revenue last year came from the Far East theater that Starr helped carpet bomb and liberate.[54]

We should start to take note of the web of connections between organizations and agencies; for example, note also that Cornelius V. Starr began a large foundation. Richard Harris Smith's book *OSS: The Secret History of America's First Central Intelligence Agency*[55] provides extensive background about this period.

Trilaterals and Other Related NGO's

That the circumvention of freedom is being carried out piece by piece through a slow and methodical process has been openly

---

[54] Mark Fritz, "The Secret (Insurance) Agent Men," *Los Angeles Times*, September 22, 2000. www.latimes.com/archives/la-xpm-2000-sep-22-mn-25118-story.html.
[55] Richard Harris Smith, *OSS: The Secret History of America's First Central Intelligence Agency* (New York: Rowman and Littlefield, 2005).

admitted. When we look around, we see frogs being slowly boiled, with no awareness of the differences in temperature between today and 50–100 years ago. Edith Kermit Roosevelt, granddaughter of Theodore Roosevelt, stated:

> The word "Establishment" is a general term for the power elite in international finance, business, the professions and government, largely from the northeast, who wield most of the power regardless of who is in the White House. Most people are unaware of the existence of this "legitimate Mafia." Yet the power of the Establishment makes itself felt from the professor who seeks a foundation grant, to the candidate for a cabinet post or State Department job. It affects the nation's policies in almost every area.[56]

The Trilateral Commission was founded in the early 1970's for the following purpose.

> The objective of the Trilateral Commission is to foster discussion and cooperation among the core democratic industrialized areas of the world. David Rockefeller defined the Commission's primary focus as bringing "the best brains in the world to bear on the problems of the future."8
>
> In the 1970's the dominance of the United States in the world community and economy was diminishing and there was a sense that a new more equitable paradigm of international affairs would be needed to address global challenges…
> In many ways the origins of the Trilateral Commission stem from the reorganization and reconstruction of the political and

---

[56] Edith Kermit Roosevelt, "Elite Clique Holds Power in US," *Indianapolis News*, December 23, 1961, p. 6.

economic order following the resolution of World War II. The United Nations Monetary and Financial Conference held July 1-22, 1944 at the Washington Hotel in Bretton Woods, New Hampshire, commonly known as the Bretton Woods Conference, brought together delegates from all the allied nations to stabilize and regulate the international monetary and financial order. The Bretton Woods accords established the International Bank for Reconstruction and Development, the General Agreement on Tariffs and Trade (GATT) and the International Monetary Fund (IMF). A period of significant economic growth followed particularly in the regions of Western Europe and Japan where the redevelopment of infrastructure and the expansion of trade exports increased their relative economic power.

The exchange rate management system established at Bretton Woods, with the U.S. dollar as its benchmark, remained in place until 1971 when U.S. President Richard M. Nixon abolished the direct convertibility of the U.S. dollar to gold and in effect abandoned U.S. participation in the Bretton Woods system. In this period of rapid change, economic and financial instability and growing nationalist tendencies discouraging the open market system established at Bretton Woods, the Trilateral Commission was conceptualized and formulated.

In March 1972, speaking before Chase Bank investment forums in Montreal, London, Brussels and Paris, David Rockefeller called for "an international commission for peace and prosperity composed of private citizens drawn from the NATO countries and Japan to examine such vital fields as international trade and investment; environmental problems; control of crime and drugs; population control; and assistance to developing nations."1 Rockefeller considered Japan as an essential member of the international community and viewed a commission as a mechanism for including the Japanese in the international dialogue. While on an airplane headed to the Bilderberg group meeting in Belgium in April 1972, David Rockefeller spoke with a like-minded colleague Zbigniew Brzezinski, Director of the Research Institute on Communist Affairs, Columbia University. Two years earlier Brzezinski had published Between Two Ages: America's Role in the Technotronic Era in which he advocated that "a community of developed nations must eventually be formed if the world is to respond effectively to the increasingly serious crisis that in different ways now threatens both the advanced world and the Third World."[57]

What this basically means is that David Rockefeller and his "best brains in the world" cronies set off to control nations and peoples with the aid of government influence. Notice Brzezinski's use of the term "shaping" in the first Trilateral director's 1970 book, *Between Two Ages*:

> To sum up: Though the objective of shaping a community of the developed

---

[57] Description of the Trilateral Commission, *Trilateral Commission (North America) Records* (Sleepy Hollow, NY, Rockefeller Archive Center). https://dimes.rockarch.org/collections/2KaqPEr3JRZv5WBQsf9mKn

nations is less ambitious than the goal of
world government, it is more attainable,⁵⁸

Since his famous book was written a long time ago, we can compare his predictions with similar newer statements. Brzezinski attended *The State of the World Forum* in 1995 sponsored by the Gorbachev Foundation and stated these remarks to his fellow globalists (except for the non-globalist journalist who was there and reported this for us).

> Brzezinski: "Yet five years after the end of the century's greatest ideological struggle and five years before the onset of the next millennium," wailed the architect and first director of the Trilateral Commission, "the end of the ideological centrality in global politics has not ushered in a new world order.... We do not have a new world order. Instead we are facing growing doubts regarding the meaning of our era and regarding the shape of our future."
>
> "We cannot leap into world government in one quick step," Brzezinski told his audience, apparently ignoring Gorbachev's caution. Such a grand goal "requires a process of gradually expanding the range of democratic cooperation as well as the range of personal and national security, a widening, step by step, stone by stone, [of] existing relatively narrow zones of stability in the world of security and cooperation. In brief, the precondition for eventual globalization — genuine globalization — is progressive regionalization, because

---

[58] Zbigniew Brzezinski, *Between Two Ages; America's Role in the Technetronic Era* (New York, The Viking Press, 1970) p.308

thereby we move toward larger, more stable, more cooperative units."[59]

A global government does not deploy democracy because these elitists want to rule by technocracy. They will use democracy as a cover story, but it does not seem they believe in nation states, people's sovereignty or true democracy. At least one famous politician explained what the true intent of the Trilateral approach was at the time of its founding. I doubt Barry Goldwater attended CFR or Trilateral meetings. In his 1979 memoir *With No Apologies*, Senator Barry Goldwater exposed its agenda.

> In my view the Trilateral Commission represents a skillful, coordinated effort to seize control and consolidate the four centers of power—political, monetary, intellectual, and ecclesiastical,[60]

> What the Trilaterals truly intend is the creation of a worldwide economic power superior to the political governments of the nation-states involved. They believe the abundant materialism they propose to create will overwhelm existing differences. As managers and creators of the system they will rule the future.[61]

Another group to consider is the International Basic Economy Corporation, formed by Nelson Rockefeller.[62]

---

[59] William F. Jasper, Global Gorby, *The New American Magazine*, October 30, 1995. https://thenewamerican.com/world-news/europe/global-gorby/
[60] Barry M. Goldwater, *With No Apologies* (New York, Morrow, 1979) p.284
[61] Barry M. Goldwater, *With No Apologies*, p.285
[62] See Robert E. Bedingfield, "Eaton Joins Rockefellers to Spur Trade with Reds," *The New York Times*, January 16, 1967. www.nytimes.com/1967/01/16/archives/eaton-joins-rockefellers-to-spur-trade-with-reds-cleveland-and-new.html

> The International Basic Economy Corporation was founded in 1947 by Nelson Rockefeller to make investments in a variety of South American enterprises, including poultry raising, supermarkets, housing, agribusiness, and textiles. Beginning with a mere $3 million from the Rockefeller brothers, and $21 million from Standard Oil companies, IBEC today is a multinational conglomerate worth several hundred million dollars. It now has interests in the United States, Canada, Western Europe, Africa, and Asia as well as South America.[63]

The suggestion that Nelson Rockefeller could serve as vice president in Gerald Ford's administration came into question because of his family background. The subsequent investigation uncovered many holdings of the Rockefeller family. The *Probing the Rockefeller Fortune* report for the US Congress, November 1974 contains extensive information on Nelson Rockefeller's International Basic Economy Corporation (IBEC) and more about the Rockefellers in general.

Is Democracy Effective Today?

By its very nature, overwhelming evidence about the influence of the elites upon society is difficult to find. Not much is reported in the newspapers or channels that these elites own. It is necessary to continue dredging up what others have already found in original sources that have sometimes long lain dormant. Sometimes, they make statements in closed settings that some journalists report on but the system is set up in a way that places obstacles in the way of research. It is difficult to go against the gravy train of funding from foundations and government agencies.

---

[63] G. William Domhoff and Charles L. Schwartz, *Probing the Rockefeller Fortune*, report for the US Congress, November 1974. Available at www.ocf.berkeley.edu/~schwrtz/Rockefeller.html.

Martin Gilens and Benjamin I. Page did important work in publishing a study into the elites' influence over the political process and impact on public policy. It is no wonder that the funding from their research did not come from mostly individual donors and not large foundations; their study was published independently by the <u>American Political Science Association</u>. An extract is reproduced here.

> By directly pitting the predictions of ideal-type theories against each other within a single statistical model (using a unique data set that includes imperfect but useful measures of the key independent variables for nearly two thousand policy issues), we have been able to produce some striking findings. One is the nearly total failure of "median voter" and other Majoritarian Electoral Democracy theories. When the preferences of economic elites and the stands of organized interest groups are controlled for, the preferences of the average American appear to have only a minuscule, near-zero, statistically non-significant impact upon public policy.
>
> The failure of theories of Majoritarian Electoral Democracy is all the more striking because it goes against the likely effects of the limitations of our data. The preferences of ordinary citizens were measured more directly than our other independent variables, yet they are estimated to have the least effect.
>
> Nor do organized interest groups substitute for direct citizen influence, by embodying citizens' will and ensuring that their wishes prevail in the fashion postulated by theories of Majoritarian Pluralism. Interest groups do have substantial independent impacts on policy, and a few groups (particularly labor unions) represent

average citizens' views reasonably well. But the interest-group system as a whole does not.

Furthermore, the preferences of economic elites (as measured by our proxy, the preferences of "affluent" citizens) have far more independent impact upon policy change than the preferences of average citizens do ... they fairly often get the policies they favor, but only because those policies happen also to be preferred by **the economically elite citizens who wield the actual influence.**

We know that interest groups and policy makers themselves often devote considerable effort to shaping opinion. If they are successful, this might help explain the high correlation we find between elite and mass preferences. But it cannot have greatly inflated our estimate of average citizens' influence on policy making, which is near zero.

In the United States, our findings indicate, the majority does not rule. When a majority of citizens disagrees with economic elites or with organized interests, they generally lose. Moreover, because of the strong status quo bias built into the U.S. political system, even when fairly large majorities of Americans favor policy change, they generally do not get it.[64]

Research like this helps us to understand why many people have given up on voting or participating in government altogether. Maybe think tanks are working secretly to make us lose interest

---

[64] Martin Gilens and Benjamin I. Page, "Testing Theories of American Politics: Elites, Interest Groups, and Average Citizens," *Perspectives on Politics* 12(3) (2014), pp. 564–581; (emphasis added).

in politics; if we remain silent, we will be more susceptible to control through collectivist illusions.

Global Public-Private Partnerships

Public–private partnerships (PPPs) are stronger than the collective power of average people when it comes to influencing politics. PPPs often work outside the political process; however, global PPPs (known as G3Ps) are even more insidious.[65]

> The G3P controls global finance and the world's economy. It sets world, national and local policy (via global governance) and then promotes those policies using the mainstream media (MSM) corporations, which are also "partners" within the G3P.
>
> Often those policies are devised by the think tanks before being adopted by governments, which are also G3P partners. Government is the process of transforming G3P global governance into hard policy, legislation and law.
>
> Under our current model of Westphalian national sovereignty ... the government of one nation cannot make legislation or law in another. However, through global governance, the G3P creates policy initiatives at the global level, which then cascade down to people in every nation. This typically occurs via an intermediary policy distributor, such as the IMF or IPCC, and national government then enact the recommended policies.
>
> The policy trajectory is set internationally by the authorised definition of problems and their prescribed solutions. Once the G3P enforces the consensus

---

[65] For more information, see Iain Davis, "What Is the Global Public-Private Partnership," The Disillusioned Blogger, October 6, 2021. https://iaindavis.com/what-is-the-global-public-private-partnership/.

internationally, the policy framework is set. The G3P stakeholder partners then collaborate to ensure the desired policies are developed, implemented and enforced. This is the oft-quoted "international rules-based system."

In this way, the G3P controls many nations at once without having to resort to legislation. This has the added advantage of making any legal challenge to the decisions made by the most senior partners in the G3P (it is an authoritarian hierarchy) extremely difficult ...

In February 2000 researchers Kent Buse and Gill Walt of the George Institute for Global Health, wrote an official history of the development of the G3P concept. They suggested the G3P was a response to growing disillusionment in the UN project as a whole as well as an emerging realisation that global corporations were increasingly key to policy implementation.

Buse and Walt acknowledged why the G3P was such an enticing prospect for the global giants of banking, industry, finance and commerce:

"Shifting ideologies and trends in globalization have highlighted the need for closer global governance, an issue for both private and public sectors. We suggest that at least some of the support for G3Ps stems from this recognition, and a desire on the part of the private sector to be part of global regulatory decision-making processes."

... Trilateral Commission founder Zbigniew Brzezinski recognised how to make this approach easier to implement. In his 1970 book Between Two Ages: Americas Role In The Technetronic Era, he wrote:

"Though the objective of shaping a community of the developed nations is less ambitious than the goal of world government, it is more attainable."

... In 1987 the Commission published the Brundtland Report, also known as <u>Our Common Future</u>. Central to the idea of sustainable development, as outlined in the report, was population control (reduction). This policy decision to get rid of people won international acclaim and awards for the authors ...

Secretary-General Kofi Annan to the WEF in 1998, as marking the transition to a G3P-based global governance model:

"The United Nations has been transformed since we last met here in Davos. The Organization has undergone a complete overhaul that I have described as a 'quiet revolution.' ... A fundamental shift has occurred. The United Nations once dealt only with governments. By now we know that peace and prosperity cannot be achieved without partnerships involving governments, international organizations, the business community and civil society ... The business of the United Nations involves the businesses of the world.[66]

It takes money to realize the Beast's world order. Average people in the USA have neither a sufficiently strong voice nor the funding to put up a good fight against the well-planned systems in place. Big NGOs, foundations, and government agencies are working together, and they also working closely with private

---

[66] Iain Davis, "What Is the Global Public-Private Partnership."

central banks and their backers. The next chapter looks at how banking constrains our lives, perhaps more than anything else.

Chapter 3: The Power of Central Banks and the Banking System

> *"It is well enough that people of the nation do not understand our banking and monetary system, for if they did, I believe there would be a revolution before tomorrow morning."*
>
> Henry Ford[1]

The Federal Reserve Corporation

We have examined how the Federal Reserve works with BlackRock. A 2022 paper describes the need for the Federal Reserve and the US government to collaborate more closely in the management of the economy even though they are completely separate entities.

> The recent fiscal interventions in response to the COVID pandemic have altered the private sector's beliefs about the fiscal framework, accelerating the recovery, but also determining an increase in fiscal inflation. This increase in inflation could not have been averted by simply tightening monetary policy. The conquest of post-pandemic inflation requires mutually consistent monetary and fiscal policies to avoid fiscal stagflation.
>
> Following the COVID pandemic, the United States, like many other countries, has implemented robust fiscal interventions. We have shown that these policy interventions facilitated the quick

---

[1] Henry Ford, as retold by Representative Charles G. Binderup of Nebraska. *Social Justice*, April 19, 1937, p. 10. www.unz.com/print/SocialJustice-1937apr19-00010

rebound observed after the pandemic recession. At the same time, they also contributed to the surge in fiscal inflation. Increasing rates, by itself, would not have prevented the recent surge in inflation, given that large part of the increase was due to a change in the perceived policy mix. In fact, increasing rates without the appropriate fiscal backing could result in fiscal stagflation. Instead, conquering the post-pandemic inflation requires **mutually consistent monetary and fiscal policies** providing a clear path for both the desired inflation rate and debt sustainability.[2]

In publishing this Working Paper, the Chicago Fed implies that the US Federal Reserve cannot control the economy by itself, since it does not control fiscal policies issued by the government. It states the need to coordinate with the government to achieve the best results. The use of separate power centers not only better serves to obscure strategy, but the method might also help keep the Beast in control. We can consider that no single actor besides the Beast controls all plans.

Congressman Wright Patman, former chairman of the House Banking Committee, said the following in a 1967 Joint Economic Committee session in Congress.

> We have a lot of confusion in that field, as you know. It occurs to me that we have reached the point when we must decide whether elected representatives of the people, like the president, should represent the people or whether unelected representatives of the people, who really have no obligation directly to the people, and the people are helpless to

---

[2] Francesco Bianchi and Leonardo Melosi, *Inflation as a Fiscal Limit*, Working Paper, Federal Reserve Bank of Chicago, August 19, 2022. (emphasis added) www.chicagofed.org/publications/working-papers/2022/2022-37.

> hold them accountable, should make these decisions.
>
> They can hold the president accountable, because he must seek reelection, or election if he wants to, but the members of the Federal Reserve Board, the unelected officials, can't be dealt with by the people if they make a mistake. The people are just helpless. So in effect, don't we have two governments here in Washington? ... We have one that is operated by elected representatives of the people ... but we have another government here which seems to have much more power sometimes than the one elected by the people; the government that controls our monetary affairs. I don't think they legally have the power to do it.
>
> My personal opinion is they have just seized that power. It was never intended to give it to them.[3]

Do we imagine that the two governments collaborate equally, or is one side mightier than the other? If the Beast is really in control, then banks and governments take orders from outside of their power centers. Perhaps the Beast keeps the management of banks, corporations and governments separate so that no single actor ever becomes too dominant.

Who controls the monetary system, if not the Fed? Absolute Fed control seems unlikely, because the monetary system is directly related to other systems, like fiscal policies. We should also understand that the entire monetary system is based on debt; as is evident from the dire situation we currently face, neither can the Fed control debt.

---

[3] Joint Economic Committee, *The 1967 Economic Report of the President*, US Congress, February 15, 16, and 17, 1967, pp. 511–512. https://fraser.stlouisfed.org/files/docs/historical/jec/jec_hearing_1967_economic_report_p3_19670215.pdf.

> If all the bank loans were paid, no one could have a bank deposit, and there would not be a dollar of coin or currency in circulation. This is a staggering thought. We are completely dependent on the commercial banks. Someone has to borrow every dollar we have in circulation, cash, or credit. If the banks create ample synthetic money we are prosperous; if not, we starve. We are absolutely without a permanent money system. When one gets a complete grasp of the picture, the tragic absurdity of our hopeless situation is almost incredible—but there it is ... our present civilization may collapse unless it is widely understood and the defects remedied very soon.[4]

That the Fed alone cannot control the monetary system seems obvious. Hemphill's remarks are a rare admission. The Federal Reserve operates on a system that is susceptible to being crushed under the immense load of debt we now have. It can be likened to a parasite that feeds off its host for a while, then kills it off when it no longer serves its purpose.

> There are only two groups of people who believe in infinite growth: mainstream economists and people awaiting the arrival of the Kurzweilian "singularity", when the merger of biological and nonbiological entities will create immortal software-based humans.
>
> Kenneth Boulding, who headed the American Economic Association in 1968, offered a pungent take on this point of view: "Anyone who believes in indefinite

---

[4] Robert H. Hemphill, *National Economy and the Banking System of the United States*, US Senate, Document no. 23, 1939, p. 102. https://archive.org/details/NationalEconomyAndTheBankingSystemOfTheUnitedStates/page/n107/mode/2up?q=concentrated. Hemphill was a former credit manager of the Federal Reserve Bank of Atlanta.

growth in anything physical, on a physically finite planet, is either mad or an economist."[5]

There is no infinite printing press. The debt machine can't and won't continue.

In the meantime, the Fed has immense power, even if it won't be able to sustain itself indefinitely. It continues to maintain influence over governments here and abroad. Congressman Louis T. McFadden warned of this very issue way back in 1932.

> Every effort has been made by the Federal Reserve Board to conceal its power but the truth is the Federal Reserve Board has usurped the government of the United States. It controls everything here and it controls all our foreign relations. It makes and breaks governments at will.[6]

The US government does not have any control over monetary policy. Former Chairman of the Federal Reserve Alan Greenspan confirmed the separation of the Fed and the US government with a direct answer to this important question.

> Well, first of all, the Federal Reserve is an independent agency, and that means, basically, that there is no other agency of government which can overrule actions that we take. So long as that is in place and there is no evidence that the administration or the Congress or anybody else is requesting that we do things other than what we think is the appropriate

---

[5] Vaclav Smil, "Infinite Growth Is a Pipe Dream," *Financial Times*, August 8, 2019. www.ft.com/content/db0a7be2-b2d2-11e9-b2c2-1e116952691a.
[6] Louis T. McFadden, speech in US Congress, Congressional Record, June 10, 1932, location 12602. https://archive.org/stream/pdfy-ed9k_Ns-KZhp3WOn/Congressional-Record-June-10-1932-Louis-T-McFadden_djvu.txt.

thing, then what the relationships are don't, frankly, matter.[7]

Greenspan emphasized that the US government cannot control the Fed, yet he did not elaborate on who does. Perhaps historian Carroll Quigley provides us with the best answer to this question, as involving a relationship between central banks and merchant banks.

> It must not be felt that these heads of the world's chief central banks were themselves substantive powers in world finance. They were not. Rather, they were the technicians and agents of the dominant investment bankers of their own countries, who had raised them up and were perfectly capable of throwing them down. The substantive financial powers of the world were in the hands of these investment bankers (also called "international" or "merchant" bankers) who renamed largely behind the scenes in their own unincorporated banks. These formed a system of international cooperation and national dominance which was more private, more powerful, and more secret than that of their agents in the central banks.[8]

In summary, central banks like the Federal Reserve are owned and controlled by private bankers. This means private banks work "behind the scenes" to control national monetary policies. Even where a central bank coordinates with a government on

---

[7] "Alan Greenspan - Federal Reserve Is an Independent Agency - In Their Own Words - 2007-09-18," YouTube, user RealRealFruit, uploaded August 26, 2023. www.youtube.com/watch?v=QPc5QgBRv9w&ab_channel=RealReal Fruit.

[8] Carroll Quigley, *Tragedy and Hope: A History of the World in Our Time* (New York: MacMillan, 1966), pp. 326–327.

some level, hidden interactions between central and private banks take place concurrently.

Perhaps this secrecy has always been the plan, since banks' power over the people would be utterly rejected if people knew about it, as Henry Ford said. It is in the interest of the owners of private banks to make it seem as though the Federal Reserve has an exclusive and transparent relationship with the government regarding monetary and fiscal policies.

The Formation of the Federal Reserve

We should go back in time to identify that while there may have always been legal separation between entities, there is nonetheless an alliance between the actors that comprise the Beast.

Frank A. Vanderlip, president of the Rockefeller-owned National City Bank and a key actor in the establishment of the Federal Reserve, recalled many years after the event about having made a secret trip that led to the formation of the Fed.

> Despite my views about the value to society of greater publicity for the affairs of corporations, there was an occasion, near the close of 1910, when I was as secretive—indeed as furtive—as any conspirator.
>
> Discovery, we knew, simply must not happen, or else all our time and effort would be wasted. If it were to be exposed that our particular group had got together and written a banking bill, that bill would have no chance whatever of passage by Congress.
>
> I do not feel it is any exaggeration to speak of our secret expedition to Jekyl Island as the occasion of the actual conception of

what eventually became the Federal Reserve System.⁹

The single person most responsible for allowing the Fed mess we find ourselves in was, in fact, President Woodrow Wilson. He was the key needed to sign the Federal Reserve Act of 1913 into law. The following quote, which is included in the Senate records, records Wilson's disgust as he later, and regretfully, signed the Act into law.

> A great industrial nation is controlled by its system of credit. Our system of credit is concentrated. The growth of the nation, therefore, and all our activities are in the hands of a few men. We have come to be one of the worst ruled, one of the most completely controlled and dominated Governments in the civilized world, no longer a Government by free opinion, no longer a Government by conviction and the vote of the majority, but a Government by the opinion and duress of a small group of dominant men.¹⁰

Saying that Woodrow Wilson had deep regrets is an understatement. The Feds, with its private owners, has certainly contributed its share to the desperate times we find ourselves in. However, it gets worse.

What Is Publicly Known about the Federal Reserve?

Regarding what is publicly known about the Federal Reserve, it is worth referring to a 1976 congressional study on corporate and

---

⁹ Frank A. Vanderlip, "From Farm Boy to Financier," *The Saturday Evening Post*, February 9, 1935, p. 70.
www.saturdayeveningpost.com/reprints/from-farm-boy-to-financier/.
¹⁰ Robert L. Owen, *National Economy and the Banking System of the United States* (Washington, DC: Government Printing Office, 1939) p.100.
https://archive.org/details/NationalEconomyAndTheBankingSystemO fTheUnitedStates/page/n105/mode/2up

banking influence in government. The report is worth viewing in full, as it presents visual representations of the relationships between key groups and actors in the sector.

> We present as our Chart V page 49 of this study, showing the interlocking directorates of David Rockefeller. As our Chart VI we reproduce page 55 of this study, showing the interlocking directorates of Frank R. Milliken, one of the Class C directors of the Federal Reserve Bank of New York. Chart VI presents all the main personages in our story of the Jekyll Island Conference: Citibank, J. P. Morgan and Company, Kuhn Loeb and Company, and many related firms.

> As Chart VII we reproduce page 53 of this study, showing the interlocking directorates of another Class C director of the Federal Reserve Bank of New York, Alan Pifer. As president of the Carnegie Corporation of New York, he interlocked with the J. Henry Schroder Trust Company, the J. Henry Schroder Banking Corporation, the Rockefeller Center, Inc., the Federal Reserve Bank of Boston, the Equitable Life Assurance Society (J.P. Morgan), and others.[11]

This August 1976 study from the House Committee on Banking, Currency, and Housing presents all our main cast of personages, functioning today just as they did in 1914.

> The three Class C Directors are appointed by the Board of Governors as

---

[11] House Committee on Banking, Currency, and Housing, *Federal Reserve Directors: A Study of Corporate and Banking Influence* (Washington, DC: Government Printing Office, 1976).

representatives of the public interest as a whole.[12]

Many of the companies on these tables, as mentioned earlier, have multiple interlocks to the Federal Reserve System. First Bank Systems; Southeast Banking Corporation; Federated Department Stores; Westinghouse Electric Corporation; Proctor and Gamble; Alcoa; Honeywell, Inc.; Kennecott Copper; Owens-Corning Fiberglass; all have two or more director ties to district or branch banks.

In Summary, the Federal Reserve directors are apparently representatives of a small elite group which dominates much of the economic life of this nation.[13]

The Bank of International Settlements

Banking interlocks and connections are very elaborate. Yet there is potentially a single power center to the central banks of the world, in the form of the Bank of International Settlements (BIS), headquartered in Switzerland. The BIS is the international bank of the national banks.

Most people had never heard of the BIS until two journalists from *The New York Times* and *The Washington Post* reported on its workings in a series of interviews with representatives. We can see that the BIS had obtained significant worldwide influence by the time of these articles, written between 1995 and 1998.

An August 5, 1995 article by Keith Bradsher of *The New York Times* stated:

> In a small Swiss city sits an international organization so obscure and secretive ...

---

[12] House Committee on Banking, Currency, and Housing, *Federal Reserve Directors*, p. 34.
[13] House Committee on Banking, Currency, and Housing, *Federal Reserve Directors*

> Control of the institution, the Bank for International Settlements, lies with some of the world's most powerful and least visible men: the heads of 32 central banks, officials able to shift billions of dollars and alter the course of economies at the stroke of a pen.[14]

On June 27, 1998, John M. Berry of *The Washington Times* wrote about "the financial barons who control the world's supply of money" in an article titled, "Banking's Key Players."

> The 13 members of this economic cabal met on the glass-walled 18th floor of the round headquarters tower of an obscure institution known as the Bank for International Settlements.
>
> The members of this secretive group are the governors of the central banks …
>
> All but 16 percent of the BIS shares are owned by its member central banks. The remainder are in private hands, as the result of the United States's failure in 1930 to pay for its shares; they were instead acquired by a group of American banks, which later sold them, mostly to individuals in Europe …
>
> "The BIS … is now too valuable to the Federal Reserve in carrying out its statutory responsibilities for the [Fed] not to be a full participant in BIS institutional deliberations," Greenspan told Congress …

---

[14] Keith Bradsher, "Obscure Global Bank Moves Into the Light," *The New York Times*, August 5, 1995, p. 31. www.nytimes.com/1995/08/05/business/international-business-obscure-global-bank-moves-into-the-light.html?searchResultPosition=19.

> The Bank for International Settlements ... is a central bank for central banks.[15]

We know little about who owns and controls the BIS, since the shares are private. Countries like the USA need to be in alliance with it because of the BIS's influence over the Fed. The BIS is part of the Beast's network of control. There are many global owners of this organization, demonstrating the Beast's need for an alignment of influential people to accomplish greater global control.

For further context, we can again look to Carroll Quigley.

> In addition to these pragmatic goals, the powers of financial capitalism had another far-reaching aim, nothing less than to create a world system of financial control in private hands able to dominate the political system of each country and the economy of the world as a whole. This system was to be controlled in a feudalist fashion by the central banks of the world acting in concert, by secret agreements arrived at in frequent private meetings and conferences. The apex of the system was to be the Bank for International Settlements in Basle, Switzerland, a private bank owned and controlled by the world's central banks which were themselves private corporations. Each central bank, in the hands of men like Montagu Norman of the Bank of England, Benjamin Strong of the New York Federal Reserve Bank, Charles Rist of the Bank of France, and Hjalmar Schacht of the Reichsbank, sought to dominate its government by its ability to control Treasury loans, to

---

[15] John M. Berry, "Banking's Key Players," *The Washington Post*, June 27, 1998. www.washingtonpost.com/archive/business/1998/06/28/bankings-key-players/88403c84-42de-445f-8e49-7ddd6b125e8f/.

manipulate foreign exchanges, to influence the level of economic activity in the country, and to influence cooperative politicians by subsequent economic rewards in the business world.[16]

At least the BIS did not aim to control the entire earth with everything in it—only governments and the monetary system. It seems we may keep control of our football teams and garden clubs.

It is worth turning here to the BIS's own stated goals, particularly a BIS description about the future of banking and money. BIS General Manager Agustín Carstens said the following in a 2022 speech on data, digitalization and digital currencies.

> Some say that in the future, money and finance will be provided by just a few big tech corporations. Others dream of a decentralised system in which blockchains and algorithms replace people and institutions. And maybe, all of this will take place in the Metaverse ...
>
> My main message today is simple: the soul of money belongs neither to a big tech nor to an anonymous ledger. The soul of money is trust. So the question becomes: which institution is best placed to generate trust? I will argue that central banks have been and continue to be the institutions best placed to provide trust in the digital age. This is also the best way to ensure an efficient and inclusive financial system to the benefit of all ...
>
> Like the legal system, this trust is a public good. Maintaining it is crucial for the effective functioning of societies ... the vision of an open and global monetary

---

[16] Quigley, *Tragedy and Hope*, p. 277.

> and financial system that harnesses technology for the benefit of all ...
>
> Imagine a global network of CBDCs [Central Bank Digital Currencies]. Different central banks would design and issue a new form of public money, tailored to their economies and societies' preferences.[17]

This may sound okay at first glance; trust is an important aspect of money. However, there is a risk that central banks will take more control via technological means. It seems that we are to trust the banks, but that they will not trust us or governments. They want "absolute control" without transparency or accountability. In the words of Carstens:

> We don't know who's using a $100 bill today and we don't know who's using a 1,000 peso bill today. The key difference with the CBDC is the central bank will have absolute control on the rules and regulations that will determine the use of that expression of central bank liability, and also we will have the technology to enforce that.[18]

Disturbingly, the BIS openly admits to market manipulation, verifying the claims of Carroll Quigley. This is one proof that private bankers constrain our ability to realize a free market. The BIS pamphlet *Promoting Global Monetary and Financial Stability through International Cooperation* clarifies who is in control of global finance.

---

[17] Agustín Carstens, "Digital Currencies and the Soul of Money," speech at the conference Data, Digitalization, the New Finance and Central Bank Digital Currencies: The Future of Banking and Money, Goethe University Institute for Law and Finance, January 18, 2022.

[18] Quoted in Samuel Wan, "The BIS Wants 'Absolute Control' of Your Money Via Central Bank Digital Currencies," Bitcoinist, 2021. https://bitcoinist.com/the-bis-wants-absolute-control-of-your-money-via-central-bank-digital-currencies/.

Banking services

We offer financial services exclusively to central banks, monetary authorities and international organisations, mainly to assist them in the management of their foreign exchange assets.

As an institution owned and governed by central banks, we are well placed to understand the needs of reserve managers – their primary focus on safety and liquidity, as well as the evolving need to diversify their exposures and obtain a competitive return.

To meet those needs, we provide credit, gold and foreign exchange intermediation, and asset management services, while administering our own capital. An integrated risk management function ensures that financial and operational risks are properly measured and controlled.[19]

The Financial Stability Board promotes international financial stability by coordinating the work of national financial authorities and international standard-setting bodies as they develop regulatory, supervisory and other policies.[20]

Notice how the BIS states that it is owned and governed by central banks, then in the next breath that it also uses its own funds and gives advice to central banks. This is like Vanguard owning a large chunk of BlackRock. We know neither the whole story behind these groups, nor whether they are driven by cronyism or secrecy.

---

[19] Bank for International Settlements, *Promoting Global Monetary and Financial Stability through International Cooperation*, July 2024, p. 3, (emphasis added). www.bis.org/about/profile_en.pdf.
[20] BIS, *Promoting Global Monetary and Financial Stability through International Cooperation*, p. 4.

> [The last objective of the BIS is] the provision of international credits and joint efforts to **influence asset prices** (especially gold and foreign exchange) in circumstances where this might be thought useful.[21]

Monetary manipulation is another way to say "influence asset prices" in this case. These central banks regulate and supervise the global banking system with little government oversight, having instead set up their own governance. (The watchdog Gold Anti-Trust Action Committee provides more information about the BIS and details such as gold price manipulation.[22])

At certain points in history, the balance between freedom and regulation has been realized. It does not appear that we are currently living in such a time. It is not hard to imagine society coming under yet greater control from even fewer unelected elites. We saw evidence that this is happening around the world during the recent pandemic. We are on a fast track back to a feudal-type system, and technology will most likely accelerate the movement toward issuing greater debt while we let them control it.

The Digital Currency Monetary Authority

There is a new sheriff in town: the Digital Currency Monetary Authority (DCMA). This group works with the BIS and the International Monetary Fund (IMF) to promote and help implement the usage of digital currency globally. Let's investigate the DCMA, starting with a paper it published on April 19, 2023.

---

[21] Bank for International Settlements, *Past and Future of Central Bank Cooperation: Policy Panel Discussion*, BIS Paper No. 27, February 2006, p. 2, (emphasis added). www.bis.org/publ/bppdf/bispap27.pdf.
[22] Gold Anti-Trust Action Committee, "BIS Official: Central Banks Cooperate to Influence Gold Price," March 9, 2006. www.gata.org/node/4279.

Bitcoin inspired a generation of cryptographic store of value and medium of exchange innovations intended to disrupt and to circumvent regulated banking and financial institutions.

The International Monetary Fund (IMF) recently published a report on the potential risks of crypto assets to the international monetary system and recommended not to provide legal tender status to crypto assets. The IMF did not consider the possibility of a new class of cryptographic innovations conceived to not only support but to strengthen the monetary sovereignty of the international banking system (i.e., Crypto 2.0).

The Digital Currency Monetary Authority (DCMA) is a world leader in the advocacy of digital currency innovations for governments and monetary authorities and has innovated a best-in-class design for international Central Bank Digital Currency (CBDC) leveraging a digital economic union. The IMF states it has a mandate to provide economic and financial stability to its member states. There are some noted encumbrances in the current international monetary system that continually challenge emerging markets, and even some advanced economies, in sustaining their monetary sovereignty.[23]

Some interesting statements are made in this white paper. To paraphrase, *Bitcoin and unregulated crypto are bad; digital*

---

[23] Digital Currency Monetary Authority, *A Best-in-Class Money Commodity for Strengthening Monetary Sovereignty with a Digital Economic Union*, April 19, 2023. https://dcma.io/whitepaper.html.

currency controlled by member states, the IMF, and central banks is good.

Robin Hood then comes along and bans CDBC's in the USA. It sounds interesting at first but then the Trump administration and Congress presented a Stablecoin plan to tie this digital currency with the USD and US Treasuries to keep the debt machine running. This led to the GENIUS Act being signed into law on July 18, 2025. The Federal Reserve is part of the GENIUS Act so banning CBDC's to favor a Stablecoin does not change the fact that the Fed is still in control of monetary policy (See the definition of "Board" in the GENIUS Act).[24]

At the time of writing this book, the BIS and the Trump administration seem to be in a battle over control of monetary policy. What is a Stablecoin you might ask? The BIS provides their answer and recommendations.

> Stablecoins are digital assets designed to maintain a stable value relative to a reference asset, such as fiat currencies. The market is dominated by stablecoins that are pegged to the US dollar, with backing assets composed mostly of dollar-denominated short-term instruments such as US Treasury securities. As of March 2025, their combined assets under management exceeded $200 billion, surpassing the short-term US securities holdings of major foreign investors. In 2024, they purchased $40 billion of US Treasury bills, similar to the largest US government money market funds and larger than most foreign purchases. Their rapid growth in recent years raises questions about the impact on the markets they invest in, with potential broader implications for monetary policy and financial stability.

---

[24] https://www.congress.gov/bill/119th-congress/senate-bill/394/text/is

> ...results suggest that stablecoins have already established themselves as significant players in Treasury markets. Their growth blurs the lines between cryptocurrency and traditional finance and carries implications for monetary policy, transparency of stablecoin reserves and financial stability – particularly during periods of market stress.[25]

A prediction by the author – the BIS will win. This will probably be due to the fact that hardly anybody in the USA saw the Unicoin coming. The GENIUS Act will allow the USD Stablecoin market to be aligned with this new nemesis.

Things will get worse with this 'Universal Monetary Unit' ('Unicoin').[26] It is the first crypto to have been created with an official monetary policy in mind. Basically, it is *one coin to rule them all*, pulled from the forge by Sauron at Mount Doom.

As has been explicitly announced by BIS general manager Agustín Carstens, there is a planned transition away from cash and toward digital-only currency. We can imagine a day when we will not be able to choose whether we want to pay with cash, credit, or debit; the only options will be digital debit or credit, with the accompanying digital controls. As pointed out in the DCMA's paper, artificial intelligence (AI) will handle everything for us, so please do not worry.

> In society, physical cash and electronic cash are the two forms of legal tender recognized by the international monetary system. With the advent of CBDC, both societal forms of legal cash will be

---

[25] Stablecoins and Safe Asset Prices, May 2025. www.bis.org/publ/work1270.htm
[26] DCMA, "Universal Monetary Unit is a Continuous Demand Money Commodity and an International Payment Currency." https://dcma.io/universal-monetary-unit.html.

represented in a cryptographic form, called Digital Cash...[27]

The paper elaborates further.

> Electronic Cash is transacted through the regulated banking system, requiring KYC, AML, and other requirements. Physical Cash can transact outside the banking system privately between two parties. Many citizens fear with the advent of retail CBDC, governments may take away private physical cash money and incorporate surveillance capabilities in retail CBDC.[28]

Citizens may fear surveillance or more government control? I do not care as much if someone is watching my internet searches, listening to my phone calls, or tracking my transactions, but I think the restrictions on making transactions is a bigger problem. It seems the war on cash will begin sooner than we thought, and will occur through a multi-phased approach.

> The DCMA suggests CBDC will augment the banking system and must co-exist and interact with legacy banking. A major function of both central banking and retail and commercial banking is the creation or minting of money. Central banks create money through purchasing government bonds from banks. Retail and commercial banks create money by issuing loans to consumers and businesses. The DCMA does not suspect this foundational layer of the banking system will be displaced by

---

[27] DCMA, *A Best-in-Class Money Commodity for Strengthening Monetary Sovereignty with a Digital Economic Union*, p. 10. https://dcma.io/whitepaper.html.
[28] DCMA, *A Best-in-Class Money Commodity for Strengthening Monetary Sovereignty with a Digital Economic Union*, p. 11. https://dcma.io/whitepaper.html.

> CBDC. In the Unicoin Network, we leverage existing traditional banking legacy systems for the creation of money, then enable to capability to transfer between legacy fiat bank accounts and CBDC bank accounts at both the central bank and commercial banking levels.[29]

The first step in the transition away from the legacy system will be a linking of cash transactions to the CBDC network, as outlined above. Central bank circuits and commercial bank circuits will be wired together with Unicoin for the creation of all money.

The BIS has confirmed the stated plans of the DCMA. BIS manager Carstens gave a keynote speech to the Monetary Authority of Singapore (MAS) on February 22, 2023, in which he stated:

> Around the world, central banks are exploring how to give money new capabilities ... But to fully realise the transformative potential of these new financial technologies, we need some way to bring them all together. In this regard, there is great promise in developing the idea of a "unified ledger" with a common programming environment. A unified ledger is a digital infrastructure with the potential to combine the monetary system with other registries of real and financial claims. It would need to be a public-private partnership with a clear division of roles, and where the central bank is tasked with underpinning the trust in money.

---

[29] DCMA, *A Best-in-Class Money Commodity for Strengthening Monetary Sovereignty with a Digital Economic Union*, p. 12. https://dcma.io/whitepaper.html.

Innovation and the future of the monetary system.[30]

The DCMA white paper presents a vision for a second phase involving linking traditional cash to its own form of digital cash. Remember that while the first phase consists of the use of digital cash while maintaining traditional cash payment systems, phase two will potentially allow governments to merge and trace all transactions if they so desire. Feel free to research this on the DCMA website. The key point is that digital cash is "programmable," and can be adapted to fit the plans of the central banks:

> [F]ull-service banking also requires more than just cash ledgers. It requires dozens of assets and liabilities ledgers for the transfer of money. Hence, ideally multiple accounting ledgers, beyond cash, should be supported by CBDC ledger technology. Even with cash, it can be nuanced into central banking cash and commercial banking cash with even further subclassifications of cash for accounting purposes.[31]

The white paper then describes the broad programmable nature of "digital ledger technology" (DLT).

> The Unicoin Network has published a money servicing DLT with over one hundred commands that could be configured to the needs of each central bank or retail or commercial bank. Levering these commands, unlimited digital banking, digital trade, and digital

---

[30] Agustín Carstens, "Innovation and the Future of the Money System," keynote speech to the Monetary Authority of Singapore, February 22, 2023. www.bis.org/speeches/sp230222.htm.
[31] DCMA, *A Best-in-Class Money Commodity for Strengthening Monetary Sovereignty with a Digital Economic Union*, p. 15, (emphasis added). https://dcma.io/whitepaper.html.

payment applications could be built without the need for any smart contracts.[32]

Of course, this system will be international.

> [Imagine] a global customer identification registry that is decentralized in every central banking jurisdiction so customer information is not passed out of the country and is not shared with any other bank. This global, yet decentralized, registry would create a unique global identifier for every person and entity for every bank account opened in the international monetary system, or at least, the participating member banks. So, if a banking customer in the United States have [sic] the same or statistically similar KYC information as banking customer in the Cayman Islands, the global KYC registry would generate the same globally unique identifier (GUID) for each customer. Although the customer is transacting in two distinct banking systems, if both banks are members of the same CBDC network or digital economic union, the GUID will be associated with all their transactions enabling network monitoring technology to monitor customers on a global basis.[33]

The white paper also provides details about why the DCMA dislikes deregulated crypto. It probably has something to do with maintaining the reserve banking system, and not wanting regular people to control how they want to trade, buy, sell, etc.

---

[32] DCMA, *A Best-in-Class Money Commodity for Strengthening Monetary Sovereignty with a Digital Economic Union*, p. 18. https://dcma.io/whitepaper.html.

[33] DCMA, *A Best-in-Class Money Commodity for Strengthening Monetary Sovereignty with a Digital Economic Union*, p. 22. https://dcma.io/whitepaper.html.

> Tokenized Deposits are a fundamental foundation to building block of a CBDC transaction network. Tokenized deposits are implemented the same as banking deposits and should fall under the same bank regulatory framework and protections for all legal tender deposits. Cryptocurrencies and stablecoins are not tokenized deposits as they are issued and governed by private sector companies and pose a threat to the future of banking because of the outflow of capital leaving the international monetary banking system. The banking industry views tokenized deposits as a safer solution than privately governed stablecoins. With tokenized deposits the funds remain on the balance sheet of the depositing institution and can be monetized according for fractional reserve lending and other banking transactions.[34]

The DCMA's bottom line appears a little later in the paper. It wants to make virtual gold, with people trusting the officially backed currencies over cryptos like Bitcoin.

> In the 1960s, the United States did not have enough gold to cover the dollars in circulation outside the United States, leading to fears of a run that could wipe out U.S. gold reserves. Following failed efforts to save the system, President Richard Nixon suspended the dollar's convertibility to gold in August 1971, marking the beginning of the end of the Bretton Woods exchange rate system. Now that the world has learned the economic strains the floating foreign

---

[34] DCMA, *A Best-in-Class Money Commodity for Strengthening Monetary Sovereignty with a Digital Economic Union*, p. 23. https://dcma.io/whitepaper.html.

exchange rate system is imposing on mainly least developed emerging markets, perhaps it is time to consider another refinement to the money system to reinforce the IMF's commitment to its economic stability mandate to member states. Absent a monetary policy change to the foundational international monetary system, complementing the money system with a monetary commodity that could sustainably mitigate against local currency depreciation and inflation, like gold has been periodically adopted, seems to be a plausible alternative ...

Some economists and investment analysts advocate Bitcoin as digital gold and purport it could serve as a hedge against inflation. Bitcoin has not proven to meet this requirement because it lacks fundamental underlying monetary utility to drive sustained usage in the economy. Further, Bitcoin lacks proper governance and monetary policies that could positively impact its performance in the financial markets. A Digital Economic Union is the perfect innovation to realizing a "digital gold" money commodity. In a digital economic union, a monetary commodity, such as UMU, is traded as a single asset and not traded in financial markets as a currency pair against other currencies.[35]

The DCMA and BIS must think we are naïve. While they might claim that each transaction will have an anonymous identifier, everything will still go through a centralized system—which they

---

[35] DCMA, *A Best-in-Class Money Commodity for Strengthening Monetary Sovereignty with a Digital Economic Union*, p. 35. https://dcma.io/whitepaper.html.

will control. This will not be stated openly. Get ready for programmable currency, coming soon to a city near you.

The Financial Stability Board, headquartered in Switzerland, has something to say about who will control decentralized stablecoin currencies.

> **Recommendation 1: Regulatory powers and tools**
>
> Authorities should have and utilise the appropriate powers and tools, and adequate resources to regulate, supervise, and oversee crypto-asset activities and markets, and enforce relevant laws and regulations effectively, as appropriate.[36]

In one wallet, the non-central-bank currencies will be highly regulated by many international and national parties, while in the other wallet, the central banks will regulate themselves. I do not think there will be much government oversight or audits.

The World Bank seems to have developed a means to accomplish the broad international goals of self-regulated digital currency: "fast payments."

> *Central banks typically play the role of overseer of payment systems (and very often the broader NPS). The overseer role is generally accompanied by a regulatory function. In some cases, depending on the institutional setting, this regulatory function may be shared with a different regulatory authority or performed independently by the*

---

[36] Financial Stability Board, *High-level Recommendations for the Regulation, Supervision and Oversight of Crypto-asset Activities and Markets: Final Report*, July 17, 2023. www.fsb.org/2023/07/high-level-recommendations-for-the-regulation-supervision-and-oversight-of-crypto-asset-activities-and-markets-final-report/.

> *latter. A fast payment arrangement is usually considered a critical national payment infrastructure. Therefore, the overseer puts in place a monitoring mechanism to try to ensure that it operates in a safe and efficient manner.*[37]

The World Bank does not hide anything here: the overseers and regulators of all transactions are mostly going to be the central banks. But how can they regulate themselves without oversight? We will simply allow it, that's how.

Yet it does give a stern warning in the same report to make us feel better about the control scheme.

> The central bank should seek to avoid any impression that it might use its role as overseer of private sector systems to support unfairly the operation of its payment systems.[38]

I don't feel any better but there is only one quote left. Finally, the option is laid out how central banks can work together with fast payments so there will be seamless integration to keep their scheme alive.

> As central banks continue to explore the development of central bank digital currencies (CBDCs), the interplay between CBDCs and fast payments is likely to receive further attention. A CBDC network

---

[37] World Bank, *Considerations and Lessons for the Development and Implementation of Fast Payment Systems*, main report, September 2021, p. 18.
https://fastpayments.worldbank.org/sites/default/files/2021-11/Fast%20Payment%20Flagship_Final_Nov%201.pdf.

[38] World Bank, *Considerations and Lessons for the Development and Implementation of Fast Payment Systems*, p. 19.
https://fastpayments.worldbank.org/sites/default/files/2021-11/Fast%20Payment%20Flagship_Final_Nov%201.pdf.

and fast payments do not necessarily have to compete. One potential option in this space would be using the FPS payment rails for CBDCs.³⁹

Insights into Banking

Let's now take some time to digest various insights into banking from the past two hundred years, in order to witness the warnings that—heeded or not—have led us to the place in which we find ourselves in today.

> When a Government, Bonaparte declared, is dependent for money upon bankers, they and not the leaders of that Government control the situation, since "the hand that gives is above the hand that takes."
>
> ...
>
> [Bonaparte's] Ambassador in London, Andréossy, warned him that — "In a country where the main interest is business, and where the merchant class is so prosperous, the Government has to appeal to the merchants for extraordinary funds and they have the right to insist that their interests should be considered in the policy which is adopted."⁴⁰

In a letter to John Taylor in 1816, Thomas Jefferson wrote:

---

³⁹ World Bank, *Considerations and Lessons for the Development and Implementation of Fast Payment Systems*, p. 70. https://fastpayments.worldbank.org/sites/default/files/2021-11/Fast%20Payment%20Flagship_Final_Nov%201.pdf

⁴⁰ R. McNair Wilson, *Monarchy or Money Power* (London: Eyre and Spottiswoode, 1934), chapter 9. Available at https://ia800507.us.archive.org/18/items/McNairWilsonRobertMonarchyOrMoneyPower/McNair_Wilson_Robert_-_Monarchy_or_money_power.pdf.

> And I sincerely believe with you, that banking establishments are more dangerous than standing armies.[41]

Quote from FDR:

> The real truth of the matter is, as you and I know, that a financial element in the larger centers has owned the government ever since the days of Andrew Jackson ...[42]

Quote from Sir Josiah Stamp, President of the Bank of England in the 1920's, and was the second richest man in Britain (who must have been drinking before his speech in 1927):

> But, if you want to continue to be the slave of the bankers and pay the cost of your own slavery, then let the bankers continue to create money and control credit.[43]

Here is another clear statement from a high level banker on November 11, 1927, *The Wall Street Journal* described the Bank of England's Montagu Norman as "the currency dictator of Europe." Norman stated:

> the Hegemony of World Finance should reign supreme over everyone, everywhere, as one whole super-national control mechanism.[44]

---

[41] Personal Letter from Thomas Jefferson to John Taylor, May 28, 1816. Quoted at:
https://founders.archives.gov/?q=%20Author%3A%22Jefferson%2C%20Thomas%22&s=1111311111&r=58&sr=taylor.
[42] Franklin D. Roosevelt, letter to Colonel House, November 21, 1933. Quoted at https://libquotes.com/franklin-d-roosevelt/quote/lbf4i8w.
[43] Josiah Stamp, Commencement Address to the University of Texas, 1927. Attributed to Josiah Stamp by Silas W. Adams in *The Legalized Crime of Banking* (1958).
http://libertytree.ca/quotes/Josiah.Stamp.Quote.69BB.
[44] John Hargrave, *Montagu Norman* (New York: Greystone Press, 1942).

Reginald McKenna, Chancellor of the Exchequer (a role at the head of the British Treasury), made a statement similar to Alan Greenspan's, in that government fiscal policies have an effect over, but do not control, monetary policies in the USA or the UK. It is reasonable to assume that the two entities need to coordinate on some level; however, he told truths in private that could not be mentioned in public.

> To define monetary policy in few words I should say that it is the policy which concerns itself with regulating the quantity of money. As I shall show later it is controlled by the Bank of England, but the action or requirements of the Government may seriously affect it.[45]

> In January, 1924, Reginald McKenna, who had been chancellor of the Exchequer in 1915–1916, as chairman of the board of the Midland Bank told its stockholders: "I am afraid the ordinary citizen will not like to be told that the banks can, and do, create money … And **they who control the credit of the nation direct the policy of Governments** and hold in the hollow of their hands the destiny of the people."[46]

Money from Nothing

We will start with a quote about the magic of money:

> The modern banking system manufactures "money" out of nothing; and the process

---

[45] Reginald McKenna, *Post-War Banking Policy* (Kingswood: The Windmill Press, 1928). https://ia903208.us.archive.org/19/items/1928-mckenna-postwar-banking-policy/1928%20McKenna%20%5BHT1%5D%20Post-War%20Banking%20Policy%20OCRe.pdf.
[46] Quigley, *Tragedy and Hope*, p.325, (emphasis added).

is, perhaps, the most, astounding piece of "sleight of hand" that was ever invented.[47]

Minnesota Congressman Charles Lindbergh, Sr. was strongly against the formation of the Fed; he petitioned against it in 1913 with sound logic during debates in Congress, but most congressmen did not heed his warnings about the immense power being granted to this new body to create money from nothing.

> Why should Congress place a controlling agency [the Fed], employed for private gain, between the people and the Government of the United States? That is what has been done by giving to the banks the exclusive privilege of the use of the Government credit. Why is it proposed that the banker should take the merchants', the manufactures', and other notes, as well as the bonds of towns, villages, cities, States, and even the Nation's bonds, to the Government and get currency, and at the same time refuse the producers themselves, the makers of the notes and obligations, an equal privilege? The absurdity of the Government giving away its own credit to corporations to exploit the people is incomprehensible. The bankers are not to blame. Congress is to blame for giving away the people's rights and bestowing them upon the banks.
>
> It is true that Congress possesses the authority and has the power to strip the banks of their exclusive monopoly, but the most of us have not the courage, and therefore we have the absurdity of the Congress of the United States giving to

---

[47] L. L. B. Angas, *Slump Ahead in Bonds* (New York: Somerset, 1937), p. 20.

> special interests the Government credit – the credit of the people – thereby forcing the people to borrow at exorbitant rates of interest the very money that their own Government issues on their own credit. The fiat of the Government is stamped upon the coins and the currency and then given to special interests and used as a means to pauperize the people. If the exclusive privilege were not given to the banks, then they would become the people's natural agents, but with the exclusive monopoly they become the people's masters.[48]

A Mr. Alexander Lassen made the following statement before the Senate Banking and Currency Committee in 1913, that the Fed would benefit from the proposed system, while the people would not.

> But the whole scheme of the Federal Reserve bank with its commercial-paper basis is an impractical, cumbersome machinery, is simply a cover, to find a way to secure the privilege of issuing money and to evade payment of as much tax upon circulation as possible, and then control the issue and maintain, instead of reduce, interest rates. It is a system that, if inaugurated, will prove to the advantage of the few and the detriment of the people of the United States. It will mean continued shortage of actual money and further extension of credits; for when there is a lack of real money people have to borrow credit to their cost.[49]

---

[48] Charles August Lindbergh, Sr., speech to the House of Representatives, September 11, 1913, *Congressional Record* 50(5), p. 4746.
[49] Alexander Lassen, Senate Committee on Banking and Currency, 63rd Congress, 1st Session, Vol. 1, on H. R. 7837.

Explicit statements about the relationship of debt to money were made during hearings of the House Committee on Banking and Currency on September 30, 1941. This was the debate for the Price-Control Bill H.R. 5479. The Chairman of the Federal Reserve Board, Marriner Eccles, was interviewed by Congressman Patman in one such hearing.

> Mr. Patman. How did you get the money to buy those $2,000,000,000 worth of Government securities?
>
> Mr. Eccles. We created it.
>
> Mr. Patman. Out of what?
>
> Mr. Eccles. Out of the right to issue credit, money.
>
> Mr. Patman. And there is nothing behind it, is there, except the Government's credit?
>
> Mr. Eccles. We have the Government bonds.
>
> Mr. Patman. That's right, the Government's credit.
>
> Mr. Eccles. That is what your money system is.[50]

Later on in another Congressional Hearing, we notice that Eccles made a remarkable statement.

> [Congressman] Mr. Fletcher. "Chairman Eccles, when do you think there is a possibility of returning to a free and open market, instead of this pegged and artificially controlled financial market we now have?"

---

https://fraser.stlouisfed.org/files/docs/historical/congressional/1913sen_bankcurr_v1.pdf.
[50] House Committee on Banking and Currency, 77th Congress, 1st Session, September 30, 1941, p. 1342.

Mr. Eccles. You mean the governments?

Mr Fletcher. That is right.

Mr. Eccles: Never, not in your lifetime or mine.[51]

All of this raises the point that persuasion is key to the creation of this illogical system. The arguments were spelled out in this 80th session of Congress during the Banking and Currency Committee's hearings on March 3, 4 and 5, 1947. How did the Federal Reserve persuade Congress to establish this system? Please read pages 47-54 of the Hearings for H.R. 2233, *Direct Purchases of Government Securities by Federal Reserve Banks*.[52] You will learn more details about how money is created, the defense of the Federal Reserve, and solutions to the same problems we still face as well. These suggestions were shot down, but they are still valid to revisit today.

The subjects of the Beast know that in order to accomplish their goals, they must argue convincingly for the creation of laws and policies. Investment banker Cyrus Eaton provides us with an example of how private banks have used lawyers to gain influence over the government and the stock market:

> Arthur H. Dean, a senior partner of Sullivan & Cromwell of No. 48 Wall Street, was one of those who assisted in the drafting of the Securities Act of 1933, the first of the series of bills passed to regulate the capital markets. He and his firm, which is reputed to be the largest in the United States, have maintained close relations with the SEC since its creation, and theirs is the

---

[51] House Committee on Banking and Currency, 80th Congress, 1st Session, March 5, 1947, p. 108.
https://fraser.stlouisfed.org/files/docs/historical/house/1947hr_directpurchgov.pdf
[52] House Committee on Banking and Currency, 80th Congress, 1st Session, March 3-5, 1947, pp. 47-54.
https://fraser.stlouisfed.org/files/docs/historical/house/1947hr_directpurchgov.pdf

dominating influence on the Commission.⁵³

Even if the outsourcing some monetary or market controls to privateers were to make sense in a restricted way, broad controls allowed by governments make neither political nor social sense. And despite the congressional reports of oversight we have looked at so far, no action has been taken to change the systems in place. Further, we should wonder why the US Treasury allowed supporters of communism to continue their subversive actions against the USA, especially in light of US financial assistance in the formation of the CCP and the interests in merging with the USSR.

Comrade Commerce

Congressman Louis McFadden, while chairman of the House Banking Committee, said in a speech on June 15, 1933:

> The Soviet government has been given United States Treasury funds by the Federal Reserve Board and the Federal Reserve Banks acting through the Chase Bank and the Guaranty Trust Company and other banks in New York City.
>
> Open up the books of Amtorg, the trading organization of the Soviet government in New York, and of Gostorg, the general office of the Soviet Trade Organization, and of the State Bank of the Union of Soviet Socialist Republics and you will be staggered to see how much American money has been taken from the United

---

[53] Cyrus Eaton, House Subcommittee on Study of Monopoly Power of the Committee on the Judiciary, hearings, 81st Congress, 1st Session, Serial No. 14, Part 2-A, p. 468. For further information about the Sullivan & Cromwell law firm that identifies far-reaching corruption and control schemes, see Nancy Lisagor and Frank Lipsius, *A Law Unto Itself: The Untold Story of the Law Firm of Sullivan and Cromwell* (New York: William Morrow and Co., 1988).

States' Treasury for the benefit of Russia. Find out what business has been transacted for the State Bank of Soviet Russia by its correspondent, the Chase Bank of New York.[54]

McFadden's above speech is quoted in Antony C. Sutton's book *Western Technology and Soviet Economic Development*, published by the Hoover Institution on War, Revolution and Peace. In the book, Sutton goes on to state:

> In 1925, negotiations between Chase and Prombank extended beyond the finance of raw materials and mapped out a complete program for financing Soviet raw material exports to the U. S. and imports of U. S. cotton and machinery.[55]

Sutton also claims:

> Chase National Bank and the Equitable Trust Company were leaders in the Soviet credit business.[56]

> Stalin paid tribute to the assistance rendered by the United States to Soviet industry before and during the war. He said that about two-thirds of all the large industrial enterprise in the Soviet Union had been built with United States help or technical assistance.[57]

The ability to issue money allows private banks a means to finance their global agendas outside of government foreign

---

[54] Louis McFadden, Congressional Record, House of Representatives, 73rd Congress, 1st Session, Vol. 77, Part 6, June 15, 1933, p. 6227. www.congress.gov/73/crecb/1933/06/15/GPO-CRECB-1933-pt6-v77-7-2.pdf.
[55] Antony C. Sutton, *Western Technology and Soviet Economic Development* (Stanford, CA: Hoover Institution, 1968), Vol. 11, p. 226.
[56] Sutton, *Western Technology*, p. 277.
[57] Sutton, *Western Technology*, p. 3.

policy. The problem is that the average person is not aware of this.

What has been the role of technology in creating and controlling the bubble we are now in? Will a controlled collapse or transition away from the current monetary system be undertaken as part of the introduction of a new digital system like that described by the DCMA and the BIS?

> There is no means of avoiding the final collapse of a boom brought about by credit expansion. The alternative is only whether the crisis should come sooner as the result of voluntary abandonment of further credit expansion, or later as a final and total catastrophe of the currency system involved.[58]

Congressman Wright Patman finishes up this section for us with provoking thoughts to ponder.

> I have never yet had anyone who could, through the use of logic and reason, justify the Federal Government borrowing the use of its own money. ...
>
> I believe the time will come when people will demand that this be changed. I believe the time will come in this country when they will actually blame you and me and everyone else connected with the Congress for sitting idly by and permitting such an idiotic system to continue.[59]

---

[58] Ludwig von Mises, *Human Action: A Treatise on Economics* (Auburn, AL: Ludwig von Mises Institute, 1998), chapter xx, section 8. https://cdn.mises.org/Human%20Action_3.pdf.
[59] Wright Patman, Congressional Record, House of Representatives, 77th Congress, 1st Session, Vol. 87, Part 7, September 29, 1941, pp. 7582-7583. www.govinfo.gov/content/pkg/GPO-CRECB-1941-pt7/pdf/GPO-CRECB-1941-pt7-27.pdf.

Since nobody acted upon Patman's advice for revising our monetary system, it looks like the best option for the Federal Reserve and its followers is to keep the current debt scheme alive by transitioning it into a new digital system. This will require the use of new technology like the AI banking software being rolled out as we speak. Thankfully, they left crumbs for us to follow.

> International banks and multinational corporations are acting and planning in terms that are far in advance of the political concepts of the nation-state.[60]

---

[60] A. Barber, *The 20th Century Renaissance*, private paper (Washington, DC: Institute of Politics and Planning, 1968), pp. 1, 8. This is a citation from Zbigniew Brzezinski's book, *Between Two Ages*. He must have read the private paper as it is not easy to find the original. It is also cited as being on pages 1 and 8.

Chapter 4: Technology Control Systems

Where would the Beast be without a body to perform its functions? It can't just hang out in the ether and control robots remotely. It needs people to carry out its mission and technology to accomplish its plans.

Now that we have learned about some of the key actors and mechanisms of the Beast's networks, we should aim to discover more about its plans to place controls on the average person.

Does the Beast need more money? Over the past centuries, it has been doing a great job of slowly gathering up the majority of the wealth on the planet. Well done, Beast! Award yourself ten gold stars to place on your refrigerator.

Gaining more wealth is probably not the only goal; the Beast seems to want something more than riches. Money is a means to an end, and *control* looks to be of more interest in the achievement of the Beast's ultimate aims.

Are you a willing participant, or are you resistant to the Beast's plans of tighter controls? A big question for society at this juncture is about reduced personal freedom resulting from an expanding control system. If the Beast tried to simply convince people to sign up to be controlled, it would be a tough sell. People need to be *lured* into giving up freedoms in exchange for controls that are presented as safeguards. Basically, in order for people to accept digital servitude, they need to be lied to. It works even better if "everybody is doing it" and it sounds socially righteous.

Fiction meets reality in the prophetic work of Aldous Huxley.

> "In the end," says the Grand Inquisitor in Dostoevsky's parable, "in the end they will lay their freedom at our feet and say to us, 'make us your slaves, but feed us.'" And when Alyosha Karamazov asks his brother, the teller of the story, if the Grand Inquisitor

> is speaking ironically, Ivan answers, "Not a bit of it! He claims it as a merit for himself and his Church that they have vanquished freedom and done so to make men happy." Yes, to make men happy; "for nothing," the Inquisitor insists, "has ever been more insupportable for a man or a human society than freedom."
>
> In my fable of *Brave New World*, the dictators had added science to the list and thus were able to enforce their authority by manipulating the bodies of embryos, the reflexes of infants and the minds of children and adults.
>
> In the past, free-thinkers and revolutionaries were often the products of the most piously orthodox education. This is not surprising. The methods employed by orthodox educators were and still are extremely inefficient. Under a scientific dictator education will really work—with the result that most men and women will grow up to love their servitude and will never dream of revolution. There seems to be no good reason why a thoroughly scientific dictatorship should ever be overthrown.[1]

The ESG mantra "fair and equitable" sounds great at first glance, but as we have learned in previous chapters, it begins as a one-sided control scheme of the elite that attempts to capture the minds of the people. Reduced freedoms do not mean life will become more fair or equitable. The grantor decides, not the recipient.

---

[1] Aldous Huxley, *Brave New World Revisited* (New York: Rosetta Books, 2000 [1958]), p. 91. www.huxley.net/bnw-revisited.pdf.

We can observe trends of the rich getting richer and the poor masses becoming poorer.[2] What about a mission to strengthen the middle class? The trends go beyond racial justice or culture wars. All people who are not part of the elite are continually being sold into debt prison. This is how it is being rolled out; the Beast has slowly gotten larger, gaining increasing control over humanity without the need for a total takeover in one fell swoop.

Eugenics, Technocracy, and Transhumanism

What are the goals of the Beast? Does it even have a brain with which to make its plans? Is it simply natural for a destroyer of the earth to exist, in order to balance and be an opposing force to good?

It doesn't matter for our purposes whether the Beast has a brain. What matters at this critical time in history is to identify its actions through the people that carry out what is either an intentional will or an unintentional driving force. Since the Beast is invisible and works behind the curtain, we can only see and engage with those actors.

One of the Beast's plans that is being carried out today is exactly like what was implemented by the technocrats of the 1930s. Quite simply, no matter what label we put on them, they are control system advocates. They fit the overall plan of the Beast

---

[2] See the following sources: Michael Diedrich, "Graph of the Day: The 1% Get Richer," *Twin Cities Daily Planet*, November 5, 2011. www.tcdailyplanet.net/graph-day-1-get-richer/; *The Washington Post*, "This Chart Explains Everything You Need to Know about Inequality." www.washingtonpost.com/news/wonk/wp/2015/04/20/this-chart-explains-everything-you-need-to-know-about-inequality/; Drew Desilver, "For Most US Workers, Real Wages HaveBarely Budget in Decades," Pew Research Center, August 7, 2018. www.pewresearch.org/short-reads/2018/08/07/for-most-us-workers-real-wages-have-barely-budged-for-decades/; howmuch.net, "Visualizing the Purchasing Power of the Dollar Over the Last Century." https://howmuch.net/articles/rise-and-fall-dollar; BMC Group, "USD: Purchasing Power and Currency in Circulation." https://bmg-group.com/usd-purchasing-power-currency-in-circulation/.

perfectly. They believe that they are smarter than you and me, and that therefore they know what is best for humanity.

We are currently experiencing a modern version of a movement that dates back to eugenics and similar ideologies. The current technological revolution is similar to the former industrial revolutions, except it is on electronic steroids; indeed, those movements of the past laid the foundations for our modern dilemma. The bad news is that recent attempts are even worse for the planet and us regular people.

Although some may think they are doing good, malevolent actors are using technology to control others. No matter what they think, their actions are detrimental for us, but not for them—unless we are happy to face more constraints in order to save the world. There are many reasons why we should not allow them to take even more control, even while some technological improvements are useful. There are other ways to save the world that are more benevolent than the current methods.

The connection between technocracy, transhumanism, and eugenics will become clear as we continue. The main point to understand is that leaders of these movements are obsessed with controlling humanity, or at a minimum believe they should utilize technological tools to lead us to a better future through their schemes.

Eugenics is defined in the American Heritage Dictionary as:

> The study or practice of attempting to improve the human gene pool by encouraging the reproduction of people considered to have desirable traits and discouraging or preventing the reproduction of people considered to have undesirable traits.[3]

Going way back, the term "eugenics" (meaning "good breeding") was coined by Sir Francis Galton in 1883, and

---

[3] The American Heritage Dictionary of the English Language, "eugenics." www.ahdictionary.com/word/search.html?q=eugenics.

prominent members of British society soon joined the official Eugenics Society. Winston Churchill was even vice president of the Eugenics Congress.[4]

> The Eugenics Education Society was founded in Britain in 1907 to campaign for sterilisation and marriage restrictions for the weak, to prevent the degeneration of the British race.[5]

Galton's ideas in the mid-1800s were partly based on the work of previous scientists like Charles Darwin, whose research Galton picked up on and linked with his own evolutionary theories.[6] Before Galton, Thomas Malthus had proposed the idea that human reproduction would consume the earth's resources. Indeed, people still use the term "Malthusian" today.[7]

Darwin himself claimed in his autobiography that his ideas came to fruition after reading Malthus. The fortress of evolutionary teaching in our modern era was built on a shaky foundation of eugenics.

> In October 1838, that is fifteen months after I had begun my systematic enquiry, I happened to read for amusement Malthus on *Population*, and being well prepared to appreciate the struggle for existence which everywhere goes on from long-continued observation of the habits of animals and plants, it at once struck me that under these circumstances

---

[4] English Heritage, "Eugenics in Britain," Blue Plaque Stories. www.english-heritage.org.uk/visit/blue-plaques/blue-plaque-stories/eugenics/.
[5] Pat Walsh, "The Eugenics Congress, London 1912," personal blog, May 26, 2017. https://drpatwalsh.com/2017/05/26/the-eugenics-congress-london-1912/.
[6] Britannica, "Francis Galton," last updated October 4, 2024. www.britannica.com/biography/Francis-Galton.
[7] Robert Zubrin, "The Population Control Holocaust," The New Atlantis, spring 2012. www.thenewatlantis.com/publications/the-population-control-holocaust.

> favourable variations would tend to be preserved, and unfavourable ones to be destroyed. The result of this would be the formation of a new species. Here, then, I had at last got a theory by which to work.[8]

Eugenics, in its connotations of "good being" or being "well born," reflects the concept of noble birth. As has been made clear throughout this book, some people think they are better than others, and feel compelled to control us—or at least cattle-prod the herd.

Renowned scientist Nikola Tesla had the following to say in support of the ideology.

> Eugenics [is] universally established. In past ages, the law governing the survival of the fittest roughly weeded out the less desirable strains. Then man's new sense of pity began to interfere with the ruthless workings of nature. As a result, we continue to keep it alive and to breed the unfit. The only method compatible with our notions of civilization and the race is to prevent the breeding of the unfit by sterilization and the deliberate guidance of the mating instinct.
>
> Several European countries and a number of states of the American union sterilize the criminal and the insane. This is not sufficient. The trend of opinion among ecumenists is that we must make marriage more difficult. Certainly no one who is not a desirable parent should be permitted to produce progeny. A century from now it will no more occur to a normal person to

---

[8] Charles Darwin, *The Autobiography of Charles Darwin* (London: Collins, 1958 [1887]), p. 61.

mate with a person eugenically unfit than to marry a habitual criminal.⁹

John Ruskin and Elite Imperialism

Eugenicists and other like-minded individuals in positions of power and influence not only used philosophical arguments to expand their efforts; science was needed to justify their beliefs. The teachings of English polymath John Ruskin helped lead the way to other movements, like the American Eugenics Society[10] and the programs implemented by the technocrats of the 1930s.

John Ruskin was an influencer of the mining magnate and politician Cecil Rhodes, famous for his brutal DeBeers diamond cartel and his activities in the African state of Rhodesia (now Zambia and Zimbabwe), named after him. (For more on Cecil Rhodes, see Chapter 5.) The influence of Ruskin on the work of Rhodes can be seen to this day.

> Two of Rhodes's biographers, who knew him most intimately, Sir Herbert Baker and Sir James McDonald, believe that Rhodes found the inspiration for that great dream of his in the teaching of John Ruskin ... Ruskin was teaching and writing in the first enthusiasm of his professorship: his Inaugural Address had been delivered and published in 1870 ... Ruskin's theme was the destiny of England ... He asks himself what are the virtues of the English and what the fate of England will be. His answer to these questions was a challenge to his youthful hearers.[11]

---

[9] Nikola Tesla, "A Machine to End War: As Told to Sylvester Viereck," Liberty, February 1937. http://tfcbooks.com/tesla/1935-02-00.htm.
[10] Rachel Gur-Arie, "American Eugenics Society (1926–1972)," Embryo Project Encyclopedia, November 22, 2014. https://embryo.asu.edu/pages/american-eugenics-society-1926-1972.
[11] Frank Aydelotte, *The Vision of Cecil Rhodes: A Reivew of the First Forty Years of American Scholarships* (London: Oxford University Press, 1946), pp. 2–3.

Ruskin stated:

> "There is a destiny now possible to us—the highest ever set before a nation to be accepted or refused. We are still undegenerate in race; a race mingled of the best northern blood. We are not yet dissolute in temper, but still have the firmness to govern, and the grace to obey. We have been taught a religion of pure mercy, which we must either now betray, or learn to defend by fulfilling. And we are rich in an inheritance of honour, bequeathed to us through a thousand years of noble history, which it should be our daily thirst to increase with splendid avarice, so that Englishmen, if it be a sin to covet honour, should be the most offending souls alive.
>
> And this is what she must either do, or perish: she must found colonies as fast and as far as she is able, formed of her most energetic and worthiest men ... seizing every piece of fruitful waste ground she can set her foot on, and there teaching these her colonists that their chief virtue is to be fidelity to their country, and that their first aim is to be to advance the power of England by land and sea: and that, though they live on a distant plot of ground, they are no more to consider themselves therefore disfranchised from their native land, than the sailors of her fleet do, because they float on distant waves."[12]

Translated for our purposes, Ruskin was proclaiming the need for a superior group of people to "guide" (read: control) the world.

---

[12] John Ruskin, quoted in Aydelotte, *The Vision of Cecil Rhodes*, pp. 3–4.

Why not the British? This was an attractive proposition for a Beast-loving Brit.

These beliefs led to prominent leaders expounding on the necessity for population control, and their favoring of like-minded believers. The concern for race was not as prominent as we might think—yet beliefs about the "degenerate" blood of certain races were certainly common. These concepts were fundamentally for the benefit of the high-minded elite who shared this same ideology. This group considered itself to consist of the smartest people on the planet who knew what was best for everyone else, happy to go beyond the Greco-Roman philosophies we inherited in the West, or even the Roman imperialism concepts that "justified" the expansion of the British empire.

The mid-1800s saw a convergence of evolutionary science, eugenics, and communism. None of these concepts were new at that time, yet they revived momentum from past teachings by utilizing different terminologies to lend themselves an air of novelty. More importantly, their timing was ripe.

These seemingly unrelated sciences and teachings are related in their overall scheme of worldwide domination. The thinkers and technocrats who subscribed to eugenics needed to base their beliefs on evolutionary teachings. Communists also liked evolutionary teachings because they enabled the bypassing of the "Divine Right" of kings and the infringement on the sovereign rights of the individual that were necessary in order for their plans to be implemented successfully.

"The Preservation of Favoured Races in the Struggle for Life"

Charles Darwin's landmark work *On the Origin of Species* was subtitled "The Preservation of Favoured Races in the Struggle for Life." Many of us were taught in school that Darwin invented the concept of evolution; yet he did not conceive it independently, but instead built upon previous ideas. In fact, the Royal Society made Darwin put disclaimers in the preface of the sixth edition of *On the Origins of Species* giving credit to previous evolutionary theories, including the work of his own grandfather.

Among other acknowledgements, this preface contains the following passage.

> Lamarck was the first man whose conclusions on the subject excited much attention. This justly celebrated naturalist first published his views in 1801; he much enlarged them in 1809 in his "Philosophie Zoologique", and subsequently, 1815, in the Introduction to his "Hist. Nat. des Animaux sans Vertébres". In these works he up holds the doctrine that all species, including man, are descended from other species ...
>
> I have taken the date of the first publication of Lamarck from Isidore Geoffroy Saint-Hilaire's ... excellent history of opinion on this subject. In this work a full account is given of Buffon's conclusions on the same subject. It is curious how largely my grandfather, Dr. Erasmus Darwin, anticipated the views and erroneous grounds of opinion of Lamarck in his "Zoonomia" ... published in 1794. According to Isid. Geoffroy there is no doubt that Goethe was an extreme partisan of similar views, as shown in the introduction to a work written in 1794 and 1795, but not published till long afterward; he has pointedly remarked ... that the future question for naturalists will be how, for instance, cattle got their horns and not for what they are used. It is rather a singular instance of the manner in which similar views arise at about the same time, that Goethe in Germany, Dr. Darwin in England, and Geoffroy Saint-Hilaire (as we shall immediately see) in France, came to

the same conclusion on the origin of species, in the years 1794–5.[13]

The concept of evolution was not new to the 1800s, but what about communism or eugenics? The use of a term like eugenics is not as important as the people carrying the belief forward; terminology changes over time, but by examining actions we can identify connections to other belief systems. We can also recognize the role of technology in accomplishing the goals of these ideologies.

Cold Springs Harbor Laboratory

What do eugenics, evolution and population control have to do with technology? Malthusianism and eugenics may seem like narrow philosophical ideas at first glance, yet they cannot operate effectively without utilizing science and technology.

The eugenics movement in the USA is believed to have begun in 1910 at the Cold Spring Harbor Laboratory on Long Island, New York. Did it just pop up out of nowhere, or had it borrowed from concepts previously developed in England? Regardless, the facility needed funding to operate. Of course, the usual suspects can be identified in the lineup.

> Cold Spring Harbor Laboratory in New York was the center of the American Eugenics Movement. Charles Davenport, a geneticist and biologist, founded the ERO, and served as its director until 1934.
>
> Davenport became the director of the Biological Laboratory at Cold Spring Harbor in 1898. In 1904 he convinced the Carnegie Institution of Washington (CIW) to fund the Station for Experimental Evolution, located on the

---

[13] Charles Darwin, *On the Origin of Species by Means of Natural Selection, or, The Preservation of Favoured Races in the Struggle for Life* (London: John Murray, 6th edition, 1872). www.gutenberg.org/files/2009/2009-h/2009-h.htm#link2H_4_0001.

same campus. Davenport was excited by the potential social benefit of studies in human heredity, as was his wife, Gertrude Crotty Davenport, also an embryologist and geneticist.

With a grant from Mary Harriman, the widow of railroad magnate Edward Henry Harriman, Davenport founded the Eugenics Record Office in 1910. In 1917, the Carnegie Institution began funding the ERO, and continued to provide its primary funding source until the ERO closed in 1939. John D. Rockefeller, John H. Kellogg, and other private wealthy philanthropists also provided funding for the organization.[14]

We can easily make connections from this summary—evolution, funding sources from foundations, participation of the elite, and social engineering. What was the role of technology?

Carrying out experiments regarding evolution, the compiling of databases of information and funding from various sources were the inputs, while social benefits were the supposed outputs. Without funding, this project would not have gotten off the ground. This attempt at playing god, to manipulate outcomes outside of nature, would not have been possible without evolution as its basis.

Why would members of the elite like Carnegie and Rockefeller support this endeavor, with its purpose of social engineering? Was it simply for the sake of money, or was there a deeper motivation, like obtaining more control over people's lives? It's unlikely that they were truly philanthropic and didn't expect anything in return; instead, through eugenics, the elite would

---

[14] Cera R. Lawrence, "The Eugenics Record Office at Cold Spring Harbor Laboratory (1910–1939)," Embryo Project Encyclopedia, April 21, 2011. https://embryo.asu.edu/pages/eugenics-record-office-cold-spring-harbor-laboratory-1910-1939.

attempt to tailor heredity, weeding out the undesirable attributes of the population. Why?

> [As] Carnegie famously argued, they believed that most previous giving had been "indiscriminate charity ... spent as to encourage the slothful, the drunken, the unworthy," without addressing the **underlying circumstances** that produced such conditions.[15]

Rockefeller had the following to say about his motives.

> What he needed, he felt, was to rationalize his philanthropy—to develop an "organized plan" based on some **"underlying principles"** of giving. The philanthropy that mattered most, he concluded, was philanthropy that struck at the root of fundamental problems: "To help the sick and distressed appeals to the kindhearted always, but to help the investigator who is striving successfully to attack the causes which bring about sickness and distress does not so strongly attract the giver of money ... The best philanthropy is constantly in search of the finalities—a search for cause, **an attempt to cure evils at their source.**"[16]

Now we know a little more about *why*. Rockefeller felt that investing in eugenics would help cure "evil" genes. Did he know that this would lead to horrific acts upon innocent people, who had no evil genes? We do not know what he believed deep

---

[15] William A. Schambra, "How the Carnegie Corporation Contributed to NC's Shameful Past," Philanthropy Daily, September 19, 2011, (emphasis added). https://philanthropydaily.com/how-the-carnegie-corporation-contributed-to-ncs-shameful-past/.
[16] Philanthropy Roundtable, "John Rockefeller Sr."
www.philanthropyroundtable.org/hall-of-fame/john-rockefeller-sr/.
(emphasis added).

down, since it is not laid out on the record and we don't know the specific orders that were given, but tragic experiments were carried out.

Carnegie and Rockefeller's claim that they intended to research the underlying problems and root causes of social ills is admirable at first glance. Excellent research should focus on this foundation. However, they were probably aware that the scientists they funded, and that they themselves, had ulterior motives in their belief that it was best to tailor the human population as they saw fit. This is speculation but it is known that funding drives research and scientists follow the money. What is clear is that they set up these programs outside the realms of transparency and accountability.

Modern times have seen various attempts at apologies for the programs carried out by these foundations. Eric D. Isaacs, president of Carnegie Institution, had the following to say about the foundation's funding of eugenics in the past.

> For the Carnegie Institution, this process of discernment requires us to grapple with our history of eugenics research. Our involvement in eugenics dates back to 1902, when zoologist Charles B. Davenport received Carnegie support to establish a "Biological Experiment Station for the study of evolution." His stated aim was the "analytic and experimental study of the causes of specific differentiation—of race change." This became the Eugenics Record Office, and for more than 30 years thereafter, Carnegie researchers helped to lead the eugenics movement, with the expressed support of America's mainstream scientific community. It was not until 1935 that a review panel convened by the Carnegie Institution concluded that our eugenics research lacked scientific merit; Carnegie closed the Eugenics Record Office in 1939 and

> wound down all eugenics-related research by 1944.
>
> I want to express my sincere and profound apologies for this organization's past involvement in these horrific pseudoscientific activities.[17]

Regardless of this recent apology, the Institute continued to fund the research for decades afterwards—despite knowing it was not scientifically valid—and kept leading eugenicist Frederick Osborn on its board until the 1960s. He was a major proponent of eugenics the entire time.

> What went unmentioned in [the documentary] "Against Their Will" was the central role the Carnegie Corporation of New York and one of its trustees, Frederick Osborn, played in the establishment of the school's medical genetics program.
>
> Like Dr. Allan and Dr. Herndon, Mr. Osborn was persuaded that a genetics-trained medical profession could promote eugenics without the taint of Nazi race purification.
>
> That did not diminish his enthusiasm for state-sponsored sterilization, however. Writing in A Preface to Eugenics in 1940, Mr. Osborn noted approvingly that "the inexcusable process of allowing feebleminded persons ... to reproduce their kind is on the way to being checked in a number of states in which such persons may be sterilized."
>
> In his capacity as a Carnegie trustee, he secured several grants from the Carnegie

---

[17] Eric D. Isaacs, "Statement on Eugenics Research," Carnegie Science, August 12, 2020. https://carnegiescience.edu/about/history/statement-eugenics-research.

Corporation for the founding of the Bowman Gray department of genetics, thereby furthering his goal of injecting eugenics into the medical profession. Osborn was as well a director of the pro-eugenics Pioneer Fund from 1937 to 1958, which also financed Dr. Herndon's work.[18]

While the knowledge and manipulation of genetic information can be useful in improving human health, for example, by reducing the risk of disease where genetic mutations have been identified, we understand that in practice this research may be rooted in, and can result in, belief systems that lend themselves to control structures. Through research in eugenics, the Beast became more modern and coordinated. We cannot say that genetic research is bad in a general sense, but obvious signs of its manipulation through various initiatives and research programs—eugenics, in particular—point toward nefarious goals. The question to ask is – what is the agenda of an elitist to fund these programs?

Population Control

Alongside generously funded experiments to control the genetics of individuals within populations, we can see clear justifications in the beliefs of the elite to subdue entire populations. For example, Henry Kissinger is quoted in a declassified National Security Study Memorandum as stating:

> In the longer run, a lower ultimate world population (say 8 to 9 billion rather than 12 to 16 billion) would require a lower annual input of depletable resources directly affected by population size as well as a much lower volume of food, forest products, textiles, and other renewable resources. Whatever may be done to

---

[18] Schambra, "How the Carnegie Corporation Contributed to NC's Shameful Past." https://philanthropydaily.com/how-the-carnegie-corporation-contributed-to-ncs-shameful-past/

> guard against interruptions of supply and to develop domestic alternatives, the U.S. economy will require large and increasing amounts of minerals from abroad, especially from less developed countries.[19]

We should expect by now that because the Beast needs more mineral resources to feed upon, it can't let the populations of undeveloped countries get in the way of the extracting resources for the benefit of the "first" world.

Yet, Kissinger's recommendations were driven by ill intent. This statement follows the same overall plan recorded over hundreds of years by many influential people. Kissinger's modern version became yet closer to being realized, since he geared his approach toward government policy and the work of NGOs. Whereas previously a handful of rich people had been working together with mad scientists, within a few decades a prominent government figure was speaking the quiet part out loud.

The quote from Kissinger continues:

> [T]he U.S. economy will require large and increasing amounts of minerals from abroad, especially from less developed countries. That fact gives the U.S. enhanced interest in the political, economic, and social stability of the supplying countries. Wherever a lessening of population pressures through reduced birth rates can increase the prospects for such stability, population policy becomes relevant to resource supplies and to the economic interests of the United States.[20]

---

[19] Henry Kissinger, *National Security Memorandum, NSSM200: Implications of Worldwide Population Growth for US Security and Overseas Interests*, December 10, 1974, pp. 41-42 http://pdf.usaid.gov/pdf_docs/PCAAB500.pdf

[20] Henry Kissinger, *National Security Memorandum, NSSM200: Implications of Worldwide Population Growth for US Security and*

As I stated previously, these Beast followers believe themselves to be smarter than everyone else. By now, we should expect them to think they know what is best for the average person. Should we have an *open* discussion about the problems that might entail from a growing global population? Certainly. Right now, it is a closed discussion, and we are not invited. Calling your Representative doesn't work well either.

In his book *Fatal Misconception*,[21] historian Matthew Connelly provides a record of various population-control conferences that took place in the twentieth century. Here is one example he found from a speaker. These people seem to speak as if the subjects of their discussions do not exist as real people.

> "Perhaps the individual patient is expendable in the general scheme of things," says one attendee at a 1962 meeting, "particularly if the infection she acquires is sterilising but not lethal."
>
> In 1969 Robert McNamara, then president of the World Bank, said he was reluctant to finance health care in other countries "unless it was very strictly related to population control, because usually health facilities contributed to the decline

---

Overseas Interests, December 10, 1974, p. 42.
http://pdf.usaid.gov/pdf_docs/PCAAB500.pdf
Kissinger is not alone in having been caught conveying these beliefs of the elite. The Population Council is a research institute founded by John D. Rockefeller; an official history of the Population Council can be found on the Wayback Machine, since the company has since deleted the post: "About the Population Council".
https://web.archive.org/web/20080129092213/http:/www.popcouncil.org/about/history.html. See also "Horrid History," *The Economist*, May 22, 2008. www.economist.com/books-and-arts/2008/05/22/horrid-history: "In 1935 one representative told India's Council of State that population control was a necessity for the masses, adding that 'it is not what they want, but what is good for them.'"
[21] Matthew Connelly, *Fatal Misconception: The Struggle to Control World Population* (Cambridge, MA: Harvard University Press, 2008).

of the death rate, and thereby to the population explosion."[22]

Let's consider more incredible statements from elite-minded people about population control. Some of these quotes may seem tame—and some might even sound logical at first—but let them sink in. The core theme is that these smart people have the answers, while the rest of us, the poor, the disenfranchised, and the oppressed, need to be educated. I would not mind having a forum for these discussions in an open setting but I get the feeling these people are not looking for my feedback.

> The primary challenge facing our species is the reproduction of our species itself ... It is time we had a grown-up discussion about the optimum quantity of human beings in this country and on this planet ... All the evidence shows that we can help reduce population growth, and world poverty, by promoting literacy and female emancipation and access to birth control.
>
> Boris Johnson[23]

> One of the things we could do about it is to change the technologies, to put out less of this pollution, to stabilize the population, and one of the principal ways of doing that is to empower and educate girls and women.
>
> Al Gore[24]

---

[22] Matthew Connelly, "How Did the 'Population Control' Movement Go So Terribly Wrong?" *The Wilson Quarterly*, summer 2008. www.wilsonquarterly.com/quarterly/summer-2008-saving-the-world/how-did-population-control-movement-go-so-terribly-wrong.
[23] "Global Over-Population Is the Real Issue," *The Telegraph*, October 25, 2007. www.telegraph.co.uk/comment/3643551/Global-over-population-is-the-real-issue.html.
[24] Al Gore, quoted by Abel Keogh, "Life Imitates the Third VII," personal blog, June 23, 2011. www.abelkeogh.com/blog/the-third/life-imitates-the-third/vii.

All of our problems are the result of overbreeding among the working class.

Margaret Sanger[25]

The problem is that the population is growing the fastest where people are less able to deal with it. So it's in the very poorest places that you're going to have a tripling in population by 2050 ... And we've got to make sure that we help out with the tools now so that they don't have an impossible situation later.

Bill Gates[26]

The human population can no longer be allowed to grow in the same old uncontrolled way. If we do not take charge of our population size, then nature will do it for us.

David Attenborough[27]

I'm pro-choice, I'm for assisted suicide, I'm for regular suicide, I'm for whatever gets the freeway moving—that's what I'm for.

---

[25] "Morality and Birth Control," *Birth Control Review* (February–March 1918), p. 11.
[26] "A Conversation with Bill Gates: Why Focus on Global Aid?" GatesNotes, February 18, 2012. www.gatesnotes.com/A-Conversation-with-Bill-Gates-Global-Aid. A transcript of this conversation is archived at https://web.archive.org/web/20200520180115/https:/media.gatesnotes.com/-/media/Files/Personal/A-Conversation-with-Bill-Gates/A%20Conversation%20with%20Bill%20Gates%20transcript.
[27] Quoted at Population Matters, "Quotes." https://populationmatters.org/quotes/.

> It's too crowded, the planet is too crowded and we need to promote death.
>
> Bill Maher[28]

There are also not so famous people providing more details about who gets to decide the fate of humanity without our input. Only one book reference is needed since it encompasses the major thrusts. Paul Ehrlich and former Obama scientific advisor John Holdren co-authored *EcoScience* in 1977. Below are some excerpts of this book that talks about forced abortions, involuntary sterilization, and government control.

> A program of sterilizing women after their second or third child, despite the relatively greater difficulty of the operation than vasectomy, might be easier to implement than trying to sterilize men.[29]

> To date, there has been no serious attempt in Western countries to use laws to control excessive population growth, although there exists ample authority under which population growth could be regulated. For example, under the United States Constitution, effective population-control programs could be enacted under the clauses that empower Congress to appropriate funds to provide for the general welfare and to regulate commerce, or under the equal-protection clause of the Fourteenth Amendment. Such laws constitutionally could be very broad. Indeed, it has been concluded that compulsory population-control laws, even including laws requiring compulsory

---

[28] StarTalk Radio, *Real Science with Bill Maher, Part 1*, October 7, 2012. https://startalkmedia.com/show/real-science-with-bill-maher-part-1/.
[29] Ehrlich, Ehrlich, and Holdren, *Ecoscience: Population, Resources, Environment* (San Francisco, CA: W. H. Freeman and Co., 1977), p. 787.

abortion, could be sustained under the existing Constitution if the population crisis became sufficiently severe to endanger the society.[30]

A Planetary Regime?

Ecoscience examines many of the questions we've looked at so far.

> Perhaps those agencies, combined with UNEP and the United Nations population agencies, might eventually be developed into a Planetary Regime—sort of an international superagency for population, resources, and environment. Such a comprehensive Planetary Regime could control the development, administration, conservation, and distribution of all natural resources, renewable or nonrenewable, at least insofar as international implications exist. Thus the Regime could have the power to control pollution not only in the atmosphere and oceans, but also in such freshwater bodies as rivers and lakes that cross international boundaries or that discharge into the oceans. The Regime might also be a logical central agency for regulating all international trade, perhaps including assistance from DCs to LDCs, and including all food on the international market.[31]

> The Planetary Regime might be given responsibility for determining the optimum population for the world and for each

---

[30] Ehrlich, Ehrlich, and Holdren, *Ecoscience: Population, Resources, Environment*. p. 837.

[31] Ehrlich, Ehrlich, and Holdren, *Ecoscience: Population, Resources, Environment*, p. 942.

> region and for arbitrating various countries' shares within their regional limits.[32]

Of course, this means a partial surrender of national sovereignty to an international police force. It is as if the name "Planetary Regime" has come straight from a science fiction movie.

> If this could be accomplished, security might be provided by an armed international organization, a global analogue of a police force. Many people have recognized this as a goal, but the way to reach it remains obscure in a world where factionalism seems, if anything, to be increasing. **The first step necessarily involves partial surrender of sovereignty to an international organization.**[33]

Various other famous elitists have discussed population control in terms of concrete numbers. Some of the mildest to most extreme cases include the following.

> First, we've got population ... The world today has 6.8 billion people. That's headed up to about nine billion. Now, if we do a really great job on new vaccines, health care, reproductive health services, we could lower that by, perhaps, 10 or 15 percent.
>
> Bill Gates[34]

Suggesting a 90-percent reduction in global population, British anthropologist Jane Goodall said at Davos:

---

[32] Ehrlich, Ehrlich, and Holdren, *Ecoscience: Population, Resources, Environment*, p. 943.
[33] Ehrlich, Ehrlich, and Holdren, *Ecoscience: Population, Resources, Environment*, p. 917, (emphasis added).
[34] "Innovating to Zero," TED Talk, February 2010. www.ted.com/talks/bill_gates_innovating_to_zero?subtitle=en.

All these [environmental] things we talk about wouldn't be a problem if there was the size of population that there was 500 years ago.[35]

Most Beast-lovers advocate in the range of a 10–90-percent reduction in global population. Yet it is obvious that population explosions self-regulate, and there are countless methods to handle any problems caused by a growth in the world's population. The issue remains that we are not supposed to contribute any of the solutions because they have all the answers it seems.

The secret gathering described in this *Sunday Times* article below was sponsored by Bill Gates, and calls itself "The Good Club." Its participants have included the late David Rockefeller, Warren Buffett, George Soros, Michael Bloomberg, Ted Turner, and Oprah Winfrey.

> Some of America's leading billionaires have met secretly to consider how their wealth could be used to slow the growth of the world's population and speed up improvements in health and education.
>
> The philanthropists who attended a summit convened on the initiative of Bill Gates, the Microsoft co-founder, discussed joining forces to overcome political and religious obstacles to change. ...
>
> Stacy Palmer, editor of the *Chronicle of Philanthropy*, said the summit was unprecedented. "We only learnt about it afterwards, by accident. Normally these people are happy to talk good causes, but this is different—maybe because they

---

[35] Video in Tweet, @tomselliott, January 24, 2020. https://x.com/tomselliott/status/1220696092532187136.

don't want to be seen as a global cabal," he said. ...

Another guest said there was "nothing as crude as a vote" but a consensus emerged that they would back a strategy in which population growth would be tackled as a potentially disastrous environmental, social and industrial threat....

"This is something so nightmarish that everyone in this group agreed **it needs big-brain answers**," said the guest ...

Why all the secrecy? "They wanted to speak rich to rich without worrying anything they said would end up in the newspapers, painting them as an alternative world government," he said.[36]

According to the logic of the Good Club, only "big-brain" people can solve difficult problems. Why do these people consider themselves to be in this unique, morally superior position? Is it because they are wealthy and they believe that their success proves their moral superiority? Does their circular reasoning justify their wealth as the result of their moral superiority, and their moral superiority as coming from their wealth? Do they believe that the financially poor are wrong, less valuable, or less capable of making decisions?

Another question to ask is whether those at-risk groups most affected by potential problems arising from population growth—groups mentioned in documents like the *World Population Plan of Action*[37]—have themselves requested any

---

[36] John Harlow, "Billionaire Club in Bid to Curb Overpopulation," *The Sunday Times*, May 24, 2009; (emphasis added). www.thetimes.com/article/billionaire-club-in-bid-to-curb-overpopulation-d2fl22qhl02.

[37] United Nations, *World Population Plan of Action*, August 19–30, 1974.

help. It seems like the smartest people on the planet are intending to give them help they have not asked for. In fact, some individuals may enjoy traditional farming and family life, and while they may ask for some aid in specific aspects of their lives, they have not requested complete intervention. Brookings has published a helpful critique of this approach:

> Africans' opinions do not always align with U.S. policy priorities, most notably regarding the attachment of economic or political conditionalities to development assistance and national control over development spending.
>
> Nationalist sentiments have increased in Africa in recent years, and with them has come an increased desire for control over domestic affairs ... a majority of those polled agree that their government should retain full autonomy over development assistance.[38]

Those who currently enjoy freedom do not wish to give it up easily. Those who have been oppressed want freedom even more. It is not as easy for the elite to implement new control structures in the form of official legislation as it is for them to use alternative methods using money to accelerate their agenda. Perhaps this has led to the rise of the thought police. Today, information management is the mechanism by which they attempt to achieve their goals.

Information versus Disinformation

What role does technology play in the philosophy of the elite? While at first appearing to be unconnected to these belief

---

www.un.org/en/development/desa/population/migration/generalassembly/docs/globalcompact/E_CONF.60_19_Plan.pdf.
[38] E. Gyimah-Boadi, Landry Signé, and Josephine Appiah-Nyamekye Sanny, "US Foreign Policy toward Africa: An African Citizen Perspective," Brookings, October 23, 2020.
www.brookings.edu/articles/us-foreign-policy-toward-africa-an-african-citizen-perspective/.

systems, we can explore how the power elite's use of technology helps them to accomplish the goals of the Beast. Does the Beast need technology?

A key use of technology that provides us with interesting connections is the attempt at social engineering through the use of databases.

Technology has not always been in the forms it takes today. The Beast's use of technology stems back to fundamental sciences, as we have explored already, and has at times involved the compilation of databases of information as a method of accomplishing control schemes. Simple genetic studies and the gathering of hereditary information have been used to build a mass of data that is required to accomplish nefarious ends. Concepts are easier to sell to the public if you have data to back up your case; partial facts, plus a partial concept, equals a total solution that the Beast can sell to the masses.

In order to sell such a solution to us, these actors need a story. Scientific and objective-sounding information is used to justify the thinning of the herd and control of the masses. The house of cards we find ourselves in today was built as follows.

- Evolutionary theory was useful, as it allowed the elimination of the possibility of a God (or gods) having creating us, and resulted in the corresponding elimination of the sovereign rights of *created* beings. This central atheistic belief system that catered to their goals was crucial.
- Once the concepts of a God (or gods) and individual rights were delegitimized at a foundational level, the elite established a scientific basis that advocated for social engineering and the use of technology to justify their methods of achieving more power.
- The new science was subjective, so it had to be repeated often to the masses until it was seen as factual and not up for debate.

What they did not tell us was that this whole scheme was just another belief system, like those that had previously been in place. Think of the priest-kings from long ago who controlled the masses. The "new" system is presented as factual to encourage followers to give up their individual rights willingly. This approach helped advance social justice causes, developed a corporate medical system over private practices, and led to the changing, over time, of other traditional ways of life. Basically, they mixed facts with opinions. It is still a deception, any way you look at it: a truth multiplied by a lie is a lie.

But blatant deceit also has a place within this agenda; many lies are told in banking, government policy, healthcare, and even ecology. While few people admit lying, there are a couple of honest liars to consider, whose means are used to justify their end goal.

The following material is extracted from a Climate Depot article about how exaggeration and manipulation are being used in the debate around global warming.

> The complete Abstract [of a peer-reviewed paper] is reproduced below:
>
> "It appears that news media and some pro-environmental organizations have the tendency to accentuate or even exaggerate the damage caused by climate change. This article provides a rationale for this tendency by using a modified International Environmental Agreement (IEA) model with asymmetric information. We find that the information manipulation has an instrumental value, as it ex post induces more countries to participate in an IEA, which will eventually enhance global welfare. From the ex anteperspective, however, the impact that manipulating information has on the level of participation in an IEA and on welfare is ambiguous."
>
> Craig Rucker of Committee for a Constructive Tomorrow CFACT (Climate Depot's parent company) noted in an

April 4 blog: "What will shock you is that two professors not only candidly admit it, but published a paper in a peer reviewed journal touting the beneficial effects of lying for pushing nations into a UN climate treaty in Paris next year!"

Rucker added: "The authors not only believe that their dubious ends justify their shady means, they institutionalize 'information manipulation' as a tactic, host panels about it at climate conferences and publish it in journals. They're shameless."

CFACT's David Rothbard noted: "Global warming skeptics have long charged that alarmists are over-hyping the dangers of climate change. Now comes a new paper from two economists in Singapore and Hong Kong that actually advocates exaggerating global warming fears to get countries on board international environmental agreements."

According to Kevin Glass of Townhall.com, the paper claims that the urgency of climate change makes it OK to deceive the public about the projected consequences of global warming. They don't actually use the word "lying," but by calling for "informational manipulation and exaggeration," they certainly think the ends justify these very questionable and over-heated means."

This is not the first time that global warming advocates have been accused of being deceptive. The late Stanford University professor Stephen Schneider wrote in 1989: "So we have to offer up scary scenarios, make simplified, dramatic statements, and make little mention of any doubts we

> might have. This 'double ethical bind' which we frequently find ourselves in cannot be solved by any formula. Each of us has to decide what the right balance is between being effective and being honest. I hope that means being both." ...
>
> Former NASA global warming scientist James Hansen conceded in a 2003 issue of Natural Science that the use of "extreme scenarios" to dramatize global warming "may have been appropriate at one time" to drive the public's attention to the issue.[39]

We could speculate that there is some reason behind the claims of these scientific articles but most likely there are control schemes involved with research funding as the carrot used to get the data needed.

Although some facts justify their means, Beast-followers tend to not explain the primary reason behind their methods, for example, their use of genetic information to accomplish control. They avoid reference to contrary belief systems in the knowledge that some people will resist their plans and opt for more freedom to practice their individual beliefs. However, sometimes they openly state their agenda.

> In searching for a new enemy to unite us, we came up with the idea that pollution, the threat of global warming, water shortages, famine and the like would fit the bill... All these dangers are caused by human intervention, and it is only through changed attitudes and behavior that they

---

[39] Marc Morano, "Shock Peer-Reviewed Paper Provides 'Rationale' for 'Information Manipulation' & 'Exaggeration' in Global Warming Debate to 'Enhance Global Welfare'," Climate Depot: A CFACT Project, April 4, 2014. www.climatedepot.com/2014/04/04/shock-peer-reviewed-paper-advocates-information-manipulation-exaggeration-in-global-warming-debate-to-enhance-global-welfare-published-in-american-journal-of-agricultural-economics/.

can be overcome. The real enemy then is humanity itself.[40]

Who is the Club of Rome that wrote this plan to unify humanity? They are the group who wrote *The Limits to Growth* in 1971.

> In 1972, the Club's first major Report, *The Limits to Growth* was published. It sold millions of copies worldwide, creating media controversy and also impetus for the global sustainability movement. This call for objective, scientific assessment of the impact of humanity's behaviour and use of resources, still defines the Club of Rome today.[41]

To be fair to the Club of Rome, they certainly helped warn everyone about the dangers of pollution such as mercury and lead poisoning. The popularity of their first report made an impression on the environmental movement and governments took notice. I would also agree with many of their arguments. However, they seem to get into trouble when they mix some science with some philosophical arguments to make dire conclusions that the Beast ends up using as justification for carrying out globalism.

Dennis Meadows, one of the co-authors of *Limits to Growth*, did an interview in 2016 to express his core views about population control. I think he boiled down the argument very succinctly – we can either have freedom if we have less people, or we can have more people if we have a smart dictatorship. He nailed it.

---

[40] Alexander King, Bertrand Schneider, *The First Global Revolution: A Report by the Council of the Club Of Rome* (New York, Pantheon Books, 1991), p.115. www.clubofrome.org/publication/the-first-global-revolution-1991/. Also quoted by The Sociable, "Globalists Outline World Govt Pathway: 76% Population Reduction, Global Truth Commission, Earth System Currency, Revised UN Charter," August 5, 2024. https://sociable.co/government-and-policy/globalists-world-govt-population-reduction-truth-commission-system-currency-un-charter/.
[41] https://www.clubofrome.org/history/

> I mean the planet can support something like a billion people, maybe two billion depending on how much Liberty and how much material consumption you want to have. If you want more Liberty and more consumption, you have to have fewer people, and conversely you can have more people, I mean we could even have eight or nine billion, probably, if we have a very strong dictatorship which is smart, that's unfortunately you never have smart dictatorships, they're always stupid, so. But if you had a smart dictatorship and a low standard of living you can have it but, but we want to have freedom and we want to have a high [standard] so we're going to have a billion people and we're now at seven, so we have to get back down. I hope that this can be slow, relatively slow, and that it can be done in a way which is relatively equal, so that people share the experience and we don't have a few rich trying to force everybody else to deal with it, so those are my hopes. These are pretty pessimistic hopes, but that's, that's what lies ahead.[42]

At least Meadows was very honest and straightforward. Sometimes the press reveals the truth about not providing us with the whole truth. Apparently, we can't handle it.

> Our job is to give people not what they want, but what we decide they ought to have.[43]

---

[42] Dennis Meadows Interview p4/4 (A 'peaceful collapse' & many revolutions...) @We Love Earth YouTube Channel. https://www.youtube.com/watch?v=Dbo6uvJBtZg

[43] Richard Salant, "Salant, Richard S.," Encyclopedia.com. www.encyclopedia.com/humanities/encyclopedias-almanacs-

There is no such thing, at this date of the world's history, in America, as an independent press. You know it and I know it.

There is not one of you who dares to write your honest opinions, and if you did, you know beforehand that it would never appear in print. I am paid weekly for keeping my honest opinion out of the paper I am connected with ...

We are the tools and vassals of rich men behind the scenes. We are the jumping jacks, they pull the strings and we dance. Our talents, our possibilities and our lives are all the property of other men. We are intellectual prostitutes.[44]

In March, 1915, the J.P. Morgan interests, the steel, shipbuilding, and powder interest, and their subsidiary organizations, got together 12 men high up in the newspaper world and employed them to select the most influential newspapers in the United States and sufficient number of them to control generally the policy of the daily press ... They found it was only necessary to purchase the control of 25 of the greatest papers. An agreement was reached; the policy of the papers was bought, to be paid for by the month; an editor was furnished for each paper to properly supervise and edit information regarding the questions of preparedness,

---

transcripts-and-maps/salant-richard-s. Salant was the former President of CBS News.
[44] John Swinton, quoted in Richard O. Boyer and Herbert M. Morais, *Labor's Untold Story* (New York: United Electrical, Radio & Machine Workers of America, 1975), p. 81.
https://archive.org/details/laborsuntoldstor0000boye/mode/2up.

militarism, financial policies, and other things of national and international nature considered vital to the interests of the purchasers.[45]

It seems like the old method of the elite was to maintain wars and disagreements about religion or politics in order to broaden the division of the masses to prevent unity so they could maintain controls. The new method looks to be geared for the control of information to increase unity of the masses. As long as the elite are in control, they probably do not care if we are unified or not. In all cases, deception is a primary tool used for the benefactors.

Pandemic Advice from Bankers?

The TV news show *Face the Nation* aired on April 5, 2020 with a very diverse group of guests. The president of the St. Louis Federal Reserve was present to speak about the use of technology in testing for COVID-19 infection. Perhaps it seemed logical at the time to explain the connection between economics and healthcare, yet upon reflection, the link seems artificial. Why was a banker giving advice on this topic? In this form of modern technocracy, health and economic advice went hand in hand.

> [T]here is a solution using available technology today to fix the economic part of this problem. The solution is universal testing. What you want is every single person to get tested every day. And then they would wear a badge like they would at a- after they voted or something like that to show that they've been tested. This would immediately sort out who's been infected and who hasn't been infected. That would help the health care sector. But it would also help the economy because

---

[45] Oscar Callaway, Congressional Record, January 27–February 12, 1917: Vol. 54, p. 2947. https://archive.org/details/sim_congressional-record-proceedings-and-debates_january-27-february-12-1917_54/page/2947/mode/1up.

we could interact with each other with a lot of confidence.[46]

Other guests on the same show continued with the same topic of technology:

> MARGARET BRENNAN: So you've mentioned technology. The Fed president from St. Louis mentioned technology. Doctor Fauci has mentioned technology and surveillance. Specifically, what does that look like in the United States of America and how far are we from getting that?
>
> SCOTT GOTTLIEB: Well, the **massive surveillance system** that we need to detect infection quickly, **we're going to have—we're hopefully going to have** in place. We should have that in place. We'll have the tools to do that. So we'll be able to identify cases when there are small outbreaks in the fall and use case-based interventions, basically, isolating people with the infection and their close contacts.
>
> SCOTT GOTTLIEB: What we need is a better toolbox, a good medicine cabinet coupled with—with **very aggressive surveillance**. That could be enough to really change the contours of the risk in the fall and allow people to feel comfortable going back out again.[47]

Whoops. Did Gottlieb make a Freudian slip? A week later, the president of the Minnesota Federal Reserve was on the show, promoting vaccines that were not available until a year later:

---

[46] CBS News, "Full Transcript of 'Face the Nation' on April 5, 2020," April 7, 2020. www.cbsnews.com/news/full-transcript-of-face-the-nation-on-april-5-2020/.
[47] CBS News, "Full Transcript of 'Face the Nation' on April 5, 2020," (emphasis added).

MARGARET BRENNAN: Your colleague James Bullard of the St. Louis Fed was with us last week, and he said that the answer lies fully in technology. It's testing and surveillance, getting people before they walk into their employer to have a test and wear a badge. I mean, is that your- your guidance here too?

NEEL KASHKARI: Oh, I would love it if that were possible. I've talked to some healthcare experts who- who say that it's a fantasy that we're gonna be able to test tens of millions of people every day, that there simply is not the equipment, there's not the supply chain. I hope they're wrong. That's a real concern. I don't think we should put all of our eggs only in the mass-testing basket. We should try to make that work. We should also invest fully in vaccines, fully in therapies. But then I think we're going to need to be smart about how we start to reopen parts of the economy with those who are at lowest risk until that capacity and that testing and those vaccines and therapies come online.[48]

It seems that alignments between unrelated groups are becoming more visible. Bankers repeat what medical bureaucrats say, and reporters repeat what scientists say. Why are non-experts confident enough in their information sources to make bold claims outside their areas of expertise? Why the solidarity?

We can either trust media-promoted stories or draw conclusions from our own research of source material. Upon closer inspection, we're seeing an obvious merger of all things

---

[48] CBS News, "Transcript: Neel Kashkari on 'Face the Nation,'" April 12, 2020," April 12, 2020. www.cbsnews.com/news/transcript-neel-kashkari-on-face-the-nation-april-12-2020/.

technocratic—but only if we look past unsupported claims. Healthcare, banking, and social justice, among other areas, are aligning in favor of the Beast.

On November 22, 2022, the US Department of Labor released a final rule concerning the fiduciary duties of savings plan managers, clearing the way for ESG investments in the name of socially acceptable beliefs. The department's new rule—which is not legislation and did not pass through Congress—basically means that fund managers do not need to consider profits alone when they make investments. Under this Act managers have free reign under executive powers, not laws, to save the world without needing to be accountable to shareholders for non-profitable ventures.

> [T]he U.S. Department of Labor released a final rule under the Employee Retirement Income Security Act (ERISA) to empower plan fiduciaries to safeguard the savings of America's workers by clarifying that fiduciaries may consider climate change and other environmental, social, and governance (ESG) factors when they make investment decisions and when they exercise shareholder rights, including voting on shareholder resolutions and board nominations.[49]

Elected government officials and non-elected agency officials can rule by Executive Order to bypass Congress. The following is an excerpt from a malicious letter sent by the Committee on Financial Services to the Office of the Comptroller of the Currency.

---

[49] US Department of Labor, "Final Rule on Prudence and Loyalty in Selecting Plan Investments and Exercising Shareholder Rights," Employee Benefits Security Administration, November 22, 2022. www.dol.gov/agencies/ebsa/about-ebsa/our-activities/resource-center/fact-sheets/final-rule-on-prudence-and-loyalty-in-selecting-plan-investments-and-exercising-shareholder-rights.

> In November 2020, the Office of the Comptroller of the Currency (OCC) released a notice of proposed rulemaking that would prohibit national banks and federal savings associations from categorically declining to provide financial services to industries engaged in lawful business activities. In one of its first official acts, however, the Biden Administration "paused publication" of the rule on January 28, 2021, and U.S. financial services providers may accordingly cut off politically disfavored customers in response to public pressure, or for no reason at all.[50]

The Securities and Exchange Commission is also in the mix.

> The proposed rules would require information about a registrant's climate-related risks that are reasonably likely to have a material impact on its business, results of operations, or financial condition. The required information about climate-related risks would also include disclosure of a registrant's greenhouse gas emissions, which have become a commonly used metric to assess a registrant's exposure to such risks. In addition, under the proposed rules, certain climate-related financial metrics would be required in a registrant's audited financial statements.[51]

---

[50] House of Representatives Committee on Financial Services, letter to Michael J. Hsu, March 1, 2022. https://financialservices.house.gov/uploadedfiles/202-03-01_pmc_bl_to_occ_re_asset_freezes.pdf.

[51] Securities and Exchange Commission, *The Enhancement and Standardization of Climate-Related Disclosures for Investors*, 17 CFR 210, 229, 232, 239, and 249. www.sec.gov/files/rules/proposed/2022/33-11042.pdf.

It is not just the SEC who is involved in this movement. Look who else is involved in working towards the Beast's plan to gobble up the earth's resources.

> October 4, 2023, the Securities Exchange Commission (SEC) issued a proposed rule to approve the creation of a new investment vehicle, the "Natural Asset Company (NAC)." (88 Fed. Reg. 68811 (Oct. 4, 2023)) This new vehicle was created by the Intrinsic Exchange Group (IEG) in partnership with the New York Stock Exchange (NYSE).
>
> The IEG was founded by the Rockefeller Foundation with supporting partners including international environmental organizations such as the World Wildlife Fund.
>
> The purpose for this new investment product is to provide a vehicle for elite investors and governments to profit from the protection of natural resources created by climate crisis policies. It is why these same proponents have been calling for the permanent protection of at least 30 percent of the world's land and oceans by 2023 – the 30×30 agenda. These same actors are also pushing the net zero and decarbonization policies.
>
> Their objective is not the conservation of the land. They seek total political and financial control of the world's natural resources particularly in the United States.[52]

---

[52] American Stewards of Liberty, *SEC Poised to Authorize "Natural Asset Companies"*, October 20, 2023. https://americanstewards.us/sec-poised-to-authorize-natural-asset-companies/

Since the process for passing laws is lengthy and complicated, attempts are often made to bypass the legislative system to achieve a new set of rules based on promoting the big brain ideas of the elite. *The Daily Signal* summarizes these battles between lawmakers and governmental agencies.

> Agencies, of course, write regulations that look like laws and have the force and effect of law. They also have the power to enforce these regulations.
>
> In addition to these legislative and executive powers, agencies also have their own courts and judges.
>
> The SEC tries many of the cases that arise under its rules in front of its in-house administrative law judges. In these cases, in essence, the SEC is not only "judge, jury, and executioner," but lawmaker, investigator, prosecutor, judge, jury, and executioner.[53]

Our next step is to uncover the individuals involved in the movements to shift cultural attitudes away from individualism or personal freedoms while accelerating more toward socialism or collectivism. It does matter if democracy is used as a cover story for these movements toward global unity. It is my belief that there should always be a balance between social concerns and individual freedoms; how this balance is determined and funded is a different story.

My departed good friend who was a brilliant inventor and entrepreneur, Dr. Mahlon Dennis, used to say he was a socially minded capitalist. I always liked that, but we are at a critical

---

[53] Joseph Postell, "Securities and Exchange Commission Case Could Take Down Administrative State's 'Home Court Advantage'," The Daily Signal, December 13, 2022.
www.dailysignal.com/2022/12/13/securities-and-exchange-commission-case-could-take-down-administrative-states-home-court-advantage/.

point in history where one side is becoming too powerful and disrupting any chance of balance.

Technocracy at Columbia University

> Technocracy – government by technicians who are guided solely by the imperatives of their technology.[54]

Antony Sutton, whose book *Western Technology and Soviet Economic Development* we looked at earlier, had a partner in exposing the crimes committed by the techno-elites. Patrick Wood, described as a critical expert on sustainable development, co-authored books and articles on technology with Sutton. Since Sutton's passing in 2002, Wood has carried this torch.[55] The duo's fascinating work, both together and as solo authors, demonstrates how the elites have maintained a baffling movement whose progression we can follow from a century ago to its fresh face today—in the form of the Fourth Industrial Revolution, or any other name they want to call it.

What is evident about technocracy is that its proponents have been transparent about their beliefs and agendas. The same cannot be said about nefarious movements of the past; for example, the real motives of Carnegie's and Rockefeller's large donations to movements like eugenics were obscured. Conversely, these open statements about the true intents of technocrats allow us to understand the bigger picture without needing to extrapolate.

The connection between technology and ideology is evident in many examples from history. New York City's Columbia University, for instance, became an international hub for the humanist movement, led in the US by John Dewey, who was named the "Most Influential Figure in American Education" over

---

[54] Britannica, "technocracy," definition. www.britannica.com/topic/technocracy.
[55] See *Technocracy Rising: The Trojan Horse of Global Transformation* (2015) and other publications at www.technocracy.news/store/.

the period from 1924 to 1974.[56] Dewey was a key signatory to the original *Humanist Manifesto*[57] and is considered to be the father of progressive education. He visited Russia and wrote about his admiration of the school systems there promoting collectivism vs. individualistic ideals.[58] This trip influenced his future work to help establish a new type of education system in the USA.

Although the original technocracy movement died off in the USA and was officially banned in Canada in 1940, the core movement exists today under new names and terminologies. Elon Musk's grandfather was heavily involved with technocracy in Canada; to what extent did these beliefs influence the multi-billionaire Tesla CEO's upbringing?

> In fitting with his independent spirit, [Musk's grandfather] Haldeman didn't align himself with a mainstream Canadian party. Between 1936 and 1941, he became involved in Technocracy, and eventually became the leader of the Canadian branch of the party.
>
> Technocracy is a political philosophy that advocates government by skill, rather than by opinion. The government is designed to use science and technology to distribute services to citizens, instead of relying on human opinions or traditions.
>
> The movement was temporarily banned by the Canadian government out of fear that its members planned overthrow the government by force.[59]

---

[56] *Saturday Review* magazine, August 10, 1974, p. 84.
[57] American Humanist Association, *Humanist Manifesto I* (1933). https://americanhumanist.org/what-is-humanism/manifesto1/.
[58] John Dewey, *The New Republic*, Impressions of Soviet Russia, 1928-12-05: Vol 57 Iss 731, pp. 64-67. https://archive.org/details/sim_new-republic_1928-12-05_57_731
[59] Postmedia News, "Before Elon Musk Was Thinking about Mars and Electric Cars, He Was Doing Chores on a Saskatchewan Farm," *Regina Leader-Post*, May 15, 2017.

The New Yorker has also drawn connections between Musk's business practices and his family's history in the technocracy movement.

> Musk has said that he bought Twitter to halt the advance of a "woke mind virus" spreading online. His grandfather wrote his tracts to raise an alarm about what he called "mind control," on the radio and television, where "an unconditional propaganda warfare is carried on against the White man."
>
> [Musk's grandfather] Haldeman was born in Minnesota in 1902 but grew up mostly in Saskatchewan, Canada. A daredevil aviator and sometime cowboy, he also trained and worked as a chiropractor. In the nineteen-thirties, he joined the quasi-fascistic Technocracy movement, whose proponents believed that scientists and engineers, rather than the people, should rule. He became a leader of the movement in Canada, and, when it was briefly outlawed, he was jailed, after which he became the national chairman of what was then a notoriously antisemitic party called Social Credit. In the nineteen-forties, he ran for office under its banner, and lost.[60]

Instead of diving deep into the past workings of technocracy, like Sutton and Wood have done, let's refer back to Columbia University and its role as the focal point of the humanist movement. Right next to Technocrat Central, in the basement

---

http://leaderpost.com/feature/elon-musk-inherited-a-lifetime-of-adventure-from-his-sask-family.
[60] Jill Lepore, "The World According to Elon Musk's Grandfather," *The New Yorker*, September 19, 2023. www.newyorker.com/news/daily-comment/the-world-according-to-elon-musks-grandfather.

of Columbia, a company emerged that was vital for providing the computing power necessary for the merger of technology and the new religion.

> A case can be made that the computer industry got its start at Columbia University in the late 1920s and early 1930s when Professors Wood and Eckert, to advance their respective sciences, began to send designs and specifications for computing machines to IBM Corporation, which until then had been a maker of punched-card tabulating machines for the business market. From those days through the 1980s, the relationship of Columbia with companies like IBM was symbiotic and fruitful.
>
> Professor Wood had convinced Watson to build special Difference Tabulators, which IBM called "Columbia machines" and delivered in 1930–31. These machines could process 150 cards per minute and were unique in their ability to rapidly accumulate sums of products or squares ... The Statistical Bureau soon became a service provider to outside organizations like the Rockefeller and Carnegie Foundations.[61]

Modern Technocrats

The founding of IBM and development of database systems arose from the necessity for the elite to keep track of what they considered to be "undesirable" populations before and during World War II, including Nazi persecution of Europe's Jewish, Non-Nazi Christians and Gypsy populations. But this was not limited to German elites; those in power in the USA and elsewhere were

---

[61] Frank da Cruz, "Columbia University Computing History," Watson Laboratory, Columbia University, last updated May 22, 2024. www.columbia.edu/cu/computinghistory/.

heavily involved in the planning of population control. For example, in *IBM and the Holocaust*, American historian Edwin Black highlights the involvement of Henry Ford, the computing giant IBM and other actors in crimes of the twentieth century.[62]

IBM CEO Thomas J. Watson's business machines helped implement eugenics programs in Poland and won the business leader recognition from Germany, which awarded him the Order of the German Eagle in 1937, an honorary award that industrialist Henry Ford would win a year later, in 1938.

> What Hitler has done to us through his economic warfare, one of our own American corporations has also done ... Hence IBM is in a class with the Nazis ... The entire world citizenry is hampered by an international monster.[63]

Today, we find that IBM is still working behind the scenes to accomplish the plans of the Beast, now with expanded computing power, in its development of New York State's digital health certificate, also known as the Excelsior Pass.

During the early stages of the COVID-19 pandemic, New York Governor Cuomo's office made a behind-the-scenes deal with IBM. The Excelsior digital health pass was stated to be the first voluntary testing program in the US, costing $2.5 million in New York taxpayer dollars. The contract was hidden from the public until it was published by the folks at the Surveillance Technology Oversight Project (STOP).[64] There was no transparency.

---

[62] Edwin Black, *IBM and the Holocaust: The Strategic Alliance Between Nazi Germany and America's Most Powerful Corporation* (New York: Little, Brown, 2001).
[63] Howard J. Carter, quoted in Savannah Cox, "How IBM Helped the Nazis Carry Out the Holocaust," All That's Interesting, March 25, 2018. https://allthatsinteresting.com/ibm-nazis-ww2/3.
[64] STOP, "STOP Condemns Cuomo for Hiding Excelsior Pass's $17M Price Tag," press release, June 9, 2021. www.stopspying.org/latest-news/2021/6/9/stop-condemns-cuomo-for-hiding-excelsior-passs-17-m-price-tag.

Cuomo announced the scheme just as the vaccines were rolling out.

> As more New Yorkers get vaccinated each day and as key public health metrics continue to regularly reach their lowest rates in months, the first-in-the-nation Excelsior Pass heralds the next step in our thoughtful, science-based reopening.[65]

Cuomo and his colleagues had their own technocratic science, and while he stated that the scheme would cost only $2.5 million, the contract says otherwise. *The New York Times* and other media caught wind of this and reported on it several times.[66] With technocrats using surveillance technology like programmable currency, passports and apps to accomplish their plans, we should pause to consider whether the purpose of digital passports is intended to save lives or help the economy.

The following contract details were not initially disclosed to the public, with Cuomo neglecting to mention the three-year term as he promoted the trial phase. While at the time few would have believed a three-year term to have been necessary, some technocrats would have known we would need passports in advance.

> 1. The term of this Contract T000685 will be from January 25, 2021 through March 19, 2024 …

---

[65] New York State, "Governor Cuomo Announces Launch of Excelsior Pass to Help Fast-Track Reopening of Businesses and Entertainment Venues Statewide," press release, March 26, 2021. www.governor.ny.gov/news/governor-cuomo-announces-launch-excelsior-pass-help-fast-track-reopening-businesses-and.

[66] Sharon Otterman, "New York's 'Excelsior Pass' Could Cost Up to $27 Million," *The New York Times*, August 19, 2021. www.nytimes.com/2021/08/19/nyregion/new-york-excelsior-pass-cost.html; Karen Weintraub and Elizabeth Weise, "New York Launches Nation's First 'Vaccine Passports,'" *USA Today*, March 26, 2021. www.usatoday.com/story/news/health/2021/03/26/covid-vaccine-passports-new-york-first-vaccination-proof-system/6976009002/

2. the estimated pricing for the full three-year term of this Contract is $16,981,000.00, consisting of fixed one-time implementation costs of $2,500,000.00.[67]

New York State paid enormous sums for IBM's development and implementation of this software. Furthermore, the IT giant can keep the intellectual property rights and sell similar software to other purchasers. (Section 26.4 of the contract states that IBM owns the technology, which it licenses to the State of New York.)

Within six months, over a million people had signed up for New York's digital heath pass, with taxpayers having funded the enormous rollout. The app was free for businesses and individuals.

The NSA and IBM: Working Behind the Scenes

Twitter's (X's) new management, after the Musk purchase, released files pertaining to the connections between the National Security Agency, IBM, and the social network. Other social media giants have also testified to Congress about their involvement with intelligence agencies.

NSA whistleblowing has long been in the media's focus.

> Thomas Drake, William Binney and J. Kirk Wiebe belong to a select fraternity: the NSA officials who paved the way.
>
> They had spent decades in the top ranks of the agency, designing and managing the very data-collection systems they say have been turned against Americans. When they became convinced that fundamental constitutional rights were being violated, they complained first to their superiors, then to federal

---

[67] STOP, "Excelsior Pass Development Contract And Amendments," updated August 18, 2021. www.stopspying.org/excelsior-pass-contract.

investigators, congressional oversight committees and, finally, to the news media.

William Binney: We tried to stay for the better part of seven years inside the government trying to get the government to recognize the unconstitutional, illegal activity that they were doing and openly admit that and devise certain ways that would be constitutionally and legally acceptable to achieve the ends they were really after. And that just failed totally because no one in Congress or—we couldn't get anybody in the courts, and certainly the Department of Justice and inspector general's office didn't pay any attention to it. And all of the efforts we made just produced no change whatsoever.[68]

The lesson to be learned from stories such as this is that the intelligence community, with its connections to the elite, can break the law, while whistle-blowers and honest individuals cannot seem to get laws enforced. Indeed, until Edward Snowden, whistle-blowers were on the sidelines, and nothing was resolved at the NSA after the fouls were whistled in this case. Since 2013, no significant improvements have been made, even in light of recent information concerning Facebook and Twitter.

How does the NSA obtain private internet information on American (or foreign) citizens? Does the agency really use "backdoor" software to access user data from all internet providers and social media platforms? Have you seen your end-user agreement, where you signed off on third-party rights? Did you willingly give the government the right to spy on you?

---

[68] See, for example, Peter Eisler and Susan Page, "3 NSA Veterans Speak Out on Whistle-Blower: We Told You So," June 16, 2013. https://eu.usatoday.com/story/news/politics/2013/06/16/snowden-whistleblower-nsa-officials-roundtable/2428809/.

In an article with Ewen MacAskill, Glenn Greenwald, the *Guardian* investigator who broke the Edward Snowden story, describes the forms of co-operation between the NSA and tech giants.

> The National Security Agency has obtained direct access to the systems of Google, Facebook, Apple and other U.S. internet giants, according to a top secret document obtained by the Guardian.
>
> The NSA access is part of a previously undisclosed program called Prism, which allows officials to collect material including search history, the content of emails, file transfers and live chats, the document says.[69]

Other major players, including Cisco Systems, have openly admitted to similar issues on their servers,[70] and another giant in the industry, Juniper Networks, has relayed security issues with the NSA.

> Juniper Networks Inc said late on Friday it would stop using a piece of security code that analysts believe was developed by the National Security Agency in order to

---

[69] Glenn Greenwald and Ewen MacAskill, "NSA Prism Program Taps in to User Data of Apple, Google and Others," *The Guardian*, June 7, 2013. www.theguardian.com/world/2013/jun/06/us-tech-giants-nsa-data.

[70] Dan Goodin, "Cisco Confirms NSA-Linked Zeroday Targeted Its Firewalls for Years," arsTechnica, August 18, 2016. https://arstechnica.com/information-technology/2016/08/cisco-confirms-nsa-linked-zeroday-targeted-its-firewalls-for-years/; on other instances, see Dan Goodin, "How 'Omnipotent' Hackers Tied to NSA Hid for 14 Years—and Were Found at Last," arsTechnica, February 16, 2015. https://arstechnica.com/information-technology/2015/02/how-omnipotent-hackers-tied-to-the-nsa-hid-for-14-years-and-were-found-at-last/.

eavesdrop through technology products.⁷¹

Eavesdropping plans have been going on for a while, whether through phone or internet surveillance. Indeed, an unclassified highlight (from a Carnegie Endowment-sponsored event), the "Third CPSR Cryptography and Privacy Conference," provides a key statement regarding a 1992 FBI proposal.

> In 1992 the Federal Bureau of Investigation introduced a proposal to require that telecommunications manufacturers and service providers redesign their systems to facilitate wiretapping.⁷²

Evidently, government agencies bypass the legal requirement for a warrant to get more information about us, perhaps justifying their actions by claiming there is too much red tape, or using other excuses about our safety.

> James Clapper, the former director of national intelligence, denied Tuesday that he lied to Congress when he falsely testified during the Obama administration that the government does "not wittingly" collect the telephone records of millions of Americans.
>
> The head of the U.S. intelligence community under former President Barack Obama, Mr. Clapper recalled his 2013 testimony in light of the National Security Agency reportedly abandoning a controversial, warrantless mass-

---

⁷¹ Joseph Menn, "Juniper Networks Will Drop Code Tied to National Security Agency," Reuters, January 9, 2016.
www.reuters.com/article/spying-juniper/juniper-networks-will-drop-code-tied-to-national-security-agency-idUSL1N14T05420160109/.
⁷² http://freedomgrid.org/wp-content/uploads/2025/07/Third-CPSR-Cryptography-and-Privacy-Conference.pdf

surveillance program he previously denied existing.

"I didn't lie, I made a big mistake, and I just simply didn't understand what I was being asked about," Mr. Clapper said on CNN. "I thought of another surveillance program, Section 702 of the Foreign Intelligence Surveillance Act, when I was being asked about Section 215 of the Patriot Act at the time, I just didn't understand that."[73]

But by looking at white-collar industry, we notice that it is not just government agencies that are trying to control information.

> The Treasury Department on Thursday slapped six Russian technology companies with sanctions for supporting Kremlin intelligence agencies engaged in "dangerous and disruptive cyber attacks."
>
> But only one of them stands out for its international footprint and partnerships with such IT heavyweights as Microsoft and IBM.
>
> IBM didn't respond to requests for comment ..."[74]

There are many issues concerning IBM.[75] Strangely enough, IBM has even sued the Internal Revenue Service (IRS), threatening

---

[73] Andrew Blake, "James Clapper Denies Lying to Congress about NSA Surveillance Program," *The Washington Times*, March 6, 2019. https://apnews.com/article/business-33a88feb083ea35515de3c73e3d854ad.

[74] Associated Press, "Sanctioned Russian IT Firm was Partner with Microsoft, IBM," Security Week, April 16, 2021. www.securityweek.com/sanctioned-russian-it-firm-was-partner-microsoft-ibm/.

[75] Arne Alsin, "The IBM Hall of Shame: A (Semi) Complete List of Bribes, Blunders and Fraud," Medium, November 27, 2016. https://medium.com/worm-capital/the-ibm-hall-of-shame-a-semi-complete-list-of-bribes-blunders-and-fraud-19e674a5b986.

that the latter would incur penalties if it did not extend its software contract. Who threatens to sue the IRS and wins?![76]

> 30. To avoid having to pay the asserted penalties, the IRS agreed to enter into a new five-year deal with IBM (the "License") for software that the IRS was not using and did not want a total cost to the United States Government and the IRS of approximately $265,000,000 because IBM represented it would wait the compliance penalties.
>
> 31. The materially false and inflated audit findings presented to the IRS and IBM's representation that it would waive those penalties if the IRS entered into a new deal caused, in substantial and material part, the IRS to enter into the License when it otherwise would not have.
>
> The Register has asked IBM for comment. [Crickets chirping.][77]

Despite IBM's corruption cases, the NSA has still publicly promoted IBM over other US microelectronics suppliers.

> Through TAPO, a contractual relationship [has been made] with IBM to produce leading-edge microelectronics parts in a trusted environment. IBM maintains world-class facilities in both Vermont and New

---

[76] MarketScreener, "International Business Machines: Whistleblower Claims IBM Defrauded IRS in Software Purchase Arising out of Audit," June 23, 2020. www.marketscreener.com/quote/stock/IBM-4828/news/International-Business-Machines-Whistleblower-Claims-IBM-Defrauded-IRS-In-Software-Purchase-Arisin-30810937/.

[77] Tim Richardson, "Ex-IBM Whistleblower's Suit Back in Court, 8 Years After He Alleged Irregularities in $265m IRS Software Deal," The Register, July 8, 2021. www.theregister.com/2021/07/08/ibm_lawsuit_whistleblower_allegations_irs/.

> York, providing a broad range of capabilities to the government in support of the Trusted Foundry contract.
>
> Who can use TAPO services? Any government-sponsored program can use TAPO to access the IBM Trusted Foundry.[78]

We can learn from past events that the leaders of companies like IBM and agencies such as the NSA have a long history of corruption. Social media sites that may once have been considered tame, like Facebook, have turned out to be responsible for massive intelligence breaches against citizens. We now know that, time and again, the US government—or actors behind it—have used social media companies to achieve their goals of database-building and surveillance. Can we do something about it?

Climate Change Technology

Another area in which technocrats have attempted to take control is climate change. Since countries like the USA and China can't agree to control emissions, it is up to those who consider themselves the *smartest people* to help set up a system for us. This ties into ESG, financing, NGOs, corporations, and influential individuals intending to use software like Climate TRACE[79] to accomplish their goals.

> Another standout development at this COP was Al Gore's announcement of Climate TRACE – a new tool for independently measuring emissions, rather than relying on self-reporting that would go a long way to address this issue.

---

[78] National Security Agency, "Trusted Access Program Office (TAPO)." Accessed at the Wayback Machine,
https://web.archive.org/web/20131127144121/http:/www.nsa.gov/business/programs/tapo.shtml.

[79] Climate TRACE uses "satellites and other remote sensing technologies" to identify emissions activities. www.climatetrace.org/.

> Climate TRACE uses A.I. and machine learning to analyse data from thousands of satellites, sensors, and public and commercial datasets from across the globe. It's an inventory that provides transparent emissions estimates for all major sources of emissions, down to an individual oil rig or power plant, on a monthly, weekly, and potentially even daily basis.[80]

> While in Glasgow for the 2021 UN Climate Change Conference, known as COP26, Al Gore elaborated on the function of this Climate TRACE coalition to hold entities and individuals accountable for climate offenses, stating, "We can now accurately determine where the greenhouse gas emissions are coming from ... and we'll have the identities of the people who are responsible for each of those greenhouse gas emission streams, and if investors, or governments, or civil society activists want to hold them responsible, they will have the information upon which to base their action in holding them responsible."[81]

Of course, we can't forget about the Council on Foreign Relations. CFR member John Kerry had this to say:

---

[80] Tahnee Burgess et al., "COP27: Rich Nations Fail to Cough Up for Climate Change," Monash University, November 15, 2022. https://web.archive.org/web/20221115041032/https://lens.monash.edu/@climate-change-rising-to-the-real-urgent-and-globa/2022/11/15/1385281/cop27-rich-nations-fail-to-cough-up-for-climate-change.

[81] The Sharp Edge, "Climate TRACE: A Framework for ESG Initiatives and Social & Climate Credit System," Corey's Digs, June 1, 2022. www.coreysdigs.com/technology/climate-trace-a-framework-for-esg-initiatives-and-social-climate-credit-system/.

Will the 122 countries that have signed the pledge to reduce methane by 30 percent globally build on a strong first year to deliver global progress quickly enough and an amazing impact? The potential of hitting that 2030 target is the reality of every ship in the world, every car in the world, every truck in the world, every airplane in the world going to zero by 2030.

I was in Seattle last week where Bill Gates' Breakthrough Energy Ventures hosted one of the world's largest gatherings of clean-tech innovators, and I left more convinced than ever that exponential progress is within our grasp—not just within this generation, but within this decade.

But key to winning this battle is securing the funding to be able to accelerate this transition. Public finance is an indispensable component, mostly to unlock private investment on a scale that is needed in order to finance the energy revolution, to de-risk, to create blended finance.

Earlier this year Secretary Yellen called for a new Bretton Woods system. And she laid out a vision for that project before this month's annual meetings that includes a modern framework for the World Bank.

There's only one way to secure the future. We have to summon the greatest effort we've ever assembled, with the greatest sense of urgency. And we must win this fight, because the alternative is beyond unacceptable.[82]

---

[82] Council on Foreign Relations, "COP27 and International Climate Action: A Conversation With John Kerry," October 25, 2022.

No sane person wants to harm the environment, and there are many improvements we can make to prevent pollution of all kinds. However, in the time ahead, the urgency of the call for such financing will probably become much more noticeable, to the point of desperation. All the planets are aligning for the Beast to introduce the biggest financing structures ever assembled. Markets are about to transform to align with ESG, AI and related efforts on a massive scale, more significant even than the investments made after World War II.

In order to maintain their financial control schemes, the likely narrative to promote the transition over to digital currencies with tight controls will be the need to save the planet from climate catastrophe.

Comments by Fink, Gore and Kerry have given us an insight into some workings of the modern technocrats, including their open statements about what is coming next (for which we need to prepare), but what about their plans behind closed doors? The Beast followers gave us their reasoning—half-truths—for these changes, yet there is the hidden agenda we need to uncover.

There are secrets buried. But some secrets can be exhumed.

---

www.cfr.org/event/cop27-and-international-climate-action-conversation-john-kerry.

Chapter 5: What Can We Really Know about Secret Societies?

> Though eighteen years have gone by, I do not feel free to give a description of this most interesting conference which Senator Aldrich pledged all participants to secrecy.
>
> Paul Warburg[1]

> [Benjamin Strong] president of the Bankers Trust Company [J.P. Morgan] was selected as the first Governor of the New York Federal Reserve Bank. An adept in high finance, Strong for many years manipulated the country's monetary system **at the discretion of directors** representing the leading New York banks. Under Strong, the Reserve System, **unsuspected by the nation**, was brought into interlocking relations with the Bank of England and the Bank of France,
>
> Ferdinand Lundberg[2]

Having never been in a secret society, I cannot share any first-hand experience. However, many books have been written by, and interviews been made with, people who were once members of these societies. They can inform us more about their inner workings. The chapter-opening quote is from Paul Warburg, a key founder of the Federal Reserve, who had first-hand experience of such circles. In this chapter, we will examine information from insiders and close outsiders of these networks of power.

---

[1] Paul Warburg, *The Federal Reserve System: Its Origin and Growth* (New York: Macmillan, 1930), Vol. I, p. 58.
[2] Ferdinand Lundberg, *America's Sixty Families* (New York: Vanguard Press, 1937), p. 122, (emphasis added).

The Bilderberg Group

The Bilderberg Group is described as an "off-the-record" annual meeting between leading figures in European and North American economics, politics, and industry. Instead of rehashing what others have said about this yearly forum, we can examine material from participants, such as the following account of a 1991 meeting.

> David Rockefeller, a longtime leader at Bilderberg conclaves, was even more explicit when addressing the 1991 meeting of the Bilderberg group. Rockefeller stated:
>
> "We are grateful to the Washington Post, The New York Times, Time Magazine and other great publications whose directors have attended our meetings and respected their promises of discretion for almost 40 years. It would have been impossible for us to develop our plan for the world if we had been subjected to the lights of publicity during those years. But the world is more sophisticated and prepared to march towards a world government. The supranational sovereignty of an intellectual elite and world bankers is surely preferable to the national auto-determination practiced in past centuries."
>
> That statement and other remarks from the Bilderberg meeting were obtained by French intelligence agents, who were tasked with monitoring the gathering, because of the obvious implications for French national interests and security. The information was then leaked to two French publications. Hilaire du Berrier, a contributing editor to The New American, verified the authenticity of the reports

through his friend, former head of French intelligence, Count Alexander de Marenches, and other sources, and provided the first account in English in his Monaco-based monthly HduB Reports in September 1991. It was then published shortly thereafter in The New American. What seemed outlandish to many people at the time, and was frequently dismissed as kooky "conspiracy theory," is being confirmed daily in unfolding events—and admissions from those who are causing the events to happen.[3]

Commentary is almost unnecessary here; David Rockefeller said that he and his elite friends should rule the world because they were superior to the sovereignty of individual nations, he thanked the media for their assistance in the cause, and he recognized that controlling information is necessary to fulfill the Bilderberg Group's plans.

Quotes about Secret Societies from Famous Leaders

On July 14, 1856, Benjamin Disraeli made the following statement to the House of Commons.

> There is in Italy a power which we seldom mention in this House, but without considering and understanding which we shall never rightly comprehend the position of Italy—I mean the secret societies. The secret societies do not care for constitutional government. They do not want existing society ameliorated, they want it changed; and they seek objects

---

[3] William F. Jasper, "Bilderberg-Picked EU Leader Van Rompuy Calls for Global Governance with Russia," *The New American*, December 27, 2012, accessed at the Wayback Machine, https://web.archive.org/web/20201030211838/https:/thenewamerican.com/bilderberg-picked-eu-leader-van-rompuy-calls-for-global-governance-with-russia/.

from such changes such as can never be obtained or secured by those enlightened institutions to which the noble Lord refers. We know something more of these societies than we did. Since the outbreak of 1848 we have had means—not sufficient, but still we have had means of obtaining a knowledge of their numbers, organisation, principles, and objects; and without some consideration of these it would be absolutely impossible for us to form a conception of what would be the consequence of our interference in the affairs of Italy. It is useless to deny, because it is impossible to conceal, that a great part of Europe—the whole of Italy and France and a great portion of Germany, to say nothing of other countries—are covered with a network of these secret societies, just as the superficies of the earth is now being covered with railroads...

The secret societies are not confined to Italy, as I have ventured to remind the House. They are at this moment more numerous, more active, and in a higher state of organisation in France than in any other State of Europe. If Italy be in flames, and if the Italian secret societies be successful, do you think that it will have no effect on the secret societies of France? They are always in a state of organisation and ready to act upon every occasion... But you will allow me to remind you that we all remember another great prince who sat upon the French throne, whose sagacity during his reign was also a proverb, who was never mentioned in this House but in terms of panegyric on both sides, who also had been schooled in adversity, and who was also seconded by an army which he and the princes of his House had themselves formed, which was fresh and flushed with victory, and which was led by able generals devoted to him and eager to prove their devotion by the assertion of his rights and the maintenance of his throne. But that great prince fell suddenly, and he fell solely and entirely by the action of the secret societies. That I apprehend is a fact which no man acquainted with the events of 1848 will deny. No doubt that terrible catastrophe was assisted by a great misfortune which then occurred to France.[4]

Many other big names such as US Presidents had similar thoughts about the difficulty in finding the details about secret societies.

That so many men, at so many separate points, should have acted in perfect concert in such business as they were engaged in, would scarcely be believed, without compelling the inference of some distinct understanding existing between them. That they should have carried into effect the most difficult part of their undertaking, a scheme of the most daring and criminal nature, in the midst of a large, intelligent and active population, without thereby incurring the risk of a full conviction of their guilt and the consequent punishment, would be equally incredible, but for the light furnished by the phraseology of the Masonic oath ["... under no less a penalty, on the violation of

---

[4] Benjamin Disraeli, Parliamentary debates, *Italy – Motion for Address* (Hansard, Volume 143: July 14, 1856).
https://hansard.parliament.uk/Commons/1856-07-14/debates/ce20adc3-1bcd-40ff-bb94-4d2cd49e57d4/Italy%E2%80%94MotionForAddress

any of them, than that of being severed in two, my bowels burned to ashes"] ...

Upon the first hasty and superficial glance, a feeling might arise of surprise that the frivolity of its unmeaning ceremonial, and ridiculous substitution of its fictions for the sacred history, should not long ago discredited the thing in the minds of good and sensible men everywhere. Yet upon closer and more attentive examination, this first feeling vanishes, and makes way for astonishment at the ingenious contrivance displayed in the construction of the whole machine. A more perfect agent for the devising and execution of conspiracies against the church or state could scarcely have been conceived.

US President John Quincy Adams[5]

Since I entered politics, I have chiefly had men's views confided to me privately. Some of the biggest men in the United States, in the Field of commerce and manufacture, are afraid of something. They know that there is a power somewhere so organized, so subtle, so watchful, so interlocked, so complete, so pervasive, that they better not speak above their breath when they speak in condemnation of it.

US President Woodrow Wilson[6]

Canadian author and mystic Manly Hall explained the following difficulties in finding information about these groups. He was

---

[5] John Quincy Adams, *Letters on the Masonic Institution* (Boston, MA: T. R. Marvin, 1847).
[6] Woodrow Wilson, *The New Freedom* (New York: Doubleday, 1913).

involved directly as an insider so he admits some truth but hides the rest.

> The foregoing may throw some light on the reason why it is so difficult to determine the position of the ancient initiates. Their reticence and humble spirit have seldom found a place on the pages of history, and yet they are the real molders of the destinies of nations. They are the invisible powers behind the thrones of earth, and men are but marionettes, dancing while the invisible ones pull the strings. We see the dancer, but the master mind that does the work remains concealed by the cloak of silence.[7]

"Providence Has Favored Our Undertakings"

Certain facts have been hidden from the American public about the founding of the USA. Perhaps we will never know what really happened. How many have heard of the Carroll family, Lorenzo Ricci, or Charles Thompson as having been influential in the formation period? Why are these names mostly hidden from history books? Certainly, some stories about American heroes are myths, like the tale about George Washington and the cherry tree, yet it seems the true backgrounds of some key actors have never been widely told.

Former Treasurer of the US Mint and Founding Father Benjamin Rush spoke in his autobiography about Charles Thom[p]son, an influential early American and secretary of the Continental Congress, who did not make it into many history books—perhaps for good reason. The conversation between Rush and Thomson is astonishing to the point where it should make us wonder how much we really know what happened behind the scenes.

> CHARLES THOMPSON. A man of great learning and general knowledge, at all

---

[7] Manly P. Hall, *What the Ancient Wisdom Expects of Its Disciples* (Los Angeles, CA: Philosophical Research Society, 1982), p. 42.

times genuine Republican, and in the evening of his life a sincere Christian. He was the intimate of John Dickinson. He was once told in my presence that he ought to write a history of the Revolution. "No," said he, "I ought not, for I should contradict all the histories of the great events of the Revolution, and shew by my account of men, motives and measures, that we are wholly indebted to the agency of providence for its successful issue. Let the world admire the supposed wisdom and valor of our great men. Perhaps they may adopt the qualities that have been ascribed to them, and thus good may be done. I shall not undeceive future generations."[8]

John Adams also had something to say about Thomson.

> We had much Conversation with Mr. Charles Thompson ... This Charles Thompson is the Sam. Adams of Phyladelphia—the Life of the Cause of Liberty, they say.[9]

Thomas Jefferson also referred people to Thomson's wide knowledge.

> [I]n an 1813 letter to John Hopkins, Jefferson suggested, "if there by any body who possesses materials either written, or on memory, I should suppose it to be Charles Thomson, who is in your

---

[8] Benjamin Rush, *The Autobiography of Benjamin Rush* (Princeton, NJ: Princeton University Press).
[9] John Adams, diary entry, August 30, 1774, quoted at "November Highlight: Charles Thomson," Harvard University Declaration Resources Project blog, November 4, 2017.
https://declaration.fas.harvard.edu/blog/november-thomson.

neighborhood. he must have retained many anecdotes at least."[10]

In a letter to Thomson on July 24, 1789, Washington wrote:

> I have to regret that the period of my coming again into public life, should be exactly that, in which you are about to retire from it. The present age does so much justice to the unsullied reputation with which you have always conducted yourself in the execution of the duties of your Office, and Posterity will find your Name so honorably connected with the verification of such a multitude of astonishing facts, that my single suffrage would add little to the illustration of your merits. Yet I cannot withold any just testimonial, in favor of so old, so faithful and so able a public officer, which might tend to sooth his mind in the shade of retirement. Accept, then, this serious Declaration, that your Services have been important, as your patriotism was distinguished; and enjoy that best of all rewards, the consciousness of having done your duty well.[11]

Charles Thomson was so highly regarded for a number of reasons; he even came up with the first seal and motto for the USA. Note that he attributed the country's formation more to "providence" than to the Founding Fathers. What invisible hand was behind it?

---

[10] Thomas Jefferson, letter to John Hopkins, August 11, 1813, quoted at National Archives, Founders Online, https://founders.archives.gov/documents/Jefferson/03-06-02-0316.

[11] George Washington, letter to Charles Thomson, July 24, 1789, quoted at National Archives, Founders Online, https://founders.archives.gov/documents/Washington/05-03-02-0171.

On June 20, 1782, Congress approved Thomson's design for both sides of the Great Seal, whose official description for the reverse side specifies:

"A Pyramid unfinished. In the Zenith an Eye in a triangle surrounded with a glory proper. Over the Eye these words 'Annuit Cœptis'."

Although Thomson did not provide an exact translation of Annuit Coeptis, he explained its meaning in conjunction with the Eye of Providence in a triangle surrounded by rays of golden light ("a glory proper") in the zenith of an unfinished pyramid:

"The Eye over it & the Motto allude to the many signal interpositions of providence in favour of the American cause."

"Signal" means unusual, notable, outstanding; to give a sign. "Interposition" means intervention; to insert between.[12]

The motto Annuit Coeptis was suggested by Charles Thomson in June 1782. He adapted it from Virgil, the renowned Roman writer's evocative instruction manual for farmers, The Georgics, written in the first century B.C.:

This sentence (Book I, line 40) has been translated as:

"Give me an easy course, and favor my daring undertakings."

It is part of Virgil's appeal to the godlike Augustus Caesar for success in his poetic

---

[12] Great Seal, "Origin and Meaning of the Motto above the Eye of Providence on the Great Seal." www.greatseal.com/mottoes/coeptis.html.

efforts to effectively convey crucial information to farmers.

"Audacibus annue coeptis" is also found in Book IX of Virgil's Aeneid, his epic masterpiece about the foundation of Rome. English translations include: "Assent to my bold attempt" and "Grant me success in this brave venture" and "Nod assent to the daring work I have in hand."

Charles Thomson, an expert in Latin, changed the second-person "annue" to its third-person form "annuit" and coined the motto: "Annuit Coeptis" – placing it above the eye of Providence where he explained it signified the "many signal interpositions of providence in favor of the American cause."

An accurate translation of Annuit Coeptis is:

"Providence Has Favored Our Undertakings."[13]

Thomson also promoted the motto "Novus Ordo Seclorum," translated as "A New Order for the Ages." This reminds me of Francis Bacon (and his unfinished novel *New Atlantis*), who we will examine in Chapter 6.

> For the reverse side of the Great Seal, Thomson used Barton's suggestion: an unfinished pyramid with the eye of Providence in its zenith.[14]

Thomson was influenced by Virgil and the prophesies of Sibyl, but why did he bring the culture of the Roman Empire to the beginnings of the USA? Why would he state the USA was

---

[13] Great Seal, "Original Source of ANNUIT COEPTIS." www.greatseal.com/mottoes/coeptisvirgil.html.
[14] Great Seal, "The Final Design of the Great Seal—June 20, 1782." www.greatseal.com/committees/finaldesign/index.html.

destined by providence vs. the work of the Founding Fathers? Why did he use the Eye of Providence in the Great Seal? We will need to explore this mystery further.

The Shadow Government

In an intriguing detail from this period, G. W. Snyder and George Washington corresponded about the Illuminati, a particularly famous secret society.

> It was some Time since that a Book fell into my Hands entituled "Proofs of a Conspiracy by John Robison," ... which gives a full Account of a Society of Freemasons, that distinguishes itself by the Name "of Illuminati," whose Plan is to overturn all Government and all Religion, even natural; and who endeavour to eradicate every Idea of a Supreme Being, and distinguish Man from Beast by his Shape only ...
>
> I send you the "Proof of a Conspiracy" which, I doubt not, will give you Satisfaction and afford you Matter for a Train of Ideas, that may operate to our national Felicity.[15]

The National Archives "Founders Online" project provides extensive notes about this "Proof of a Conspiracy" (for more information, see the link in footnote 15 on this page).

When presidents and prime ministers tell us about those behind the curtain, perhaps we should listen to their warnings.

> At the grand convention of Masonry held at Wilhelmsbad in 1782 the Order of the

---

[15] G. W. Snyder, letter to George Washington, August 22, 1798, quoted at National Archives, Founders Online, https://founders.archives.gov/documents/Washington/06-02-02-0435#GEWN-06-02-02-0435-fn-0002.

Strict Observance was suspended, and Von Knigge disclosed the scheme of Weishaupt to the assembled representatives of the masonic and mystical fraternities. Then and there disciples of Saint-Martin and of Willermooz, as well as the statesmen, scientists, magicians, and magistrates of all countries, were converted to Illuminism.[16]

What passed at this terrible Congress will never be known to the outside world, for even these men who had been drawn unwittingly into the movement, and now heard for the first time the real designs of the leaders, were under oath to reveal nothing.[17]

These real threats were reported a long time ago, but we also have evidence that people are working behind closed doors to threaten us today. Indeed, while the Illuminati may have gone underground, the Beast's trail is apparent even in modern times.

During the closing remarks of the congressional Iran-Contra committee hearings in 1987, Senator Daniel Inouye (HI) described the existence of "a shadowy government."

One vision was described in the testimony of Admiral Poindexter, Lieutenant Colonel North, General Secord, and Mr. Hakim: That of a secret government, directed principally by NSC staffers, accountable to not a single elected official, including apparently the President himself—a shadowy government with its own air force, its own navy, its own fund-raising

---

[16] "Illuminism and the French Revolution," *Edinburgh Review* (July 1906), p. 57.
[17] Nesta H. Webster, *World Revolution: The Plot against Civilization* (Boston, MA: Maynard Small, 1921), p. 31. https://archive.org/details/worldrevolutionp00webs.

mechanism, and the ability to pursue its own ideas of the national interest, free from all checks and balances and free from the law itself.

It is an elitist vision of government that trusts no one, not the people, not the Congress, and not the Cabinet.[18]

The idea of select groups of individuals in bodies such as the National Security Council with major influence in—and the ability to act outside of—the US government and military should make us stand up and take notice.

Cecil Rhodes and the Rise of the Modern Secret Societies

We have already looked at how individuals and their foundations, including Rockefeller and Carnegie, have funded nefarious projects over the years. Did they come up with these ideas independently, or were they following a pattern that had already been established?

Cecil Rhodes is the precursor to the twentieth-century playbook we examined so far. Yet even Rhodes' ideas were not new, as he learned from John Ruskin and others before him, expanding these ideas through the modern movement of philanthropy to drive an agenda of social engineering. Part of this process involved recruiting other influential individuals to the same cause. Rhodes' Wikipedia entry contains the following details.

> Financed by N M Rothschild & Sons, Rhodes succeeded over the next 17 years in buying up all the smaller diamond mining operations in the Kimberley area.
>
> His monopoly of the world's diamond supply was sealed in 1890 through a strategic partnership with the London-based Diamond Syndicate. They agreed

---

[18] Daniel Inouye, "Iran-Contra Hearings Closing Statement," August 3, 1987. https://dkii.org/speeches/august-03-1987/.

to control world supply to maintain high prices.[19]

While there is no need to recount his life here, we can focus on the information pertinent to our discussion, which is that through the company he established, De Beers, Rhodes initiated many subversive efforts in southern Africa. Among his many wills, testaments, and confessions, a couple in particular are worth noting. First, an 1877 document known as Rhodes' "Confession of Faith" explains a lot about his beliefs.

> I contend that we [The British] are the finest race in the world and that the more of the world we inhabit the better it is for the human race. Just fancy those parts that are at present inhabited by the most despicable specimens of human beings what an alteration there would be if they were brought under Anglo-Saxon influence, look again at the extra employment a new country added to our dominions gives.
>
> I look into history and I read the story of the Jesuits I see what they were able to do in a bad cause and I might say under bad leaders.
>
> At the present day I become a member of the Masonic order I see the wealth and power they possess the influence they hold and I think over their ceremonies and I wonder that a large body of men can devote themselves to what at times appear the most ridiculous and absurd rites without an object and without an end.
>
> The idea gleaming and dancing before ones eyes like a will-of-the-wisp at last frames itself into a plan. **Why should we not**

---

[19] Wikipedia, "Cecil Rhodes." https://en.wikipedia.org/wiki/Cecil_Rhodes.

form a secret society with but one object the furtherance of the British Empire and the bringing of the whole uncivilised world under British rule for the recovery of the United States for the making the Anglo-Saxon race but one Empire.

It is our duty to seize every opportunity of acquiring more territory and we should keep this one idea steadily before our eyes that more territory simply means more of the Anglo-Saxon race more of the best the most human, most honourable race the world possesses.

To forward such a scheme what a splendid help a secret society would be a society not openly acknowledged but who would work in secret for such an object.

Let us form the same kind of society a Church for the extension of the British Empire. A society which should have members in every part of the British Empire working with one object and one idea we should have its members placed at our universities and our schools and should watch the English youth passing through their hands just one perhaps in every thousand would have the mind and feelings for such an object, he should be tried in every way, he should be tested whether he is endurant, possessed of eloquence, disregardful of the petty details of life, and if found to be such, then elected and bound by oath to serve for the rest of his life in his County.

For fear that death might cut me off before the time for attempting its development I leave all my worldly goods in trust to S. G. Shippard and the Secretary for the Colonies at the time of my death to try to form such a Society with such an object.[20]

Rhodes implemented many of his monstrous ideas in his younger years, and while he wrote wills and confessions with less overt language in later years, these core beliefs made it into the twentieth and twenty-first centuries due to the wealth he had amassed and put toward funding his efforts. Equally important were the personal connections he used to lure other influential individuals to join the secret club. Newspaper editor William Thomas Stead recounted his personal involvement with Rhodes.

> Mr. Rhodes executed a third will in 1888, in which, after making provision for his brothers and sisters, he left the whole of the residue of his fortune to a financial friend, whom I will call "X.," in like manner expressing to him informally his desires and aspirations. This will was in existence when I first made the acquaintance of Mr. Rhodes.
>
> Finding that I sympathised with his ideas about English-speaking reunion and his Society although I did not see eye to eye with him about the tariff war Mr. Rhodes superseded the will, which he had made in 1888, on a sheet of notepaper, which left his fortune to " X.," by a formal will, in which the whole of his real and personal estate was left to " X." and to " W. Stead, of the REVIEW OF REVIEWS." This will, the fourth in order, was signed in March, 1891.[21]

---

[20] Cecil Rhodes, "Confession of Faith," 1877, (emphasis added). https://pages.uoregon.edu/kimball/Rhodes-Confession.htm.
[21] William Thomas Stead (ed.), "The Last Will and Testament of Cecil John Rhodes: With Elucidatory Notes to which are Added Some Chapters Describing the Political and Religious Ideas of the Testator," 1902. https://archive.org/stream/lastwilltestamen00rhodiala/lastwilltestamen00rhodiala_djvu.txt.

To whom did Rhodes wish to leave his immense wealth? Who was "Mr. X"?

> What an awful thought it is that if we had not lost America, or if even now we could arrange with the present members of the United States Assembly and our House of Commons, the peace of the world is secured for all eternity! We could hold your federal parliament five years at Washington and five at London. The only thing feasible to **carry this idea out is a secret one (society) gradually absorbing the wealth of the world** to be devoted to such an object ...
>
> [S]uch an idea as this [requires] the devotion of the best souls of the next 200 years. There are three essentials: (1) The plan duly weighed and agreed to. (2) The first organisation. (3) **The seizure of the wealth necessary.**[22]

While Stead summarized the general instructions, he tried to keep some portions of the testament secret. Rhodes envisioned that a 200-year plan was needed to achieve world domination; his followers have probably expanded his vision and have been seizing the wealth of the world ever since. The goal is now closer, less than 150 years on. Unless people wake up to stop it, at this rate, the Rhodes plan will become a reality. Just follow the money and see who is buying up the earth.

Again, we can turn to Carroll Quigley for some nuggets about the plan's inner workings, based upon his unprecedented access to secret information. In his book *The Anglo-American Establishment* (1981), Quigley states the identity of Mr. X from the third and fourth Rhodes wills.

> In each of his seven wills, Rhodes entrusted his bequest to a group of men to carry out

---

[22] "The Last Will and Testament of Cecil John Rhodes," p. 73, (emphasis added).

his purpose. In the first will, as we have seen, the trustees were Lord Carnarvon and Sidney Shippard. In the second will (1882), the sole trustee was his friend N. E. Pickering. In the third will (1888), Pickering having died, the sole trustee was Lord Rothschild. In the fourth will (1891), W. T. Stead was added, while in the fifth (1892), Rhodes's solicitor, B. F. Hawksley, was added to the previous two. In the sixth (1893) and seventh (1899) wills, the personnel of the trustees shifted considerably, ending up, at Rhodes's death in 1902, with a board of seven trustees: Lord Milner, Lord Rosebery, Lord Grey, Alfred Beit ... L. L. Michell, B. F. Hawksley, and Dr. Starr Jameson. This is the board to which the world looked to set up the Rhodes Scholarships.[23]

Here, we notice that Lord Rothschild was the Mr. X that Stead mentioned, and that he was the sole trustee from the third will. This claim is supported by other sources, with Rhodes having received a major portion of his financing to start De Beers from the Rothschilds. It is most interesting that the Rothschild name was not included in the wills that were made public, which anyone can now view, thanks to their establishment of the scholarships used to attract younger generations to continue the plan. Even Bill Clinton was a Rhodes scholar and Quigley's student at Georgetown.

The Rothschild Connection to the Secret Society

How did it come to be that the Rothschild name was removed from Rhodes' later wills? The answer may be that the Rothschilds used Alfred Beit as their agent, or indeed that the final wills did not supersede their earlier position.

---

[23] Carroll Quigley, *The Anglo-American Establishment* (New York: Books In Focus, 1981), p. 29.

> Beit's involvement with Jules Porges and Company provided Rhodes with links to foreign banks needed to finance any takeover.
>
> Through Beit, he obtained an introduction to Nathaniel de Rothschild, head of Europe's wealthiest financial house and an active speculator in diamond shares.[24]

A common misconception is that the Rothschilds were the masterminds, and Rhodes worked for them. Instead, we find from the historical records that Rhodes came up with the ideas, then convinced others to join his efforts. In *The Anglo-American Establishment*, Quigley provides an extract from diary of Lord Esher and a letter from Stead to his wife.

> His ideas are federation, expansion, and consolidation of the Empire ... He took to me [Stead]. Told me some things he has told no other man—save Lord Rothschild—[25]
>
> The evidence for this is to be found in the Journals of Lord Esher (at that time R. B. Brett), who had obviously been let in on the plan by Stead. Under the date of 3 February 1890, we read in these Journals: "Cecil Rhodes arrived last night from South Africa. I was at Stead's today when he called. I left them together. Tonight I saw Stead again. Rhodes had talked for three hours of all his great schemes ... Rhodes is a splendid enthusiast. But he looks upon men as 'machines.' This is not very penetrating." Twelve days after this, on 15 February, at Lord Rothschild's country

---

[24] Martin Meredith, *Diamonds, Gold, and War: The British, the Boers, and the Making of South Africa* (Washington, DC: PublicAffairs, 2007), chapter 15.
[25] Quigley, *The Anglo-American Establishment*, pp. 37.

> house, Brett wrote in his journal: 'Came here last night. Cecil Rhodes, Arthur Balfour, Harcourts, Albert Grey, Alfred Lyttelton. A long talk with Rhodes today. He has vast ideas. Imperial notions. He seems disinterested. But he is very ruse and, I suspect, quite unscrupulous as to the means he employs." ... The secret society, after so much preliminary talk, took form in 1891, the same year in which Rhodes drew up his fourth will and made Stead as well as Lord Rothschild the trustee of his fortune. It is perfectly clear from the evidence that he expected Rothschild to handle the financial investments associated with the trust, while Stead was to have full charge of the methods by which the funds were used.[26]

We can also find evidence of intimate dealings with Rhodes in official Rothschild records. One letter from Lord Rothschild to Cecil Rhodes openly states support for Rhodes' vision of the future, but offers no hint of being in the lead.

> [Y]ou should be able to carry out that great Imperial policy which has been the dream of your life—I think you will do us the justice to admit that we have always loyally supported you in the carrying out of that policy, and you may rest assured that we will continue to do so.[27]

We know the Rothschilds financed Rockefeller, J. P. Morgan, Rhodes and many more of the richest people on earth. Scholars

---

[26] Quigley, *The Anglo-American Establishment*, pp. 38.
[27] Lord Rothschild, letter to Cecil Rhodes, January 15, 1892, RHA Rhodes MSS C3B/201A, as published in S. D. Chapman, "Rhodes and the City of London: Another View of Imperialism," *The Historical Journal* 28(3) (1985), p. 657.

like J. A. Hobson[28] have considered bankers to be the true heads of imperialism, working toward the seizure of all wealth on earth. The Rothschilds have been just one of many families participating in the overall scheme.

The Plans of Cecil Rhodes

The execution of Rhodes' public plan was carried out by the Society of the Elect, a little-known inner-circle group. Rhodes' vision for the model was to be carried out by external groups because a massive effort was required. Not everything could be kept secret. However, the inner circle was secretly feeding the outer circles, so his planning was deceptive (and effective, for admirers of the Beast).

> About the same time, in February 1891, Stead and Rhodes had another long discussion about the secret society. First they discussed their goals and agreed that, if necessary in order to achieve Anglo-American unity, Britain should join the United States. Then they discussed the organization of the secret society and divided it into two circles: an inner circle, "The Society of the Elect", and an outer circle to include "The Association of Helpers" and The Review of Reviews (Stead's magazine, founded 1890). Rhodes said that he had already revealed the plan for "The Society of the Elect" to Rothschild and "little Johnston."

> This association was formally established on February 5, 1891, when Rhodes and Stead organized a secret society of which Rhodes had been dreaming for sixteen years. In this secret society Rhodes was to be leader; Stead, Brett (Lord Esher), and Milner were to form an executive

---

[28] J. A. Hobson, *Imperialism: A Study* (New York: James Pott & Co., 1902).

committee; Arthur (Lord) Balfour, (Sir) Harry Johnston, Lord Rothschild, Albert (Lord) Grey, and others were listed as potential members of a "Circle of Initiates"; while there was to be an outer circle known as the "Association of Helpers" (later organized by Milner as the Round Table organization). Brett was invited to join this organization the same day and Milner a couple of weeks later, on his return from Egypt. Both accepted with enthusiasm. Thus the central part of the secret society was established by March 1891. It continued to function as a formal group, although the outer circle was, apparently, not organized until 1909-1913.[29]

The Roundtable Group

After Rhodes' death, the implementation of his plans by the Society of the Elect and other related groups, such as Milner's Roundtable, led to the creation of the Council on Foreign Relations. Groups like the Pilgrims Society[30] and CFR are not secret societies but visible groups whose members include the biggest names in transatlantic politics and economics. These people continue to carry out Rhodes' vision of exploiting the world's wealth to accomplish the master plan. Based on the modern Beast plan, and supported by the research of Carroll Quigley, we can assume that the inner circle is in control, while the outer circles, consisting of groups like the CFR, take orders. The White House is after the CFR apparently.

After Rhodes led the way with major investments, we know the biggest celebrities of the Anglo-American establishment attempted to formalize stronger relations outside of their

---

[29] Quigley, *The Anglo-American Establishment*, pp. 38–39.
[30] The Pilgrims of Great Britain, "Welcome."
https://pilgrimsociety.org/new_site_03/index.php.

governmental politics. A list of Pilgrims Society members[31] includes names such as Thomas Watson Jr. of IBM, Rockefeller, Rothschild, Carnegie, and Morgan, as well as many US presidents and British royalty.

While author Stephen Bowman does not consider the Pilgrims to be a secret society ("This book contends that concepts surrounding the role of elite non-state actors are central to understanding the development of the Pilgrims, just as they help explain the activities of other, better-known, and more recent groups. Indeed, the argument here is that the early activities of the Society were a form of nascent public diplomacy"[32]), the words of Minnesota Representative Thorkelson in the 1940 Congressional Record suggest otherwise. He provides vast sources of documentation, including a short excerpt of statements made by a member of the Pilgrims Society called "Mr. Choate."

> Mr. Choate then makes his most extraordinary statement, upon which every Member of Congress and the people of this Nation should ponder—particularly in view of the happenings since 1912 ...
>
> In making this statement, Mr. Choate takes the position that Great Britain or England is our mother country; the same position that was taken by Cecil Rhodes over 50 years ago and by Andrew Carnegie in 1893, when he wrote a book entitled, "Triumphant Democracy."
>
> I want you to note particularly that this was in 1913, and that 1913 was the very year we changed our Government from a republic to a semidemocracy; the year in

---

[31] NNDB, "Pilgrims Society: Organization." www.nndb.com/org/207/000134802/.
[32] Stephen Bowman, "Public Diplomacy Conceptualised," In *The Pilgrims Society and Public Diplomacy, 1895–1945* (Edinburgh: Edinburgh University Press, 2018), pp. 19–36.

> which we destroyed constitutional government, international security, and paved the road for us to become a colony of the British Empire. It was also the same year in which we, by adopting the Federal Reserve Act, placed our Treasury under the control and domination of the Bank of England.[33]

It is apparent that most people do not read the Congressional Record; more sadly, people hear the truth but do not act.

Quigley uncovered more about Cecil Rhodes' spin-off groups. This demonstrates how people can carry on with the tradition of Rhodes as his plans expand over the first few decades after his death.

> This society has been called by various names. During the first decade or so it was called "the secret society of Cecil Rhodes," or "the dream of Cecil Rhodes." In the second and third decades of its existence it was known as "Milner's Kindergarten" (1901–1910) and as "the Round Table Group" (1910–1920). Since 1920 it has been called by various names, depending on which phase of its activities was being examined. It has been called "The Times crowd," "the Rhodes crowd," the "Chatham House crowd," "The All Souls group," and "the Cliveden set."[34]

> At the time the president of Swarthmore College was Frank Aydelotte, the most important member of the Milner Group in

---

[33] Jacob Thorkelson, Congressional Record, 76th Congress, 3rd Session, Appendix Vol. 86, Part 17, pp. 5108–5112. www.govinfo.gov/app/details/GPO-CRECB-1940-pt17-v86/GPO-CRECB-1940-pt17-v86-1.

[34] Quigley, *The Anglo-American Establishment*, p. 4.

the United States since the death of George Louis Beer. Dr. Aydelotte was one of the original Rhodes Scholars, attending Brasenose in 1905–1907. He was president of Swarthmore from 1921 to 1940; has been American secretary to the Rhodes Trustees since 1918; has been president of the American Association of Rhodes Scholars since 1930; has been a trustee of the Carnegie Foundation since 1922; and was a member of the Council on Foreign Relations for many years. In 1937, along with three other members of the Milner Group, he received from Oxford ... the honorary degree of Doctor of Civil Law.[35]

Communism or Capitalism?

While Rhodes might not have been unique in his ideas, he was famous and rich. Emperors and kings of the past have made plenty of attempts at global domination, but the modern approach is different in that it does not utilize a single state religion, economic system, or war machine, but many. Interestingly, both communism and capitalism have been recently used to accomplish the goal. It does not matter to the beast if the State confiscates all property ownership or if the Corporate Trust buys up all the real estate because people can't afford property as debt keeps inflating prices. Indeed, in the desire for a secular government that abolished private ownership, the Illuminati were ahead of Karl Marx.

> Doctor Adam Weishaupt, professor of the Canon law in the University of Ingolstadt, a city of Bavaria (in Germany) formed, about the year 1776, the order of Illuminati. This order is professedly a higher order of Masons, originated by himself, and grafted on ancient Masonic Institutions. The secresy, solemnity, mysticism, and

---

[35] Quigley, *The Anglo-American Establishment*, p. 283.

correspondence of Masonry, were in this new order preserved and enhanced; while the ardour of innovation, the impatience of civil and moral restraints, and the aims against government, morals, and religion, were elevated, expanded, and rendered more systematical, malignant, and daring. [In] the societies of Illuminati doctrines were taught, which strike at the root of all human happiness and virtue; and every such doctrine was either expressly or implicitly involved in their system. [The] being of God was denied and ridiculed. [Government] was asserted to be a curse, and authority a mere usurpation. [Civil] society was declared to be the only apostasy of man. [The] possession of property was pronounced to be robbery. [Chastity] and natural affection were declared to be nothing more than groundless prejudices. [Adultery], assassination, poisoning, and other crimes of the like infernal nature, were taught as lawful, and even as virtuous actions. [To] crown such a system of falshood and horror all means were declared to be lawful, provided the end was good. [In] this last doctrine men are not only loosed from every bond, and from every duty; but from every inducement to perform any thing which is good, and, abstain from any thing which is evil; and are set upon each other, like a company of hellhounds to worry, rend, and destroy. Of the goodness of the end every man is to judge for himself; and most men, and all men who resemble the Illuminati, will pronounce every end to be good, which will gratify their inclinations. The great and good ends proposed by the Illuminati, as the ultimate objects of their union, are the

> overthrow of religion, government, and human society civil and domestic. These they pronounce to be so good, that murder, butchery, and war, however extended and dreadful, are declared by them to be completely justifiable, if necessary for these great purposes.[36]

In one sense, the elite can look for consent through socialist or democratic ideals, while in another they are attempting to realize world control without consent by using their vast capital, made through the free market. Perhaps they like to enroll volunteers as a first line of defense, then just deal with the unbelievers.

> We shall have world government, whether or not we like it. The question is only whether world government will be achieved by consent or by conquest.[37]

Even though some of their plans are in the open, the secret goals of the elite are being realized behind the scenes. The elite have utilized capitalism while providing a false sense of the freedom of markets as a tool of deception. While they will never disclose all their plans, we can certainly substantiate our theories by observing what is going on around us. The world has slowly been made smaller by fewer and fewer companies and individuals controlling more and more interests.

> Secrecy has been maintained because the robber barons have been able to use their monopoly over money to buy up major media, educational institutions, and other outlets of public information. While Rockefeller was buying up universities,

---

[36] Timothy Dwight, "The Duty of Americans, at the Present Crisis, Illustrated in a Discourse," sermon to the citizens of New Haven, CT, July 4, 1798. https://quod.lib.umich.edu/e/evans/N25378.0001.001/.
[37] James Warburg before the Committee on Foreign Relations, US Senate, on Revision of the United Nations Charter, February 17, 1950. https://en.wikisource.org/wiki/James_Warburg_before_the_Subcommittee_on_Revision_of_the_United_Nations_Charter.

medical schools, and the Encyclopedia Britannica, Morgan bought up newspapers ... By 1983 ... fifty corporations owned half or more of the media business. By 2000, that number was down to six corporations, with directorates interlocked with each other and with major commercial banks.[38]

In pre-World War I Germany, German Foreign Minister Walther Rathenau stated that a select group of people guided the economies of all Europe. In a 1909 article for *Neue Freie Presse*, he wrote:

> Three hundred men, all of whom know one another, guide the economic destinies of the Continent and seek their successors from their own milieu.[39]

The Rosicrucian Order

In order to plot the development of later groups such as the Freemasons and the Illuminati, it is vital to understand the history of older groups, particularly the Rosicrucian Order. Further, we can examine the relations between the belief systems of such ancient orders and identify connections to modern groups. This will lead us to ask if people like Ruskin and Rhodes received secrets carried down through predecessors over hundreds of years in England (Rhodes admitted he got ideas from Jesuits and Masons).

We can gain useful information about the hidden mysteries of the Rosicrucian Order through the work of people like the astronomer-mathematician John Dee and the philosopher Francis Bacon. Peter Dawkins, one of the world's leading experts

---

[38] Ellen Hodgson Brown, *The Web of Debt: The Shocking Truth about Our Monetary System* (Baton Rouge, LA: Third Millennium Press, 2007), second edition, p. 130.

[39] Walther Rathenau, *Zur Kritik der Zeit* (Berlin, S. Fischer, 1922), chapter "Geschäftlicher Nachwuchs," p. 207, reprinted from *Neue Freie Presse*.

on Francis Bacon, believes the philosopher was the leader of the Rosicrucian Order in England as it became visible in the early 1600s. Why did a group that had previously been secret become visible at this time, unless it became so on purpose?

Referencing Bacon's contemporary philosopher John Wilkins, Dawkins suggests that Bacon not only instituted the famous Royal Society in England, but was also associated with the Rosicrucians.

> John Wilkins, a Freemason and principal founder of the Royal Society, whose declared "Instaurator" was Francis Bacon, states in a footnote on pages 236–7 of his *Mathematical Magick* (1648):
>
> "Ludovicus Vives tells us of another lamp that did continue burning for 1050 years, which was found a little before his time. Such a lamp is likewise related to be seen in the sepulcher of Francis Rosicrosse, as is more largely expressed in the confession of that fraternity."[40]

We can learn directly from Francis Bacon's writings that mysteries and hidden knowledge were critical to his thought processes. Some believe that Bacon's work *New Atlantis*, published posthumously in 1626, shortly after the arrival of the Pilgrims of the *Mayflower* in the "New World," describes plans to expand the British Empire to the Americas.

> This is summed up by a Father of Salomon's House, who declares in the book that "the end of our foundation is the knowledge of causes and secret motions of things, and the enlarging of the bounds of human empire, to the effecting of all things possible".

---

[40] Peter Dawkins, "Secrets of the Rosy Cross," Francis Bacon Research Trust. www.fbrt.org.uk/wp-content/uploads/2020/06/Secrets_of_the_Rosy_Cross.pdf.

Bacon's legal and Parliamentary work was extremely significant and ultimately very influential. For instance, his formulation of a 'double majesty' state became the basis for the unwritten constitution described by John Locke in the *Two Treatises*, and for the written constitution created by the American Founding Fathers that provided for the dual sovereignty of the American Federal system.[41]

Peter and Sarah Dawkins' Francis Bacon Research Trust highlights many interesting details about the philosopher that most people are not aware of.

In his *Advancement of Learning* Bacon identifies two distinct methods: Magistral and Initiative. In explaining what he means, he says that:

"... (borrowing the word from sacred Ceremonies) we call that Initiative Method, which discloses and unveils the Mysteries of Knowledges. For Magistral teaches, Initiative insinuates: Magistral requires our belief to what is delivered, but Initiative that it may rather be submitted to examination. The one delivers popular sciences fit for learners, the other sciences as to the Sons of Science ..."

To this he adds two further methods, Exoteric (open, revealed) and Acroamatic (enigmatic, concealed), the latter being so that:

"... by the intricate envelopings of delivery the profane vulgar may be removed from the secrets of sciences, and they only admitted which had either acquired the

---

[41] Francis Bacon Research Trust, "New Atlantis." www.fbrt.org.uk/hermes/new-atlantis/.

> interpretation of parables by tradition from their teachers, or by the sharpness and subtlety of their own wit could pierce the veil."
>
> "These words shalt thou declare and these shalt thou hide ..."[42]

Don't worry if you don't understand what he wrote. What we find in Bacon's work is a network of close relationships between science, esoteric knowledge, mystery schools and related philosophies. By now, it should not surprise us that this father of modern science believed in secret sciences and hidden knowledge. The key question to ask is if he openly published his knowledge, or taught his initiated the good stuff through symbols and hidden messages. He did both.

Indeed, the sciences of the past have often been closely related to occult teachings, and by examining how modern sciences got their beginnings we can identify similarities to the sciences of today. Eugenics was contrived as a scientific justification for plans of gene pool manipulation, and new versions of population control are constantly emerging under the guise of science—some of which are not as obvious as in the past.

We are trained to think that science is based on the scientific method, as popularized by Francis Bacon. We rarely realize that many of the beliefs of the elite that are promoted as scientific may in fact be secret schemes by which they intend to influence our lives.

---

[42] Francis Bacon Research Trust, "Myths & Archetypes." www.fbrt.org.uk/mysteries/myths-archetypes/.

Chapter 6: The Influence of Science

> Not everything that can be counted counts, and not everything that counts can be counted.
>
> William Bruce Cameron[1]

This is point of the book at which diverse concepts will fit into the overall scheme. We've investigated corrupt collaboration among governments, banks, and corporations, and now we need to expand our focus to include scientific mysteries. Is science connected to the Beast as well? By gaining a glimpse into the workings of the scientists of old, our eyes will begin to open regarding how science operates today, albeit with different terminologies.

At the end of the previous chapter, we looked at one of the most famous scientists of all time and the part he potentially played in a semi-secretive society, the Rosicrucian Order, yet we did not finish the story of Francis Bacon, nor how he relates to the Beast system. In this chapter, we'll explore the beginnings of modern science around 500 years ago, and we'll look to see if certain fields have maintained close ties with Beast lovers.

US Founding Father Thomas Jefferson named Francis Bacon at the head of his top-three most influential people of all time.

> Bacon, Locke and Newton ... I consider them as the three greatest men that have ever lived, without any exception, and as having laid the foundations of those superstructures which have been raised in the Physical & Moral sciences ... Bacon at top: Locke next then Newton.[2]

---

[1] *Informal Sociology: A Casual Introduction to Sociological Thinking* (New York: Random House, 1963).
[2] Thomas Jefferson, letter to John Trumbull, February 15, 1789. www.loc.gov/exhibits/jefferson/18.html.

We have all heard of Isaac Newton, and we know that Jefferson borrowed a lot of concepts from legal philosopher John Locke for the US Declaration of Independence. But how could Francis Bacon have been more important than the others to Jefferson? Jefferson must have knew about Bacon's influence upon Locke. Let's see what others have reported, since we know very little of Bacon today.

> Charles Darwin claimed in his own writings that he "worked on true Baconian principles" ... and Alexander Pope stated that "Lord Bacon was the greatest genius that England (or perhaps any other country) ever produced."[3]

> [Francis Bacon] is the man who drafts the programme of the modern world-view.[4]

> Francis Bacon possessed, to quote Macaulay, "the most exquisitely constructed intellect that has ever been bestowed on any of the children of men." Hallam described him as "the wisest, greatest of mankind," and affirmed that he might be compared to Aristotle, Thucydides, Tacitus, Philippe de Comines, Machiavelli, Davila, Hume, "all of these together," and confirming this view Addison said that "he possessed at once all those extraordinary talents which were divided amongst the greatest authors of antiquity."[5]

---

[3] Florian Cajori, "The Baconian Method of Scientific Research," *The Scientific Monthly* 20(1) (1925), pp. 85–91.
[4] Albert Schweitzer, *The Philosophy of Civilization, Part II: Civilization and Ethics* (London: Adam and Charles Black, 1949), p. 64.
[5] William T. Smedley, *The Mystery of Francis Bacon* (London: Robert Banks & Son, 1912), p. 103.

> Edmund Burke said: "Who is there that hearing the name of Bacon does not instantly recognise everything of genius the most profound, of literature the most extensive, of discovery the most penetrating, of observation of human life the most distinguished and refined."[6]
>
> "Money is like muck, not good except it be spread." Francis Bacon was a profound economist.[7]

George Soros in the above quote highlights the important point that Bacon was not only involved with science, called philosophy in his day; he was also involved with government and finance. Bacon was involved on many fronts for the Beast.

Sir Francis Bacon was a knight, a lawyer, a philosopher, the Keeper of the Great Seal, Viscount St Alban, and Lord Chancellor of England (effectively second-in-command to the king). Most importantly for our discussion, he was an occultist who dabbled in magic. We should take notice of how his core beliefs were related to the philosophy of science—after all, they may have been foundational to modern science.

The *Encyclopedia Britannica* reports different views about Bacon than experts like Peter Dawkins. However, we should notice the "natural magic" reference below, as this requires clarification:

> In 1609 his *De Sapientia Veterum* ("The Wisdom of the Ancients"), in which he expounded what he took to be the hidden

---

www.gutenberg.org/cache/epub/36650/pg36650-images.html#Page_103.

[6] Francis Bacon Society, *Baconiana*, Vol. IX, Third Series, January 1911, p. 218. https://francisbaconsociety.co.uk/wp-content/uploads/2021/03/1911_-Baconiana_No-33-36.pdf

[7] George Soros, "The Capitalist Threat," *The Atlantic*, February 1997. www.theatlantic.com/magazine/archive/1997/02/the-capitalist-threat/376773/.

> practical meaning embodied in ancient myths, came out and proved to be, next to the *Essayes*, his most popular book in his own lifetime. In 1614 he seems to have written *The New Atlantis*, his far-seeing scientific utopian work, which did not get into print until 1626.
>
> The major occupation ... must have been the management of James, always with reference, remote or direct, to the royal finances. The king relied on his lord chancellor but did not always follow his advice.
>
> Bacon himself has often been held to have been some kind of occultist, and, even more questionably, to have been a member of the Rosicrucian order, but the sort of "natural magic" he espoused and advertised was altogether different from that of the esoteric philosophers.[8]

In short, in Bacon's time natural magic was considered to be the study of the hidden processes of nature that Renaissance scientists searched for, as distinct from the *supernatural*, which was reserved for beings like angels.

Yet in my view, the field of "natural magic" does indeed relate to esoteric knowledge and is a bridge to helping us understand our modern definitions of empirical sciences. Our great microscopes and telescopes reveal what we can observe, but we still struggle to know the deeper meanings behind these glimpses of what is knowable. What is magic, then?

---

[8] Anthony M. Quinton and Peter Michael Urbach, "Francis Bacon," Britannica. www.britannica.com/biography/Francis-Bacon-Viscount-Saint-Alban.

The Connections of Francis Bacon

To comprehend the context of Bacon's era, it is helpful to examine the lives of Renaissance polymaths Paolo Sarpi and John Dee, both of whom influenced Bacon. Amazingly, much of modern science is based on the work of such individuals, who dabbled with the occult.

> Francis Bacon's *Great Instauration*, published in 1620, three years before the death of Sarpi, described a philosophy of scientific discovery that was consistent with [Sarpi's work] the *Pensieri* [*Philosophical Thoughts*], and it is significant that Sarpi and Bacon were in correspondence since 1616. Like Galileo, whom he often met in Venice, Sarpi believed that knowledge came about principally not by philosophical deduction but by induction, that is by observation and experiment.[9]

Surprisingly, not much is known about Sarpi. Bacon is generally credited with the inductive method, which Sarpi had described years before in his work *Pensieri*, placing Bacon among the most famous instigators of modern scientific methodology. Having lived a somewhat secretive life, and working behind the scenes of the Church, Sarpi is credited with being the modern founder of atheism.

> Paolo Sarpi, the first philosopher to develop systematic arguments for atheism, is now hardly known except by historians of ideas. Once he was famed throughout Europe. John Donne kept his portrait in his study. Boswell called him a genius. Both Gibbon and Macaulay praised him. He was well ahead of his time, since it was not until half a century after he

---

[9] Gerald Curzon, "Paolo Sarpi (1552–1623)," Philosophy Now. https://philosophynow.org/issues/101/Paolo_Sarpi_1552-1623.

died that Matthias Knutzen, the first widely mentioned atheist in modern history, distributed three handwritten atheist pamphlets at Jena in 1674.

He was a life-long sceptic who lived in many worlds—the worlds of Catholic monks, Venetian patriots, and European radicals. He called himself "a chameleon [who] had to wear a mask like everyone else in Italy." And in fact, what he really believed only became public long after he died in 1623.[10]

In the context of his close connections to Venice, this reference to Sarpi having worn a mask—a symbol of hiding one's true identity—is significant, and we will look to uncover some famous Venetian masks later.

Isaac Newton, John Dee, and Francis Bacon were all heavily involved with alchemy, alongside their work in mathematics, the creation of tools, and many other areas. They were interested in magic, esoteric knowledge, and other related topics that we would not dare to confuse with science today.

John Dee claimed to have gained his knowledge—and perhaps the resulting notoriety—from communicating with angels.

John Dee (1527–1609) was a philosopher and scholar whose work during the Tudor period has been overshadowed by his alleged sorcerous and occultist activities. He is best known for having conversations with angels through his scryer Edward Kelley's interests in astrology, alchemy, calendar reform and suggesting the date for Queen Elizabeth's coronation. What John Dee may not be as well known for is his influence on English navigation and

---

[10] Curzon, "Paolo Sarpi (1552–1623)." https://philosophynow.org/issues/101/Paolo_Sarpi_1552-1623.

being the first person to coin the term "British Empire."[11]

This period saw the continuous development of useful scientific tools and methods, at the same time as what today looks like completely unscientific research by the very same scientists. John Dee had the largest library of his time, was very famous, yet may have also been instrumental in the formation of the Rosicrucian Order in England, having also had many meetings with the younger Francis Bacon.

Where did Dee really get his knowledge from? The answer to this question will further our cause of finding links from the past to the present.

The Order of the Magi and Hermetic Tradition

Enter Heinrich Cornelius Agrippa von Nettesheim (aka Agrippa), author of the much-celebrated book *The Occult Philosophy* (1531). Agrippa's group the Order of the Magi may have been the influential predecessor to the Rosicrucian Order, having been founded a half-century before the suspected formation of the Rosicrucians (although the Rosicrucians did not start becoming somewhat public until the early 1600s).

> Agrippa declared that magi were able to perform miracles through the occult wisdom revealed to them by supernatural beings.[12]

Regarding the perceived difference between the "supernatural" and "natural magic," those who divined the supernatural realm openly were mostly shunned by the culture of their day. As a result, in the 1500s they used other terms that

---

[11] Alex Grover, "Mathematics, Navigation and Empire," Royal Museums Greenwich, July 8, 2019. www.rmg.co.uk/stories/blog/curatorial-library-archive/mathematics-navigation-empire-reassessing-john-dees-legacy.

[12] Encyclopedia of the Unusual and the Unexplained, "Magi: Agrippa (1486–1535)." www.unexplainedstuff.com/Magic-and-Sorcery/Magi-Agrippa-1486-1535.html.

sounded better in public, openly discussing "natural" philosophy. It seems that by Bacon's time, pre-eminent scientists had learned to keep certain beliefs hidden, as is suggested by his writings and in the wide use of symbols.

Dee and earlier occultists were daring in seeking the unseen realm, while later philosophers like Bacon claimed to focus on nature. Had Agrippa lived at a different time or under a different jurisdiction, he would have been burned at the stake. Indeed, he traveled a lot to avoid the fiery pole, just as Dee left England for Bohemia for a while to find support in his occult efforts from Holy Roman Emperor Rudolf II.

> Agrippa was heir to a tradition that began with two Florentines, Marsilio Ficino and Pico della Mirandola ...
>
> Although natural magic may seem unscientific to modern eyes, it was in fact an important precursor to 17th-century experimental science, because Agrippa and other magi had to do a lot of observation and experimenting in order to determine how the forces of nature operated, at a time when few natural philosophers were doing any experiments at all.[13]

This knowledge came from the East into the mix of Western thought via the Greeks, and Agrippa eventually obtained this tradition from the Florentines Ficino and Mirandola.

During the rise of magical science, the wealthy Medici family of Florence received hermetic writings from Byzantium—the capital city of the Eastern Roman Empire—which had preserved what remained of Greek writings from almost two millennia before. There was already great interest in Plato and Aristotle at the time, and the revival of knowledge from Greece was underway. When hermetic writings came to Italy, there was an

---

[13] Linda Hall Library, "Scientist of the Day: Cornelius Agrippa," September 14, 2016. www.lindahall.org/about/news/scientist-of-the-day/cornelius-agrippa/.

expanded interest in alternative knowledge. Highly occultic practices were even briefly permitted in certain locations.

Marsilio Ficino's Latin translation of the Greek *Corpus Hermeticum* was carried out in 1463 at Cosimo de' Medici's request and first printed in Treviso in 1471 without Ficino's consent. This translation, together with Ficino's preface running through Trismegistus's life and writings, was the starting point of modern Hermetism.[14]

Michael Psellus in the eleventh century knew of the *Corpus Hermeticum*, but in the medieval mind the name of Hermes Trismegistus was usually associated with alchemy and magical talismans. Albertus Magnus condemned the diabolical magic in some Hermetic works, but Roger Bacon referred to Hermes Trismegistus as the "Father of Philosophers." Medieval chemistry was often called the "hermetic science."

The magical and philosophical literature attributed to Hermes Trismegistus received widespread currency in the Renaissance.

The Latin Asclepius was printed in 1469, and Marsilio Ficino published his influential Latin translation of the first fourteen books of the Corpus in 1471.

Both philosophical and magical Hermetism declined rapidly in the seventeenth century after Isaac Casaubon showed in 1614 that the Hermetic writings were of the post-Christian era. Hermetism continued

---

[14] Maurizio Campanelli, "Marsilio Ficino's Portrait of Hermes Trismegistus and Its Afterlife," *Intellectual History Review* 29(1) (2019), pp. 53–71.

thereafter only among the Rosicrucians and other secret societies and occult groups.[15]

Hermetic tradition seemed to have died out. However, Isaac Newton and others still held on to these beliefs, which we will examine later in this chapter.

> Ficino considered himself a Platonist, but a Platonist in a very specific mold: as part of a long tradition of which Plato was a key part but which needed interpreters to keep it going. This "ancient theology" included figures who, divinely inspired, advanced true philosophy. One of the key figures in this sequence was the ancient sage Hermes "Trismegistus" ("thrice great," because he was considered the greatest king, philosopher, and priest).
>
> Ficino described the ancient theology in this fashion in his Preface to his Latin translation of the *Hermetic Corpus*, discussing Hermes as first in this chain of sages ...
>
> Among philosophers he first turned from physical and mathematical topics to contemplation of things divine, and he was the first to discuss with great wisdom the majesty of God, the order of demons, and the transformations of souls. Thus, he was called the first author of theology, and Orpheus followed him, taking second place in the ancient theology. After Aglaophemus, Pythagoras came next in theological succession, having been initiated into the rites of Orpheus, and he was followed by Philolaus, teacher of our

---

[15] Encyclopedia.com, "Hermes Trismegistus." www.encyclopedia.com/people/philosophy-and-religion/ancient-religion-biographies/hermes-trismegistus.

> divine Plato. In this way, from a wondrous line of six theologians emerged a single system of ancient theology, harmonious in every part.
>
> After the year 1469, Ficino changed the order and placed Zoroaster first, linking him to the Magi who visited the infant Christ.[16]

Belief systems are handed down as we know. What is harder to realize is how science was handed down since we think of it differently than in the past. While the *Hermetic Corpus* was eventually discovered to have not been written as long ago as suspected, ancient Magi, Brahmans, and mystical sources from Egypt had recorded similar beliefs, which were then brought to Greece by Pythagoras. Ancient Greece influenced the thinkers of the Roman Empire, and these traditions were kept safe in Byzantium during the era of the Byzantine Empire (the Eastern Roman Empire), before finding their way back to Italy and the West through the Medici's during the Renaissance.

Remember being taught the Pythagorean theorem? Pythagoras brought some early math to Greece from places such as Persia and it has been suggested that he learned the principles of trigonometry named after him from the Egyptians. He did not invent it just like Bacon did not invent the inductive method since it was handed down. Pythagoras was also heavily influenced Plato and others with his deep knowledge of occultism and his own very secret society. These concepts go back as far as we can look.

> Pythagoras left Samos for Egypt in about 535 B.C. to study with the priests in the temples. Many of the practices of the society he created later in Italy can be traced to the beliefs of Egyptian priests, such as the codes of secrecy.[17]

---

[16] Stanford Encyclopedia of Philosophy, "Marsilio Ficino," June 9, 2011. https://plato.stanford.edu/entries/ficino/#OthWor.
[17] Math Open Reference, "Pythagoras." www.mathopenref.com/pythagoras.html.

You are probably sick of ancient history by now, so let's get back to modern science.

Modern Science as Magic

The catchy concept of "modern science as magic" needs some clarification. We should consider how modern science will be viewed 100 years from now. We may think we are technologically advanced, but perhaps people in the future will laugh at our archaic beliefs and methods. Consider the medical act of bloodletting—it must have seemed logical at the time, but now it seems ridiculous, and we believe our own methods to be far superior.

Millions of people today still believe in esoteric knowledge, hermeticism, Gnosticism and other mystical traditions, and as science delves into the quantum realm, belief in these areas is only increasing. Now, once again, there is serious talk of a blend of religion and science, and of cosmic consciousness. This is similar to the time of Bacon and the natural philosophers. Perhaps we are transitioning from a secular period back to a hybrid.

Let's think about the interplay between magic and science, while sticking to the useful concepts of the "natural" and "supernatural" world. For this discussion, we can define "magic" as equating to the supernatural. Belief in the supernatural posits that trained humans can create magic by reaching into the unseen realm and distorting natural reality, and that unseen beings like angels or demons can also create these distortions. Magic is therefore not *natural* under this definition, as it bends known laws.

Science can be viewed as the understanding of *fixed, natural* laws, and does not allow for a belief in the manipulation of nature by unseen beings or human intervention to bend these laws (the supernatural). In the context of our discussion, science and magic are therefore opposing concepts.

Let's consider that some modern scientists are "natural" magicians; they may tell us to believe something based only on limited evidence, and it may sound fascinating, so we may believe it. How much money is funneled toward scientific programs that amaze or comfort us by matching science with our belief systems? More than we probably think. Just consider the amount of funding that goes toward universities and government labs. We pay a lot as a society because when we do not know the trick, we are willing to spend dearly for the solution.

Regardless, it does not really matter what we think about either science or magic, because we have little say in the functioning of the world. The elite know how to manipulate us, whether by amazement or by convincing us of arguments supposedly based in natural law. Either way, their beliefs affect us and influence us. Even Darwin had preconceived notions that he used to reach conclusions.

Science helps us to reveal things that were once hidden. Science can uncover things that were once unknown. Until we gain an understanding of them, some observations are not magical, but rather mysterious. Science has revealed many previously hidden aspects of nature. However, many more mysteries remain veiled and hidden. The following are some examples.

The Center of the Universe

How does the mystery of the center of the universe relate to the Beast? I've learned one point about modern scientists that is worth sharing, and it will end up relating indirectly to the topics we are discussing—we'll get back to the Beast later.

A few themes will become clear after reading the following short extracts from a range of academic and scientific publications. Notice the repetition of certain information stemming from a source that these authors may not have investigated themselves.

> According to all current observations, there is no center to the universe. For a

center point to exist, that point would have to somehow be special with respect to the universe as a whole.[18]

The universe, in fact, has no center. Ever since the Big Bang 13.7 billion years ago, the universe has been expanding. But despite its name, the Big Bang wasn't an explosion that burst outward from a central point of detonation. The universe started out extremely compact and tiny. Then every point in the universe expanded equally, and that continues today. And so, without any point of origin, the universe has no center.

"If the universe is infinite," Ryden told Live Science, "there is no center."

That the universe has no center—and, by extension, no edge—is consistent with the cosmological principle, the idea that no place in the universe is special.[19]

Time was created in the Big Bang—we do not know if it existed before the Big Bang.[20]

This is like saying "time was created at the time that time was created." How long ago was that? At what

---

[18] Christopher S. Baird, "Where Is the Center of the Universe?" West Texas A&M University, Science Questions with Surprising Answers, September 17, 2013. www.wtamu.edu/~cbaird/sq/2013/09/17/where-is-the-center-of-the-universe/.
[19] Marcus Woo, "Where Is the Center of the Universe?" Live Science, May 14, 2018. www.livescience.com/62547-what-is-center-of-universe.html.
[20] "The Big Bang and the Expansion of the Universe," Atlas of the Universe, Durham University. www.icc.dur.ac.uk/~tt/Lectures/Galaxies/LocalGroup/Back/bigbang.html.

location was time created if there is no point of reference?

> There is no centre of the universe! According to the standard theories of cosmology, the universe started with a "Big Bang" about 14 thousand million years ago and has been expanding ever since. Yet there is no centre to the expansion; it is the same everywhere. The Big Bang should not be visualised as an ordinary explosion. The universe is not expanding out from a centre into space; rather, the whole universe is expanding and it is doing so equally at all places, as far as we can tell.[21]

The quote below finally gives us a better explanation of the mystery.

> The Universe is centered on us in the sense that the amount of time that's passed since the Big Bang, and the distances that we can observe out to, are finite. The part of the Universe we can access is likely only a small component of what actually exists out there. The Universe could be large, it could loop back on itself, or it could be infinite; we do not know.[22]

The bottom line, as is evident from these extracts, is that scientists do not yet know much about the universe. Hundreds of years from now, people will laugh at our limited knowledge. Thankfully,

---

[21] Philip Gibbs, "Where Is the Center of the Universe?" University of California Riverside Math Department, 1997. https://math.ucr.edu/home/baez/physics/Relativity/GR/centre.html.
[22] Ethan Siegel and Starts With A Bang, "Where, Exactly, Is the Center of the Universe?" *Forbes*, July 29, 2021. www.forbes.com/sites/startswithabang/2021/07/29/where-exactly-is-the-center-of-the-universe/?sh=4c371fc7f1a5.

there are changes happening now that put into question what we were taught as fact in school.

> The big bang hypothesis itself originally emerged as an indirect consequence of general relativity undergoing remodeling. Einstein had made a fundamental assumption about the universe, that it was static in both space and time, and to make his equations add up, he added a "cosmological constant," for which **he freely admitted there was no physical justification.**
>
> In 1998, when a set of supernova measurements of accelerating galaxies seemed at odds with the framework, a new theory emerged of a mysterious force called dark energy, calculated to fill circa 70 percent of the mass-energy of the universe.
>
> The crux of today's cosmological paradigm is that in order to maintain a mathematically unified theory valid for the entire universe, we must accept that 95 percent of **our cosmos is furnished by completely unknown elements and forces for which we have no empirical evidence whatsoever.** For a scientist to be confident of **this picture requires an exceptional faith** in the power of mathematical unification.[23]

The point of all this is simply to show that scientists do not know everything. Sciences that try to explain "Big Picture" stuff still require *faith*. In our technocratic age, we should not allow

---

[23] Bjørn Ekeberg, "Cosmology Has Some Big Problems," *Scientific American*, April 30, 2019, (emphasis added). www.scientificamerican.com/blog/observations/cosmology-has-some-big-problems/.

ourselves to be tricked by the use of science to control our lives if it means having faith in half-baked science.

Who funds the scientists and programs that support and promote the elite's ideologies? The elite. These researchers are often hired as salespeople to sell a product for the elite. Scientists need a salary, so they are not to blame, and funding may be used unwittingly to help sell the narrative. (The *Forbes* article above is an exception.) What is the product being sold?

Obviously, many good scientists benefit society in many areas as we can just look around. We should simply be very careful not to be mesmerized by science with an elitist viewpoint that ends up controlling us in adverse ways, especially when the media—or, sadly, even textbooks funded by a foundation with an agenda—spin the narrative.

The established scientific method may be used by paid media and government actors to convince us to accept restrictions to our freedoms ("necessary limitations" or "sacrifice for the common good"). Threats can accomplish goals, based upon the use of fear-inducing scientific research that persuades us to give up basic human rights. For example, we should pay attention to how mechanisms like Executive Orders can promote potentially harmful science in the name of safety and the achievement of "societal goals." An Executive Order signed by US President Biden provides a pertinent example. Without an awareness of the potential use of these mechanisms as control schemes, they may even sound convincing at first. The following is a dream coming true for the technocrats.

> For biotechnology and biomanufacturing to help us achieve our societal goals, the United States needs to invest in foundational scientific capabilities. We need to develop genetic engineering technologies and techniques to be able to write circuitry for cells and predictably program biology in the same way in which we write software and program computers; unlock the power of biological data, including through computing tools

and artificial intelligence; and advance the science of scale-up production while reducing the obstacles for commercialization so that innovative technologies and products can reach markets faster ...

Sec. 4. Data for the Bioeconomy. (a) In order to facilitate development of the United States bioeconomy, my Administration shall establish a Data for the Bioeconomy Initiative (Data Initiative) that will ensure that high-quality, wide-ranging, easily accessible, and secure biological data sets can drive breakthroughs for the United States bioeconomy ...

[The] data types and sources [are] to include genomic and multiomic information, that are most critical to drive advances in health, climate, energy, food, agriculture, and biomanufacturing, as well as other bioeconomy-related R&D, along with any data gaps.[24]

Multiverse or Parallel Universe?

Since we do not yet understand our own universe, it is unclear how scientists are going to find other universes. In any case, billions of dollars are being spent looking for them.

> The discovery of the Higgs boson was a landmark in the history of physics. It explained something fundamental: how elementary particles that have mass get

---

[24] President Biden, Executive Order on Advancing Biotechnology and Biomanufacturing Innovation for a Sustainable, Safe, and Secure American Bioeconomy, September 12, 2022. www.whitehouse.gov/briefing-room/presidential-actions/2022/09/12/executive-order-on-advancing-biotechnology-and-biomanufacturing-innovation-for-a-sustainable-safe-and-secure-american-bioeconomy/.

their masses. But it also marked something no less fundamental: the beginning of an era of measuring in detail the particle's properties and finding out what they might reveal about the nature of the universe.

In a paper just published in Physical Review Letters, Raffaele Tito D'Agnolo of the French Alternative Energies and Atomic Energy Commission (CEA) and Daniele Teresi of CERN propose a new theory to explain both the lightness of the Higgs boson and another fundamental physics puzzle.

In broad brushes, the duo's theory works like this. In its early moments, the universe is a collection of many universes each with a different value of the Higgs mass, and in some of these universes the Higgs boson is light. In this multiverse model, universes with a heavy Higgs boson collapse in a big crunch in a very short time, whereas universes with a light Higgs boson survive this collapse. Our present-day universe would be one of these surviving light-Higgs universes.[25]

Here is another view, from cosmologist George F. R. Ellis, which does not simply advocate for funding a multibillion-dollar supercollider in Switzerland. Indeed, it does not seem like he is selling anything.

> A particle takes all the paths it can, and what we see is the weighted average of all those possibilities. Perhaps the same is true of the entire universe, implying a multiverse. But astronomers have not the

---

[25] Ana Lopes, "A Crunching Multiverse to Solve Two Physics Puzzles at Once," CERN, January 13, 2022. https://home.cern/news/news/physics/crunching-multiverse-solve-two-physics-puzzles-once.

slightest chance of observing this multiplicity of possibilities. Indeed, we cannot even know what the possibilities are. We can only make sense of this proposal in the face of some unverifiable organizing principle or framework that decides what is allowed and what is not—for example, that all possible mathematical structures must be realized in some physical domain (as proposed by Tegmark). But we have no idea what kinds of existence this principle entails, apart from the fact that it must, of necessity, include the world we see around us. And we have no way whatsoever to verify the existence or nature of any such organizing principle. It is in some ways an attractive proposition, but its proposed application to reality is pure speculation.

Parallel universes may or may not exist; the case is unproved. We are going to have to live with that uncertainty. Nothing is wrong with scientifically based philosophical speculation, which is what multiverse proposals are. But we should name it for what it is.[26]

The Science of Money

John Maynard Keynes is perhaps the most famous economist of the twentieth century. He directed the redesign of the German economy after World War I and tried to help the Americans get out of the Great Depression. Yet economists can also have baffling elitist beliefs. The work and advice of John Maynard Keynes have many determined aspects of our modern lives, and we are all still affected by the decisions made by officials who

---

[26] George F. R. Ellis, "Why the Multiverse May Be the Most Dangerous Idea in Physics," *Scientific American*, August 1, 2014. www.scientificamerican.com/article/why-the-multiverse-may-be-the-most-dangerous-idea-in-physics/.

listened to this world-leading "expert" a century ago. Keynes' core beliefs influenced his extremely influential recommendations about monetary policy.

> [Keynes] sacrifices the individual liberties of each citizen for the sake of the general welfare (or at least some oligarch's definition of what that should be).

> This will be seen clearly in 1) his devotion to the theories of Thomas Malthus, 2) his promotion of eugenics as a science of racial purification and population control, and 3) his general devotion to World Government as a leading member of the Fabian Society.

> Where the real solution to the hyperinflationary money printing and economic industrial shutdown of Germany during the post WWI years was to be found in the German-Russian Rapallo Agreement (destroyed with the assassination of American System Foreign Minister Walter Rathenau), Keynes and his ilk merely called for economic integration of the German banking and military system under Bank of England/League of Nations control.

> A new breed of think tanks was created to shape the Empire's grand strategy in the face of this growth of independent sovereign nations: these were T.H. Huxley's X Club (c.1865), the Fabian Society (c.1884), and the Roundtable Group (c.1902). Where Huxley's X Club coordinated with Cambridge, and the Roundtable Group/Rhodes Trust interfaced with Oxford, the Fabian Society created a new school called the London School of Economics. All three worked together as one unit.

Defining his misanthropic belief in overpopulation, Thomas Malthus (a British East India Company economist) stated in his famous 1799 Essay on Population:

"The power of population is so superior to the power in the earth to produce subsistence for man, that premature death must in some shape or other visit the human race."

By 1937, Keynes' *General Theory of Employment* was published in Nazi Germany. If anyone wishes to defend the idea that the economist was somehow an anti-fascist defender of "liberal values", let them read his own words in the preface and then either redefine "liberal values" or their naïve idea of Keynes:

"I may perhaps expect to find less resistance among German readers than among English ones, when I put before them a theory of employment and production as a whole ... The theory of production as a whole which is the object of this book, can be much better adapted to the conditions of a totalitarian state, than the theory of production and distribution of wealth under circumstances of free competition."[27]

Since money, politics and science seem to go hand in hand for the elite, there is also a connection of interest between Keynes and Isaac Newton. Keynes purchased unpublished works of Newton at a Sotheby's auction that included some embarrassing writings.

---

[27] Matthew Ehret, "Keynes' Sleight of Hand: From Fabian Eugenicist to World Government High Priest," FRN, January 10, 2021. https://fort-russ.com/2021/01/keynes-sleight-of-hand-from-fabian-eugenicist-to-world-government-high-priest/.

> Given how much labor went into Newton's chymistry, why did none of it come to light until the Sotheby's auction? It wasn't all genteel scholarly embarrassment. English alchemists had to veil their true interests because alchemy had been illegal in England since 1404. The crown feared alchemy because transforming lead into gold would have destabilized the country's economy, through counterfeit coins. The general ban on alchemy—the Act Against Multipliers—was lifted in 1689, thanks to Boyle's lobbying, but alchemists were still tainted by association, and counterfeiting remained a capital crime in England.
>
> Chymistry was one grand body of work to him, the grandest, and he'd coveted knowing nature's secrets since boyhood. He labored so long and so secretly because chymistry seemed the most promising path to obtaining near-magical powers and near-mystical insights into nature—discoveries that would, if only he could make them, vault him into the first rank of geniuses who ever lived.[28]

Even though alchemy was illegal in England for a couple hundred years, scientists like Bacon and Newton still sought after the Philosopher's Stone and solutions to many other occult mysteries. They did a great job keeping their magical work secret for such a long time, with Newton's unpublished alchemical works only being revealed, after their purchase by Keynes, in the 1930s (though some contemporaries knew of Newton's work). Bacon's interests were hidden in the open, through his use of symbols and cyphers that were interpreted after his death.

---

[28] Sam Kean, "Newton, The Last Magician," *Humanities* 32(1) (January/February 2011).
https://web.archive.org/web/20250516053634/https://www.neh.gov/humanities/2011/januaryfebruary/feature/newton-the-last-magician.

The problem for us is that these types of sciences did not die with Newton, Bacon, and the other alchemists of old. Such elite science lives on in the modern version of the eugenics movement, in economics, and in other seemingly unrelated sciences. They tie everything together, allowing the Beast-loving elite to accomplish their schemes of world domination.

The elite can utilize the work of a scientist like Newton over another like Leibniz because the Newton's fits the narrative. Both Leibniz and Newton claimed to have invented calculus, sparking enormous debate. Newton was the apparent winner, and his legacy is promoted over that of Leibniz in the English-speaking world today. We can learn something from Leibniz's reaction to Newton's "discovery" of gravity.

> How is gravity, key to the entire achievement of the *Principia*, to be understood? Leibniz charged that it was an occult quality, occult in the sense that it purported to explain but did not explain, at least as Leibniz understood that term. To attribute a "dormitive virtue" to a particular substance (to recall Voltaire's later taunt), does not explain how the powder acts as its does.
>
> Leibniz allows that attributing gravity universally to matter is helpful as information; thus, to say that Earth gravitationally attracts and is attracted by the sun can be construed as saying simply that earth and sun behave in a certain way when in a particular conjunction with one another. What Leibniz objects to is the implication that attributing gravity in this context somehow explains how these effects are brought about.
>
> Newton's indignant response (articulated in some detail in Cotes' Preface to the second edition of the *Principia*) is that gravity is a cause of motion, though the

cause of gravity itself he does not presume to know.

The only possibility left was some kind of non-mechanical agency, taking the term "mechanical" in the contact-action sense demanded by the "mechanical" philosophy of the day. Newton never gave up hope that he might be able to hit upon such an agency and tried out "active principles" (perhaps inspired by his alchemical readings).[29]

The Great Isaac Newton perhaps performed a little magic trick on us. Thankfully, Leibniz highlighted that Newton did not understand the fundamental forces at work in his explanation of gravity. While knowledge of gravitational forces has allowed us to make further progress, some things are still missing from this picture. The study of electromagnetic fields came much later, and scientists are still looking into causality.

If Leibniz's revelations about Newton's lack of complete understanding had become generally known to the public, would we still be so impressed with the genius of Isaac Newton? Would he still be considered one of the greatest minds of all time? Science does not tell us everything.

The Human Mind Has Yet to Understand Itself

If you ask Christof Koch, Ph.D., Chief Scientist and President of the Allen Institute for Brain Science, how close we are to understanding our own brains, he scoffs. "We don't even understand the brain of a worm."[30]

---

[29] Ernan McMullin, "Review: Isaac Newton: Philosophical Writings," Notre Dame Philosophical Reviews, June 14, 2005. https://ndpr.nd.edu/reviews/isaac-newton-philosophical-writings/.
[30] Rachel Tompa, "5 Unsolved Mysteries about the Brain," Allen Institute, March 14, 2019. https://alleninstitute.org/news/5-unsolved-mysteries-about-the-brain/.

Science is always a work in progress. The elite fund scientific studies to support their preconceived beliefs, claiming such research to be for the betterment of humanity, when it might instead be for their own benefit.

The wording of many grant applications often forces scientists into a cycle of perpetual research. In the conclusion of scientific publications, researchers usually suggest the "need for further research," indicating that the study is not conclusive. Nonetheless, the media and politicians often quote studies and report on findings as if they were conclusive.

Rocket-Man Science

The occult has even made its way into the work of rocket scientists at NASA, such as Jack Parsons, who was famous at the very beginning of the rocket age.

Associated with the California Institute of Technology (Caltech), Parsons was one of the principal founders of both the Jet Propulsion Laboratory (JPL) and the Aerojet Engineering Corporation. He invented the first rocket engine to use a castable, composite rocket propellant, and pioneered the advancement of both liquid-fuel and solid-fuel rockets.

In 1939, Parsons converted to Thelema, the English occultist Aleister Crowley's new religious movement. At Crowley's bidding, he replaced Wilfred Talbot Smith as the leader of the California branch of the Thelemite Ordo Templi Orientis' leader in 1942 and ran the Lodge from his mansion on Orange Grove Avenue. Parsons was expelled from JPL and Aerojet in 1944 due to the Lodge's infamous reputation and his hazardous workplace conduct.[31]

Parsons came to believe in magic, a force that he felt could be explained through quantum physics.[32]

As for NASA, just ask why the astronaut patches use highly occultic symbols and Latin phrases like those that the Vigilant Citizen has uncovered.[33]

Science Working Together with Religion, Philosophy, and Magic

[P]hilosophy, religion, astrology, magic, mythology, literature, art, war, commerce, government ... will of necessity afford some obstacle to readers unfamiliar with the study of religion.[34]

Belgian archaeologist and historian Franz Cumont's belief was that everything is connected. Whether these connections are used for altruistic motives is what we need to find out. Beast-lovers think they are working toward the good of humanity.

---

[31] American Institute of Bisexuality, "Jack Parsons." https://bi.org/en/famous/jack-parsons/.
[32] Olivia Solon, "Occultist Father of Rocketry 'Written Out' of NASA's History," WIRED, April 23, 2014. www.wired.com/story/jpl-jack-parsons/. For more on Jack Parsons, see Phillip Keane, "Jack Parsons and the Occult Roots of JPL," Space Safety Magazine, August 2, 2013. www.spacesafetymagazine.com/aerospace-engineering/rocketry/jack-parsons-occult-roots-jpl/.
[33] The Vigilant Citizen, "Top 10 Most Sinister Psyops Mission Patches," June 20, 2011. https://vigilantcitizen.com/vigilantreport/top-10-most-sinister-psyops-mission-patches/.
[34] Grant Showerman, "Introduction: The Significance of Franz Cumont's Work," Internet Sacred Text Archive. https://sacred-texts.com/cla/orrp/orrp02.htm.

Not only are there relationships between corporations, banks, and governments, but also a broad spectrum of interrelated functions. How does the Beast work as a system? It is likely that the core beliefs of the Beast unite these strands, all run by elite groups, with different disciplines, across centuries.

Does Banking Promote Science?

We return here to a modern example. We have already seen Federal Reserve presidents give advice about how COVID-19 lockdown control measures relate to central banking. How else are banks partnering with science these days? One area may be behavioral modification.

> [W]ith the aim to help inform—and change—customer
> thinking and behaviours … [g]iven the wealth of data they hold, banks are very well placed to provide timely and personalised advice on sustainability of our purchases. Moreover, because financial difficulties pose a major barrier in the adoption of green technologies—like electric cars or heat pumps—banks have a natural role to play in this space. That is why … banks should go about nudging their customers to go green.
>
> 6 in 10 support their bank helping them reduce their environmental impact and 7 in 10 support their bank reducing their own environmental impact. The biggest barriers to accepting advice or support were that it's not banks' responsibility (33%), data privacy concerns (25%) and availability of support elsewhere (20%).[35]

---

[35] Behavioural Insights Team, "Should Banks Encourage Green Behaviours?" October 13, 2022. www.bi.team/blogs/should-banks-encourage-green-behaviours/.

This sounds exactly like something the Beast would say—"Let's bypass governments and democracies and let for-profits incentivize us on how to live." A banking app can fast-track a thought to the mind, while a government cannot do it quickly enough. It seems that for changing citizen behavior, governance and traditional methods simply no longer provide a fast enough mechanism.

Who supports the Behavioural Insights Team (BIT), self-described as the "world's first 'nudge unit'," which is attempting to change the world by "nudging" citizen behavior? The usual suspects: the United Nations, philanthropists, and Big Tech corporations such as Facebook-Meta.[36]

Public–private partnerships (PPPs) are the relationship-building bond between scientific institutions, banks, governments, corporations, and NGOs. We will explore more below.

Certainly, it is a duty to take care of the earth. The big question to ask is: Who is driving climate change, all the way down to banking apps? Why are PPPs finally able to roll full-steam ahead where the UN and governments have not been able to make huge inroads before? Funding must be coming from somewhere. Oh, I almost forgot—you and I are now helping to fund climate change initiatives through our retirement accounts, without any say in the matter. Remember?

A report by the Independent High-Level Expert Group on Climate Finance titled *Finance for Climate Action* really nails it. Remember, fear sells. A bunch of scientists and bankers are needed to make this happen.

> Our world is in peril: the climate crisis is accelerating. Current action is too weak and too slow; to delay is dangerous. This is also a moment of great opportunity. One path leads to attractive growth and development, the other to destruction, catastrophe and loss of lives and

---

[36] Behavioural Insights Team, "Who We Work With." www.bi.team/partners/.

livelihoods on a massive scale, especially for the vulnerable.[37]

The report continues:

> The failure to deliver the climate finance commitment of $100 billion per year by 2020 made by developed countries at successive COPs has eroded trust. According to the latest assessment of delivery plans, the $100 billion commitment will be met only in 2023, three years past the target date, and only then mainly because of increased financing from the multilateral development banks (MDBs). Bilateral public finance, which is the most important indicator of the direct contribution by developed countries, has not increased measurably since 2016 and there remain important shortfalls in its quality. The delivery of the $100 billion is an immediate task, but governments of developed countries need to go well beyond that, starting now. The world needs a breakthrough and a new roadmap on climate finance that can mobilise the $1 trillion per year in external finance that will be needed by 2030 for emerging markets and developing countries (EMDCs).[38]

This confirms what we previously suspected: governments are not moving fast enough, so the Beast needs an updated plan.

---

[37] Independent High-Level Expert Group on Climate Finance, *Finance for Climate Action: Scaling Up Investment for Climate and Development*, November 2022, p. 5. www.lse.ac.uk/granthaminstitute/wp-content/uploads/2022/11/IHLEG-Finance-for-Climate-Action.pdf.

[38] Independent High-Level Expert Group on Climate Finance, *Finance for Climate Action*, p. 5. www.lse.ac.uk/granthaminstitute/wp-content/uploads/2022/11/IHLEG-Finance-for-Climate-Action.pdf.

The report claims that new opportunities are available for financing. Climate change will be met head-on with a bonus investment deal. For partners of the Beast, it looks like a win–win situation.

> The present trajectory is one of slow growth, low investment and public spending, and rising debt service burdens in many, if not most, EMDCs. These economies are at a juncture where high debt and slow recoveries are tilting the balance towards so-called fiscal prudence, with real risks of economic stagnation. At the same time, the urgency and opportunity of tackling climate change is becoming ever clearer. As shown by each successive report from the Intergovernmental Panel on Climate Change, climate change is occurring at a faster pace and with ever more severe impacts than previously anticipated and the time for remedial action is rapidly narrowing.
>
> There is a real opportunity to make a breakthrough on both development goals and climate, building on the progress achieved by EMDCs and new technological options that can deliver improved results.[39]

We need to come to a conclusion about science and how it has benefited us. Even with marvelous breakthroughs and improvements in certain areas, the elite have not channeled the ability of science to solve some of the most important problems of life. In 1992, Democrat Representative George Brown showed that not much had really been achieved in these areas as our example that still holds true today (unless you consider living an

---

[39] Independent High-Level Expert Group on Climate Finance, *Finance for Climate Action*, p. 14. www.lse.ac.uk/granthaminstitute/wp-content/uploads/2022/11/IHLEG-Finance-for-Climate-Action.pdf.

extra few years beyond the life expectancy average of 1992 as a big improvement). While there have been some improvements since then, there have also been declines in the other areas he referenced.

> [O]ur global leadership in science and technology has not translated into leadership in infant health, life expectancy, rates of literacy, equality of opportunity, productivity of our workers or efficiency of resource consumption. Neither has it overcome a failing education system, decaying cities, environmental degradation, unaffordable health care and history's largest national debt.[40]

I agree with Brown. People are hungry, there are widows, orphans, and wounded vets, and issues like the decline in children's education are worsening. Are these not more worthy of funding than some of the big elitist initiatives out there, like going to Mars or smashing atoms in a supercollider? Certainly, there are some good philanthropic organizations out there, but some are suspect of being technocratic and do not deserve tax exemption or other benefits.

So where do we go from here? Where will this road we are traveling on take us?

---

[40] George E. Brown Jr., "Perspective on Science Research: It's Down to the Last Blank Check," *Los Angeles Times*, Sptember 8, 1992. www.latimes.com/archives/la-xpm-1992-09-08-me-15-story.html.

Chapter 7: All Roads Lead to...?

It used to be that all roads led to Rome. Where do they lead us in the modern age? Where is the central hub linking all the networks we have looked at?

An obscure theory posits that the Roman Empire never fell; instead, Rome morphed into widespread sub-empires, ultimately leading to a modern-day elite plutocracy. The evidence supporting this theory is interesting—I promise. If you made it this far through the book, you obviously don't mind history. Perhaps we will now begin to understand where the elite get their ideas from.

> There was Winston Churchill's 1946 speech in Zurich calling for a United States of Europe; the plan in 1950 by Robert Schuman, France's Foreign Minister, to pool European coal and steel the muscle of war under a multinational authority; the emotion at the signing of the Treaty of Rome, which established the European Economic Community, in 1957. On the BBC TV series The Poisoned Chalice a few years ago, an aide to Belgian Foreign Minister Paul-Henri Spaak recalled the mood: "Spaak turned to us and said: 'Do you think we have today been putting the first stone of a new Roman Empire, and this time without firing a shot?' We all felt like Romans that day."[1]

It will come as no surprise that a Rothschild was involved in the formation of the European Union. The same names come up often as you have noticed in this book.

---

[1] Michael Elliot, "The Decline and Fall of Rome," *Time*, June 13, 2005. https://time.com/archive/6954034/the-decline-and-fall-of-rome-2/.

In 1954, Rothschild was appointed chef de cabinet of Paul-Henri Spaak at the Belgian foreign ministry. For the next two years, he worked together with Spaak and Jean Charles Snoy et d'Oppuers on the Treaty of Rome before the final signing of the treaty in 1957. Shortly before the treaty was signed, Rothschild was standing beside Spaak gazing over the Forum Romanum in Rome, when Spaak said "I think that we have re-established the Roman Empire without a single shot being fired."[2]

The Founding of Rome's Power Center

Even today, there are mumblings of the Roman Empire in events such as the formation of the EU. But what can we learn from the foundation of the Roman Empire in relation to our topic at hand? In the preface of his chronicle of the founding of Rome, Roman historian Livy focused on an important aspect: the ruling elite. The same old story seems to have recurred over the thousands of years since.

> Such traditions as belong to the time before the city was founded, or rather was presently to be founded, and are rather adorned with poetic legends than based upon trustworthy historical proofs, I purpose neither to affirm nor to refute. It is the privilege of antiquity to mingle divine things with human, and so to add dignity to the beginnings of cities; ... and if any people ought to be allowed to consecrate their origins and refer them to a divine source, so great is the military glory of the Roman People that when they profess that their Father and the Father of their Founder

---

[2] Wikipedia, "Robert Rothschild." https://en.wikipedia.org/wiki/Robert_Rothschild.

was none other than Mars, **the nations of the earth may well submit to this also with as good a grace as they submit to Rome's dominion.**[3]

The following is another translation of the same story, introduced by some additional context.

> Livy ... uses stories about the gods, essential to Roman legend but incompatible with the genre of history, to introduce what amounts to a programmatic statement instructing the reader how to approach his text:

> "Those things recorded about the time before the founding of the city and about its founding that are more suited to poetic legends than to the incorruptible monuments of history, I intend neither to affirm nor refute. This pardon is given to antiquity in order that by mixing human and divine things, it might make the origins of cities more august ... and if it ought to be granted to any people to consecrate its origins, and to carry them back to divine creators ... such martial glory belongs to the Roman people, so that when they claim Mars as their own parent and the father of their founder, **the human races will tolerate this with equanimity as they tolerate our imperium.**[4]

We learn from Livy that the elite at Rome's power center claimed the right to rule the world. The truth of their claim was irrelevant; what mattered was whether the citizens accepted the claim. The same concept exists today, with the elite having

---

[3] Livy, *The History of Rome, Book I*, ed. by Benjamin Oliver Foster (Cambridge, MA: Harvard University Press, 1919), (emphasis added).
[4] Andrew Feldherr, *Spectacle and Society in Livy's History* (Berkeley, CA: University of California Press, 1998), (emphasis added).

given themselves the right to rule over us. The claim becomes a reality only if we accept and follow their schemes, without an understanding of how they established their power.

But why did the people of Rome accept the claim and acquiesce to being ruled by this elite? Livy provides us with the background story of what happened after the founder of the city passed. Witness the crucial unleashing of Rome's Beast.

> And the shrewd device of one man is also said to have gained new credit for the story ... This was Proculus Julius, who, when the people were distracted with the loss of their king and in no friendly mood towards the senate, being, as tradition tells, weighty in council, were the matter never so important, addressed the assembly as follows: "Quirites, the Father of this City, Romulus, descended suddenly from the sky at dawn this morning and appeared to me. Covered with confusion, I stood reverently before him, praying that it might be vouchsafed me to look upon his face without sin ... 'Go,' said he, 'and declare to the Romans the will of Heaven that my Rome shall be the capital of the world; so let them cherish the art of war, and let them know and teach their children that no human strength can resist Roman arms.' ... So saying," he concluded, "Romulus departed on high." It is wonderful what credence the people placed in that man's tale, and how the grief for the loss of Romulus, which the plebeians and the army felt, was quieted by the assurance of his immortality.[5]

The above passage explains how the transition was effected from Rome's founder Romulus (the so-called son of Mars) to the

---

[5] Livy, *The History of Rome, Book I*, chapter 16.

next king of Rome, Numa. After Romulus' death, the city's leaders were looking for a story to tell that would maintain their position at Rome's power center. They felt it was very important that the people—the plebs, or *plebeians*—had something to grasp onto, and that the Beast system would fail if it were not supported by a narrative of the handing over of power. The story worked, with the people and the army believing that Rome really was destined to rule the world.

As Livy's story continues to build, it helps explain the most important theme of *Money and the Beast*.

> Murmurs then arose among the plebs that their servitude had been multiplied; that a hundred masters had been given them instead of one. No longer, it seemed, would they endure anything short of a king, and a king, too, of their own choosing ... Perceiving that such ideas were in the wind, the senators thought it would be well to proffer spontaneously a thing which they were on the verge of losing, and **obtained the favour of the people by granting them supreme power on such terms as to part with no greater prerogative than they retained** ... For they decreed that when the people should have named a king, **their act should only be valid in case the senators ratified it.** Even now, in voting for laws and magistrates, the same right is exercised, but is robbed of its significance; before the people can begin to vote, and when the result of the election is undetermined, the Fathers ratify it ... On the present occasion the interrex summoned the assembly and spoke as follows: "May prosperity, favour, and fortune attend our action! Quirites, choose your king. Such is the pleasure of the Fathers, who, in their turn, if your choice fall upon one worthy to be called Romulus' successor, will confirm your election." ...

> This so pleased the plebs, that, unwilling to appear outdone in generosity, they merely resolved and ordered that the senate should decree who should be king in Rome.[6]

Notice that the senators only pretended to grant the people the power of electing their own leader. As reported by Livy, this was a false democracy. Is this any different from today? We call it "consent of the governed." By retaining the right to determine the outcome of leadership contests, the senators were gatekeepers for the Beast. Instead of confirming the choice of the people, the senators chose who they wanted, vetoing the will of the people with claims about the "will of the gods."

> A great reputation for justice and piety was enjoyed in those days by Numa Pompilius. Cures, a town of the Sabines, was his home, and he was deeply versed, so far as anyone could be in that age, in all law, divine and human …
>
> When Numa's name had been proposed, the Roman senators perceived that the Sabines would gain the ascendancy if a king were to be chosen from that nation; yet nobody ventured to urge his own claims in preference to those of such a man, nor the claim of any other of his faction, nor those, in short, of any of the senators or citizens … And so they unanimously voted to offer the sovereignty to Numa Pompilius. Being summoned to Rome he commanded that, just as Romulus had obeyed the augural omens in building his city and assuming regal power, so too in his own case the gods should be consulted.[7]

---

[6] Livy, *The History of Rome, Book I*, chapter 17, (emphasis added).
[7] Livy, *The History of Rome, Book I*, chapter 18.

> When he [Numa] had thus obtained the kingship, he prepared to give the new City, founded by force of arms, a new foundation in law, statutes, and observances ... And perceiving that men could not grow used to these things in the midst of wars, since their natures grew wild and savage through warfare, he thought it needful that his warlike people should be softened by the disuse of arms, ... And fearing lest relief from anxiety on the score of foreign perils might lead men who had hitherto been held back by fear of their enemies and by military discipline into extravagance and idleness, he thought **the very first thing to do, as being the most efficacious with a populace which was ignorant and, in those early days, uncivilized, was to imbue them with the fear of Heaven** ... As he could not instil this into their hearts without inventing some marvellous story, he pretended to have nocturnal meetings with the goddess Egeria, and that hers was the advice which guided him in the establishment of rites most approved by the gods, and in the appointment of special priests for the service of each.[8]

Rome was founded on schemes used by leaders to control the people. Do the states of today follow a similar system? Livy reports how another story was required by Numa to establish the Beast of Rome. The plebs were ignorant, so a fear factor was used to control them. This is a common theme throughout history. Fear is a control scheme used to sway the masses.

Our lesson in the history of Rome concludes with Livy's summary of Numa's reign.

---

[8] Livy, *The History of Rome, Book I*, chapter 19, (emphasis added).

> The consideration and disposal of **these matters diverted the thoughts of the whole people** from violence and arms. Not only had they something to occupy their minds, but their constant preoccupation with the gods, now that it seemed to them that concern for human affairs was felt by the heavenly powers, had so tinged the hearts of all with piety, that the nation was governed by its regard for promises and oaths, rather than by the dread of laws and penalties ... And while Numa's subjects were spontaneously imitating the character of their king, as their unique exemplar, the neighboring peoples also, who had hitherto considered that it was no city but a camp that had been set up in their midst, as a menace to the general peace, came to feel such reverence for them, that they thought it sacrilege to injure a nation so wholly bent upon the worship of the gods.[9]

Rome's formation began with a brilliant plan to imbue the populace with the belief that imperialism was honorable—to such an extent that even foreigners recognized its importance. This allowed Rome to grow as it assumed the territories of other gods in other regions. When Rome became the ultimate ruler over a city, it permitted the local people's worship of their own gods, and left their temples standing.

Esteemed popular historian Mary Beard has written extensively on Rome and assimilation. The following is an interesting passage from a review of Beard's landmark bestseller *SPQR*.

> Rome was tremendously open about its gods and religion. This had two aspects.
>
> 1. One was the free and easy way the Romans assimilated foreign gods into the

---

[9] Livy, *The History of Rome, Book I*, chapter 21, (emphasis added).

> original Roman pantheon so that by the time of the empire the city was packed with temples not only to Rome's own original gods and imports from Greece, but to deities borrowed from all over the Mediterranean. Like many of Beard's points, this one is repeated half a dozen times, on pages 179, 205 and:
>
> "The range of deities worshipped in Rome was proudly elastic." (p.207)
>
> "Roman religion was not only polytheistic but treated foreign gods much as it treated foreign peoples: by incorporation ... As the Roman Empire expanded so did its pantheon of deities." (p.519)
>
> 2. The second aspect was the authorities' relaxed attitude to religious practice in the lands they conquered and assimilated.[10]

Perhaps an unbroken chain has run through time, with the same control methods as were used in Rome. Maybe the Beast forged a link in ancient times that has extended to this day. Continued expansion is the key for global conquest. There is no need for royal bloodlines; the concept could have been passed down from leaders to pupils such from the school of Pythagoras to students. Whether a state in which the concept is implemented is a democracy, a republic, or a monarchy is irrelevant. The plans spread across cultures and nations because of the shared human tendency to submit to power.

Many powerful people like to trace their bloodline to prominent Romans in order to legitimize their own position. While it is extremely difficult to track a bloodline so far back, many, including FDR's family, have tried to claim a famous family history.

---

[10] "SPQR: A History of Ancient Rome by Mary Beard (2015) 8. Assimilation," Books & Boots blog. https://astrofella.wordpress.com/2022/02/14/spqr-a-history-ancient-rome-mary-beard-8-assimilation/.

> The genealogy, history, and alliances of the American house of Delano, 1621 to 1899. Compiled by Major Joel Andrew Delano, with the history and heraldry of the maison de Franchimont and de Lannoy to Delano, 1096 to 1621, and the royal ancestry of Lannoy from Guelph, prince of the Scyrri, to Phillippe de Lannoy, 476 A. D. to 1621, including other royal lines and a list of the Lannoy chevaliers de la toison d'or [golden fleece].[11]

Perhaps it does not matter if you have royal blood. People just need to believe you do if you want to impress someone. Apparently, Napoleon was interested in this same question for obvious reasons. Even if someone's bloodline goes back to Rome, they obtained their elite status in questionable ways.

> When asked by General Napoleon Bonaparte, with whom he was negotiating the Treaty of Tolentino (signed Feb. 19, 1797), if the story of the family's descent from Fabius Maximus was true or not, the then Prince Massimo famously replied: "Je ne saurais en effet le prouver, c'est un bruit qui ne court que depuis douze cents ans dans notre famille" ("I cannot actually prove it, but it's a rumor that has been going around our family for twelve hundred years."[12]

---

[11] Joel Andrew Delano, *The Genealogy History and Alliances of the American House of Delano 1621 to 1899* (New York, 1899). https://archive.org/details/genealogyhistory13dela/page/n7/mode/2up; see also Daniel W. Delano Jr., *Franklin Roosevelt and the Delano Influence* (Pittsburgh, PA: Nudi Publications, 1946), p. 53.
[12] Napoleon Meets the Tradition of Prince Massimo. https://nobility.org/2014/05/napoleon-meets-the-tradition-of-prince-massimo/

The Influence of the Beast upon Western Culture

Philosophers like Plato and Pythagoras were incredibly influential upon Greco-Roman culture, and that influence lasts to this day. They passed their knowledge down to Marsilio Ficino and Francis Bacon, who carried the torch forward. While this sheds light on some of their progress in science and philosophy, it doesn't explain their link to the ruling elite.

That democracy could be a deceptive measure used by the elite is a disturbing thought. Perhaps politicians have claimed they represent "power for the people" while themselves remaining in control. A billionaire politician with a private jet still claims to speak for the common person; not much has changed. As the powerful still need debt-servants to rule over, the sleight of hand might be in letting the servants think they have freedom, for example, allowing them to vote in elections, while in fact they have no true freedom.

What if all the system is rigged so that the elite win whoever is in office? No matter who has been in office as US president, whether Democrat or Republican, numerous CFR members have been placed into cabinet and agency posts.[13]

In previous chapters, we learned that ordinary people have very little or no influence in public policy or monetary systems through representation or voting. Does our vote affect the biggest issues of our day? While we disagree about various minor issues, the biggest problem affecting us almost never comes up for debate. The elite let us fight over scraps from the table in order to divert our attention, just like in Livy's Rome. In any case, the true ruling class maintains its power regardless of which political party wins the election.

We can return to Carroll Quigley. Due to Quigley's unparalleled access to inside information, we should take the following statement seriously. We are free as long as we stay in the box.

---

[13] www.rummagingglobalism.com/2017/01/19/cfr-members-in-past-presidential-administrations/

Regardless of the outcome of the situation, it is increasingly clear that, in the twentieth century, the expert will replace ... the democratic voter in control of the political system. This is because planning will inevitably replace laissez faire in the relationships between the two systems. This planning may not be single or unified, but it will be planning, in which the main framework and operational forces of the system will be established and limited by the experts on the governmental side; then the experts within the big units on the economic side will do their planning within these established limitations. Hopefully, the elements of choice and freedom may survive for the ordinary individual in that he may be free to make a choice between two opposing political groups (even if these groups have little policy choice within the parameters of policy established by the experts) and he may have the choice to switch his economic support from one large unit to another. But, in general, his freedom and choice will be controlled within very narrow alternatives by the fact that he will be numbered from birth and followed, as a number, through his educational training, his required military or other public service, his tax contributions, his health and medical requirements, and his final retirement and death benefits.[14]

Researcher Joseph Plummer provides a summary of Quigley's research, along with his own commentary, in *Tragedy and Hope*

---

[14] Quigley, *Tragedy and Hope*, p. 866.

101.[15] He provides similar answers about the place we find ourselves in today.

But what if our so-called representative government is all a carefully crafted illusion? What if the Network chooses the candidates that we get to vote for? What if the Network's "experts," not the figureheads placed in official positions of power, are the ones who ultimately determine government policy? What if both political parties, right and left, are controlled by the exact same people?[16]

What about the illusion of the money system? We can't forget about debt and climbing interest. We need to dive deeper into the history of the control scheme behind interest rate control and debt creation. In an interview, American economics professor Michael Hudson[17] lays out a sweeping history of the topics we have been examining. He also illustrates how the Greeks and Romans connect to earlier civilizations.

> My theory, and it has now become the accepted theory, is that interest was brought to Greece and Rome, by Phoenician (Syrian) traders around 750 BC. They were trading, they brought the whole practice of charging interest. They would trade with presumably the chieftains or the wealthy families, and the Aegean in the Greek city states, in Italy, Rome and the other city-states. ...
>
> But you had an oligarchy developing throughout the whole ancient world, in Greece and especially in Rome. Aristotle wrote that the constitutions of many cities seem to be democratic but actually were oligarchic. Both he and Plato described how, if you do have a democracy, you're

---

[15] Joseph Plummer, *Tragedy and Hope 101: The Illusion of Justice, Freedom, and Democracy* (Brushfire Publishing, 2014).
[16] Plummer, *Tragedy and Hope 101*, chapter 1.
[17] I highly recommend Hudson's books, especially *The Collapse of Antiquity* (Islet, 2023) and *Killing the Host* (Islet, 2015).

going to have wealthy people developing, they're going to take over, and the democracy is going to turn into an oligarchy, and the oligarchy is going to make itself hereditary, into an aristocracy, and it's going to essentially stifle economic growth, grab all the wealth and all the land for itself, until someone among the ruling families is going to fight against the other ruling families. They're going to take the people into their camp (that was Aristotle's phrase) and have a revolution and have democracy all over again.

So, it was like an eternal triangle: democracy, oligarchy, aristocracy, overthrowing it with a new democracy and the whole cycle begins all over again. And that's pretty much how Greek history seemed to be developing.

In Rome, you had an oligarchy ruling from the very beginning. The kings were overthrown and the oligarchies were pretty much in control from the 5th century, end of the 6th century and onward. What you had was five centuries of repeated revolts, walkouts, secessions of the plans and civil wars. The common demand of all of the rebels was: cancel the debts, redistribute the land.

They were all killed, the Romans believed in the kind of free market that the University of Chicago believed in. "We can't have a free market, if you don't assassinate everybody who wants to challenge our power."

The oligarch's "free market" is, "Liberty for us is the liberty to enslave our debtors. Liberty for us is the ability to do what we want to other people." That was a free

> market as the Romans defined, and of course that's Milton Friedman's free market, and what libertarian economics is all about: Freedom for the wealthy.[18]

Hudson touches upon many topics in his work, debt control being among the most important. Today, our entire economy is based on the debt system. Rulers invented the debt system thousands of years ago; however, we still haven't learned how to tame it. It is unbelievable that this Beast still ensnares us today. The bottom line – we pay interest to feed the ever-larger Beast and become more enslaved to it.

The Greatest Traders of History

Who were the Phoenicians, from whom the Minoans, Greeks, and Romans received their Beast knowledge? And where did the Phoenicians get their knowledge from?

Hannibal, a military general famous for having almost conquered the Roman Empire, was a Phoenician, from the city of Carthage in present-day Tunisia. The Phoenicians were the most famous seafaring traders in all ancient history, and they dominated the most important trade routes—a method of mastering commerce that is still vital for today's ruling elite. Further, the Phoenicians introduced to Greece, and later Rome, the practice of charging interest on a loan.

> Plato referred to [the Phoenicians] as "lovers of money."
>
> According to Pliny, the Roman historian, "Phoenicians invented trade."
>
> Along with fine products, the Phoenicians brought with them more sophisticated means of transacting in business. By the 8th century, they'd introduced interest-

---

[18] Michael Hudson, "Webinar with Michael Hudson: A 4000-Year Perspective on Economy, Money and Debt," Positiva Pengar. https://positivapengar.se/michael-hudson-4000-years/.

> bearing loans to the Western Mediterranean.
>
> This practice of usury came to them from the ancient Sumerians by way of the Babylonians. And it was later popularized in the Roman Empire and spread across Europe that way.[19]

We can trace the charging of interest as far back as the Sumerian civilization in what is known as the Fertile Crescent, or Mesopotamia, at the beginning of recorded time.

> No indications of commercial or agrarian debts have been found in Early Bronze Age Egypt, the Indus valley, or even in Ebla, much less in Mycenaean Greece. They are first documented in a particular part of the world—Sumer—in the third millennium …
>
> The archaeological record shows that Assyrian traders introduced interest – bearing debt to their Asia Minor colonies such as Kanesh in Cappadocia around 2000 BC …
>
> [A] Phoenician role is the fact that the weights and measures used by Greeks and Italians seem to have been brought by Phoenician merchants. A. E. Berriman's *Historical Metrology* … points out that the carat originally was the weight of a carob grain, *ceratonia siliqua*, a tree native to the Mesopotamian meridian, weighing 1/60th of a shekel. The Greek term is *keration* …
>
> [T]emples played so great a role in archaic trade, and indeed in all types of contact

---

[19] Michael Arnold, "Banking, Trade & Commerce in Ancient Phoenicia," The Collector, December 25, 2020. www.thecollector.com/trade-in-ancient-phoenicia/.

> with foreigners. Hence, we would expect the most active traders to establish temple embassies and commercial cults ... and also for these institutions to sponsor the ligaments of credit necessary for commercial trade. It probably was under such circumstances that the idea of interest was introduced as a payment for time.
>
> Phoenicians were the chieftains and landed proprietors, and perhaps some of the [temples] probably played a role in legitimizing this trade ...
>
> [P]ersonal debts became part of an evolving patron/client relationship, serving as levers to reduce erstwhile free but poor individuals and their families to a state of dependency. This no doubt is how oligarchies came to build up their power in Corinth, Etruria and other regions.[20]

An important connection between Rome and Phoenicia carried the Beast system forward.

> [When] Romans freed themselves from their Etruscan king in 509 B.C., one of their first acts was to declare themselves a Republic ... Another immediate action, taken that same year, was to sign a trade treaty with the Phoenicians—to gain a piece of the lucrative commerce which would enable them to grow.[21]

---

[20] Michael Hudson, "Did the Phoenicians Introduce the Idea of Interest to Greece and Italy; and If So When?" Phoenician.org, 2005. https://phoenicia.org/interest.html.

[21] Phoenician.org, "Origins of the Phoenicians." https://phoenician.org/origin_of_phoenicians/#_edn57.

The Babylonian Beast System

There were records found in clay tablets from the Fertile Crescent in the ruins of Babylon that correlate to this theme. As a side note that we do not want to develop here, is that the Phoenicians were descendants from the same tribes as the Babylonians. The Phoenicians must have learned charging interest from their ancestors.

> During the Ur III period, the state was the main creditor. The state supplied so much land or so many animals to the individual, who then had to pay the state back ...
>
> In Babylon at the time of Hammurabi, there are records of loans made by the priests of the temple. Temples took in donations and tax revenue and amassed great wealth. Then, they redistributed these goods to people in need such as widows, orphans, and the poor ...
>
> After a thousand years, the priests who ran the temples had so much money that the concept of banking came up as an idea. Around the time of Hammurabi, in the 18th century B.C., the priests allowed people to take loans. Old Babylonian temples made numerous loans to poor and entrepreneurs in need. Among many other things, the Code of Hammurabi recorded interest-bearing loans.[22]

The ruling elite's control of trade and the monetary system through loans and interest began thousands of years ago. The same system has been passed on to many leaders, from Babylon, to Phoenicia, to Greece, then Rome. By the time of the Greco-Roman era, we find a blend of philosophy and law

---

[22] Ellen Lloyd, "Modern Banking Concept Started in Ancient Babylonian Temples," AncientPages.com, March 7, 2016. www.ancientpages.com/2016/03/07/modern-banking-concept-started-ancient-babylonian-temples/.

supporting these control schemes. Aristotle and Plato used language to justify systems that favored the rich and made them sound reasonable to ordinary people. They supported the ruling elite while speaking as if regular people had meaningful involvement in government.

Without a monetary system, the elite would have no way of paying for armies with which to protect trade routes and maintain their profit-making schemes. Who protects trade routes today? European countries once played a great role in maintaining physical trade routes, but eventually the USA became the largest defender of trade globally. The Council on Foreign Relations states the following.

> Like the British Royal Navy more than a century before it, the U.S. Navy has a command of the sea that affords the United States unrivaled international influence. For decades, its size and sophistication have enabled leaders in Washington to project American power over much of the earth, during times of both war and peace.
>
> "The crucial enabler for America's ability to project its military power for the past six decades has been its almost complete control over the global commons," wrote U.S. Joint Forces Command in a 2010 strategy document.[23]

We have inherited the results of ancient trade developments. Age-old principles of trade and monetary control still dominate today's governments, even those that appear to be presented as more modern or democratic. The same situation remains of an elite that rules over the plebs.

---

[23] Jonathan Masters, "Sea Power: The US Navy and Foreign Policy," Council on Foreign Relations, June 12, 2024. www.cfr.org/backgrounder/sea-power-us-navy-and-foreign-policy.

Imperial Rome Revisited

There has been a tradition of rulers throughout the world, for example, in Germany during the Third Reich and in Russia today, making claims about their continuation of a Roman legacy in order to legitimize their rule. Why not bring Rome's myth to their country?

Is there any fundamental difference between Cecil Rhodes and some Roman senator, considering the issue at hand? Both needed some claim of superiority that enabled them to take charge over common people. The senator would have believed in a god having called him to power; while Rhodes may not have shared the same belief, both trusted in the legitimacy of their power to rule over others. While the justifications may vary, the outcome is the same.

Leaders have used various cultural mechanisms to persuade the majority they should be in charge, such as the Divine Right of kings to rule, or "democracy" for the benefit of the masses. Communism was conveyed as a noble purpose, being for the benefit of the public and with a sense of fairness for all.

Russia and other states have made claims of themselves being Rome's successors in order to unite the masses under a common banner. Even the symbols of Rome are still in use today.

> The imperial monarchy established by Augustus [Rome's first emperor] at the turn of the millennium became a model repeatedly imitated into the 20th century. The Slavic title Czar is a distant echo of Caesar. Its Eagles soared over the empires of Austria, France and Mexico. The Roman fasces, an axe enclosed in a bundle of rods, were not only brandished by Mussolini and Hitler, but continue to adorn the U.S. House of Representatives.[24]

---

[24] Greg Woolf, "Top 10 Books about the Roman Empire," *The Guardian*, December 8, 2021.

A very useful Wikipedia article contains many examples about claims of succession from the Roman Empire, a few of which are worth quoting here.

> The coronation of Charlemagne by Pope Leo III, in Rome on Christmas Day 800, was explicitly intended as establishing continuity with the Roman Empire that still existed in the East …
>
> During the Middle Ages in Spain, some iberian monarchs, mostly from Kings of Castile and Kings of Leon, used the title of Imperator totius Hispaniae … in which there were claims, not only of the suzerainty over the other kings of the peninsula (both Christian and Muslim), but also the king's equality with the rulers of the Byzantine Empire and Holy Roman Empire …
>
> The last titular holder heir to the rank of Eastern Roman emperor, Andreas Palaiologos, sold his imperial title, along with his domains in Morea … to the Catholic Monarchs of Spain (Ferdinand II of Aragon and Isabella I of Castile) … in his will, written on 7 April 1502 … designating them, and their successors (the future Spanish monarchs) as his universal heirs …
>
> Even today there are opinions in which Philip VI of Spain is considered the nearest heir of Rome …
>
> The Austrian Empire, and after it the Austrian Republic, borrowed from the imagery and symbolism of the Holy Roman Empire following its demise in 1806.

---

www.theguardian.com/books/2021/dec/08/top-10-books-about-the-roman-empire-greg-woolf-rome-an-empire-s-story.

> The German Empire in 1871 claimed lineage from the Holy Roman Empire, reinterpreted as a national (German) rather than universalist endeavor – thus the lingering historiographical question on whether it started with the coronation of Charlemagne in 800, or (according to the nationalist version) in 962 with the coronation of the more unambiguously German Otto I.[25]

The same source provides more interesting details about claims at various times by the rulers of Bulgaria, Serbia, the Ottoman Empire, and countless others to be in direct succession from the Roman Empire. That so many monarchs and leaders have wanted to lay hold to Rome's legacy in order to build up their own prominence is noteworthy. Don't forget about Russia being the Third Rome.[26] We should remember from Livy and other Roman historians how Rome established its own legitimacy: Mythology. Our current world is the fruit of these fables, planted long ago.

The Emperor's New Clothes

As we consider the succession of the Roman Empire and its many spin-offs, we can see how certain terms, symbols, and schemes from ancient times have made it into our recent era. Not that long ago, czars and *Kaisers* were still running around Europe. Corroborating what Greg Woolf highlighted in his *Guardian* article above,[27] Merriam-Webster dictionary states the following in its definition of the word "emperor."

> The words *emperor*, *caesar*, *czar*, and *Kaiser* all go back to one source: the title

---

[25] Wikipedia, "Succession of the Roman Empire."
https://en.wikipedia.org/wiki/Succession_of_the_Roman_Empire.
[26] https://nationalinterest.org/feature/third-rome-rising-the-ideologues-calling-new-russian-empire-16748
[27] Woolf, "Top 10 Books about the Roman Empire"
www.theguardian.com/books/2021/dec/08/top-10-books-about-the-roman-empire-greg-woolf-rome-an-empire-s-story.

of the first Roman emperor, Imperator Caesar Augustus. Augustus was the adopted son of the Roman general and ruler Julius Caesar and he took the name Caesar as part of his official name. Later Roman emperors did the same, and thus *caesar* came to mean "an emperor of Rome." The word *caesar* was borrowed into German and other Germanic languages as *Kaiser*, which is how we get the word *kaiser* for "a ruler in Germany." Through the Russian word *tsar*, which also came from *kaiser*, we got our word *czar*, meaning "a ruler in Russia." The word *emperor* can be traced through French to Latin *imperator*. *Imperator* was a title given to great Roman generals and meant "commander," from the verb *imperare* "to command." [28]

Although the world no longer has many emperors, we have titles like commander-in-chief. It's important to consider how we shifted from divinely appointed rulers to elected officials. We find that many of the emperors were not really wearing any clothes, as their claims were based on myths. What about today's leaders? Are they naked too?

The later dislike for overbearing monarchs eventually led to abdications, revolutions, losses in war, and the establishment of democracies ruled by presidents and prime ministers. If we return to the above quotes from famous democratic leaders like Benjamin Disraeli, Winston Churchill, Franklin Delano Roosevelt, and Woodrow Wilson, we can consider the potential existence of puppet masters, hidden from our view, that they admitted were superior to them. To whom does the president of the USA answer? The people, or the Beast?

---

[28] Merriam-Webster, "emperor." www.merriam-webster.com/dictionary/emperor.

Money is the force that projects from a center of power to influence politicians and governments. In the USA and UK, central bank owners have the power to create money through the creation and arrangement of debt in cooperation with commercial banks. Non-bank corporations also have a lot of influence over governments, but they are in step with the banks and fund managers, since they require money to operate and grow.

Bank owners trump both corporations and governments, and it is the shareholders of banks and fund managers that influence corporations who are reported to be the major powerholders, above presidents and prime ministers. Even if the shareholders of the index funds do not directly control companies they own, the managers of these funds have enormous power.

The Incorporation of the Beast

Banks are corporations, and it is therefore important to understand the history of corporations. US author and journalist Edward Bellamy predicted over a century ago that corporations would gobble up the earth.[29] This is occurring before our eyes. The biggest shareholders of banks and megafunds manage centralization and globalization for the Beast.

The city-state of Venice carried the ancient methods of Babylon and the Phoenicians through a transition period and into the modern era. The need for the traditional methods—divine rulers and deities—declined as merchants and bankers took over as gatekeepers of the Beast.

To understand how shareholders operate, let's consider the Beast's need to continue its plans through the establishment of corporations. This need arose after kingdoms and empires started giving up more control over trade to the merchants. This shift saw merchants supporting government officials in return, creating two power centers that were reliant on one another, instead of a single monopoly power.

---

[29] Edward Bellamy, *Looking Backward* (New York: Dover Publications Inc., 1888 (republished 1996)), p. 15.

The most important change caused by the resulting influx of wealth was the end of hereditary absolute monarchy in Venice. The Doge (the Venetian head of state), was popularly elected only in the loosest sense before 1036. The Doges had come from one of three families, had absolute power, and could appoint their own successor.

As merchants became increasingly wealthy and powerful, the Doges became increasingly constrained. In 1036, a wealthy merchant was elected, leading to real elections and explicit limits on Dogal powers.[30]

Notice the shift from blood lineage to wealth in determining who ruled. This process has occurred over hundreds of years, putting us in our current position. All over the world, the power of the Doge has decreased, while the rule of the wealthy has increased.

Let's now look at how modern corporations got their start—and how this concept is still being used today.

By the early fourteenth century, financial innovations included: the appearance of limited liability joint stock companies; thick markets for debt (especially bills of exchange); secondary markets for a wide variety of debt, equity and mortgage instruments; bankruptcy laws that distinguished illiquidity from insolvency; double-entry accounting methods; business education (including the use of algebra for currency conversions); deposit banking; and a

---

[30] Max Nisen, "How Globalization Created and Destroyed the City of Venice," *Business Insider*, September 8, 2012. www.businessinsider.com/the-economic-history-of-venice-2012-8.

reliable medium of exchange (the Venetian ducat). All these innovations can be related directly back to the demands of long-distance trade.³¹

> [A] contract known as the colleganza [is] one of the first examples of a joint stock company. At its simplest, it was an arrangement between two parties, one an investor, and the second, a traveling merchant. The investor provided goods to the traveling merchant who sailed abroad to sell them, bought new goods with the proceeds, and returned to Venice to sell them. Profits were split in a pre-arranged manner.
>
> It introduced economic mobility to Venice, and allowed a larger section of the population to access international trade, wealth, and political power. There was no hereditary route to power, it was earned through wealth and commercial prowess ...
>
> These institutions and the mobility they provided let talent rise to the top, and ensconced a series of egalitarian economic institution that allowed Venice become a commercial and maritime power.
>
> The wealthiest and most powerful families feared erosion of their status. In 1297, they managed to pass the first of a series of laws (known as the Serrata) that gave control

---

³¹ Diego Puga and Daniel Trefler, *International Trade and Institutional Change: Medieval Venice's Response to Globalization*, NBER Working Paper (Cambridge, MA: National Bureau of Economic Research, 2012), p. 10.

of Great Council elections to a few powerful families.

A series of subsequent votes and laws further ensconced a legally ensconced Venetian nobility that had not existed before. The populace did not take it lying down, there were succession of revolts and protests, culminating in an armed insurrection in 1310 that was nearly successful.

In response, the Great Council was enlarged to co-opt would be revolutionaries, and the state's coercive powers were dramatically increased.

After they consolidated power, the now oligarchs embarked on a campaign of regulation, restriction and rent seeking. They essentially cut off the poor from engaging in long distance trade by limiting the most lucrative routes and goods to a select few, most notably with a 1324 law called the Capitulare Navigantium.[32]

The Beast is smart. When at risk of losing its control, it shifts or transitions to maintain its power center. Why not include some plebs in the system, if they follow the scheme of control? The Beast knows how to survive and adapt. Bloodlines may not matter anymore, but there are many Beast-lovers out there, and our job today is to identify them and reduce their power of control over us.

England as a Trade and Banking Power

Modern trade concepts reached Amsterdam and London from Venice, as noted by Michael Hudson (see above), eventually

---

[32] Nisen, "How Globalization Created and Destroyed the City of Venice." www.businessinsider.com/the-economic-history-of-venice-2012-8.

leading to the US's development of contemporary corporate and banking systems.

The Venetian system transitioned to the rest of Europe through the use of private corporations, versus traditional trade that was government-owned. England ended up becoming the world's superpower, after the power of Spain, France and Holland waned. This is because England adapted and adjusted, like Venice had before—and like the Beast always does. After individuals like Marco Polo had famously explored massive trade opportunities along new routes, corporations like the East India Company were established to enable vast international ventures.

> It was from Venice that Marco Polo, himself a Venetian, set off on his famous expedition to the east in 1271, returning in 1295.[33]

As Venice's geographic location became less important due to expanding international trade routes, the city-state's influence constantly bombarded England, which learned lessons from its competitor. The Beast needed to spread out, and international banking and the establishment of multiple trade centers became a widespread concern for maintaining the system.

> William the Fourth lived in just fear and blunt defiance of that "Venetian oligarchy" which ever since 1704 had been the recurrent ideal of the place-engrossing, great revolution families.[34]

The whistleblower Disraeli had more to say about England's inheritance of the Venetian system in his novel *Coningsby*.

---

[33] UNESCO, "Venice," Silk Roads Programme. https://en.unesco.org/silkroad/content/venice.
[34] Walter Sichel, *Disraeli: A Study in Personality and Ideas* (New York: Funk and Wagnalls, 1904), chapter 5. www.gutenberg.org/files/53917/53917-h/53917-h.htm#CHAPTER_V.

The great object of the Whig leaders in England from the first movement under Hampden to the last most successful one in 1688, was to establish in England a high aristocratic republic on the model of the Venetian, then the study and admiration of all speculative politicians. Read Harrington; turn over Algernon Sydney; then you will see how the minds of the English leaders in the seventeenth century were saturated with the Venetian type. And they at length succeeded. William III. found them out. He told the Whig leaders, "I will not be a Doge." He balanced parties; he baffled them as the Puritans baffled them fifty years before. The reign of Anne was a struggle between the Venetian and the English systems. Two great Whig nobles, Argyle and Somerset, worthy of seats in the Council of Ten, forced their Sovereign on her deathbed to change the ministry. They accomplished their object. They brought in a new family on their own terms. George I. was a Doge; George II. was a Doge; they were what William III., a great man, would not be. George III. tried not to be a Doge, but it was impossible materially to resist the deeply-laid combination. He might get rid of the Whig magnificoes, but he could not rid himself of the Venetian constitution. And a Venetian constitution did govern England from the accession of the House of Hanover until 1832. Now I do not ask you, Vere, to relinquish the political tenets which in ordinary times would have been your inheritance. All I say is, the constitution introduced by your ancestors having been subverted by their descendants your contemporaries, beware of still holding Venetian principles of government when you have not a Venetian constitution to govern with.[35]

The important lesson to take from Disraeli is that the *form* of government that is in power does not matter as much as the principles behind it. Today, we have a similar situation, with superficial facades of representative governments covering the deeply rooted plutocratic systems behind.

England copied the concept of joint-stock companies from Venice, where it had been established centuries earlier.

> During a period of rapid commercial growth in 16th century England, the Muscovy Company was granted a charter by Queen Mary Tudor in 1555, giving it a monopoly over trade routes to Russia ...
>
> At the time, companies needed a charter from the Crown to operate, and this licence for operations was time-limited and subject to the caprice of the King or Queen. It was not a right to form a corporation then, it was a privilege.
>
> Chartered companies were organised as *partnerships* or *guilds*, which were owned by closed groups such as families or associations of businessmen.
>
> But the Muscovy Company popularised what would prove a revolutionary innovation: it was able to raise enough money to finance the long journey to Russia by selling tradable shares.
>
> "Joint-stock" companies, as they became known, was a new concept in English law.

---

[35] Benjamin Disraeli, *Coningsby* (1844), Book 5, chapter 2.

> The corporate form has existed as far back as the Roman Republic, and likely before.[36]

As a result of the new corporate structure, the English state strongly supported the British East India Company—a joint-stock company—in its new ventures, as the Beast spread ever wider over the globe.

> We know that the East India Company eventually grew to control almost half the world's trade and become the most powerful corporation in history, as Edmund Burke famously put it, "a state in the guise of a merchant."[37]

> We still talk about the British conquering India, but that phrase disguises a more sinister reality. It was not the British government that seized India at the end of the 18th century, but a dangerously unregulated private company headquartered in one small office, five windows wide, in London …

> For all the power wielded today by the world's largest corporations—whether ExxonMobil, Walmart or Google—they are tame beasts compared with the ravaging territorial appetites of the militarised East India Company. Yet if history shows anything, it is that in the intimate dance between the power of the state and that of the corporation, while the latter can be

---

[36] Matt Kennard, "How the Modern Corporation was Invented in England," Declassified UK, May 18, 2023. www.declassifieduk.org/how-the-modern-corporation-was-invented-in-england/.

[37] William Dalrymple, "Before the East India Company," *Lapham's Quarterly*, September 27, 2019. www.laphamsquarterly.org/roundtable/east-india-company.

regulated, it will use all the resources in its power to resist.[38]

On the very last day of 1600, Queen Elizabeth I granted a charter to a group of London merchants for exclusive overseas trading rights with the East Indies, a massive swath of the globe extending from Africa's Cape of Good Hope eastward to Cape Horn in South America. The new English East India Company was a monopoly in the sense that no other British subjects could legally trade in that territory …

The monopoly granted by the royal charter at least protected the London merchants against domestic competition while also guaranteeing a kickback for the Crown, which was in desperate need of funds.

The exploits of the East India Company didn't end in India. In one of its darkest chapters, the Company smuggled opium into China in exchange for the country's most prized trade good: tea. China only traded tea for silver, but that was hard to come by in England, so the Company flouted China's opium ban through a black market of Indian opium growers and smugglers. As tea flowed into London, the Company's investors grew rich and millions of Chinese men wasted away in opium dens.

---

[38] William Dalrymple, "The East India Company: The Original Corporate Raiders," *The Guardian*, March 4, 2015. www.theguardian.com/world/2015/mar/04/east-india-company-original-corporate-raiders.

When China cracked down on the opium trade, the British government sent warships, triggering the Opium War of 1840. The humiliating Chinese defeat handed the British control of Hong Kong, but the conflict shed further light on the East India Company's dark dealings in the name of profit.[39]

Many more historical examples of extremely powerful corporations exist, but the East India Company's exploits form a sharp outline. We need to conclude. Will the plebs rally to kill the dragon, or will it remain dominant, like it has over the past thousands of years?

While we can point to times in history when average people had fair monetary policies and freedom to trade without paying the heavy fees through the control grids of the Phoenicians, Venetians or East India Company. This is not one of those times. It is getting harder and harder to conduct business and perform simple transactions without first jumping through hoops like setting up a payment App on our phones.

My former business partner, Dr. Benjamin Dorfman, lived in St. Petersburg and Moscow in the Soviet era. He said there was more freedom in the 1950's USSR than in modern America. That should make us take notice.

Can we do anything today to prevent the future plan to ban cash where we would be forced to conduct all transactions through a control grid?

There are many tasks we can accomplish. We should prioritize and pick the right battles, addressing high-level issues such as the debt-control system and realizing our strengths to combat the Beast. Can we utilize our constitutional rights to affect change?

---

[39] Dave Roos, "How the East India Company Became the World's Most Powerful Monopoly," History.com, June 29, 2023. www.history.com/news/east-india-company-england-trade.

Chapter 8: Life and Liberty, or Laziness?

Life and liberty need to be constantly worked for. We do not have a hands-off government so that we can rest upon our laurels or take it for granted. What can we do to protect any freedom that we have, while others sit back and let the Beast run wild, or, worse yet, ride the Beast? We know the Beast will devour the earth if we let it. For the sake of our discussion, we should first define "freedom."

Freedom covers a broad spectrum of things that we may take for granted. Its definition can become complicated when considering religious boundaries or other controversial areas. Through everyday experience, we can understand the meaning of freedom in the USA to practice religion, or free speech, as enshrined in the Bill of Rights or our state constitution.

Only an insider can know exactly how the complex system of the Beast operates. So far, we have surveyed many external facets of its power center, yet we have not looked in the mirror to see how we relate to, and enable, the Beast. Without people, it cannot survive. It certainly has its followers. The opposite of a follower is an opponent. We can rebel against it individually but as a group is far better.

We naturally assume an entitlement to a happy life. Does the law grant us this right, or is it a privilege, and do we have rights inherent at birth that cannot be stripped away by the government?

Freedom is the unrestricted ability to do what we should, not the right to do anything we want. "Should" is the key word, which we can stumble over. We need to narrow in on the meaning of "should" as it presents limitations within civic life. Civility relates to individual freedoms interacting with others.

Freedom resides under certain constraints. We do not have complete freedom as a whole, or as individuals. A big question to answer about limited freedoms is whether we have unalienable rights to them, or not. If they are inherent, where do they come from? Another task is to determine how to balance the tension between constraints on our rights and our freedoms to practice them.

Are Life, Liberty, and Happiness Guarantees?

The rights to life, liberty, and property are granted by the government and protected in the Fourteenth Amendment to the US Constitution. Let that sink in for a second. The government grants us our rights. Aren't they unalienable? Don't we naturally have rights, while the government only grants privileges?

Section 1 of the Fourteenth Amendment contains the following statement.

> All persons born or naturalized in the United States, and subject to the jurisdiction thereof, are citizens of the United States and of the State wherein they reside. No State shall make or enforce any law which shall abridge the privileges or immunities of citizens of the United States; nor shall any State deprive any person of life, liberty, or property, without due process of law; nor deny to any person within its jurisdiction the equal protection of the laws.[1]

Our rights are not as clear as we might think. For example, the government cannot take our life, liberty, or property without due process. This means it can, and does, take life, liberty, and property *with* due process. Thousands of US citizens have therefore lost these rights in court, because they were never expressly granted in the first place. The intentions of the Founding Fathers seem to have been forgotten by the time of the post-Civil War period and the Fourteenth Amendment.

The Ninth Amendment provides another example, as in it the Founding Fathers stated that "The People" would retain rights

---

[1] Fourteenth Amendment to the US Constitution: Civil Rights (1868), National Archives. www.archives.gov/milestone-documents/14th-amendment.

not expressly written elsewhere. Having been drafted at the beginning of the Republic, it is too probably broad for modern people, who think differently. Since then, the meaning has been forgotten, or it is interpreted differently from the original intent by today's leading minds.

> Overall, the Court has generally treated the Ninth Amendment as a rule of construction for the Constitution rather than a freestanding guarantee of any substantive rights.[2]

> Since its enactment, scholars and judges have argued about both the Ninth Amendment's meaning and its legal effect, and the courts have rarely relied upon it. During his failed confirmation hearing to become a Supreme Court justice in 1987, Robert Bork analogized the Amendment to an "inkblot," which hid the constitutional text that was under it. Just as judges should not guess what was under an inkblot, he argued, so too they should not guess at the Ninth Amendment's meaning. Bork's very public denial that any meaning of the Amendment could be discovered fueled intense academic interest in the original meaning of the text.[3]

We can think of analogies with which we can compare our rights and freedoms. I have the *ability* to take a candy bar from the store without paying, but I do not have the *right*. Imagine I was never taught that stealing is wrong; if I do not get caught, I might

---

[2] Cornell Law School, "Amdt9.1 Overview of Ninth Amendment, Unenumerated Rights," Legal Information Institute. www.law.cornell.edu/constitution-conan/amendment-9/overview-of-ninth-amendment-unenumerated-rights.
[3] National Constitution Center, "The Ninth Amendment," Interpretation and Debate. https://constitutioncenter.org/the-constitution/amendments/amendment-ix/interpretations/131.

think it is my right to take that candy bar. However, if I get caught, then I will learn otherwise.

Our rights under the Constitution are realized in this same way. We can practice freedom until we get caught and are told we can't. We might assume we have certain freedoms, only to get involved in some wild legal battle, like in the case of *Wickard v. Filburn*.

> In 1942, in the case of *Wickard v. Filburn*, the Supreme Court unanimously approved an agricultural regulation that capped how much wheat a farmer could produce—even though the farmer in question grew wheat only to feed his livestock and family. Although farmer Filburn's wheat never left his home state (or indeed, his own farm), the justices reasoned that any wheat grown anywhere in the country could affect the price of wheat in the interstate market. Even private production for home consumption was therefore part of interstate commerce, and Congress could validly regulate it.
>
> The *Wickard* case gave Congress and regulators a green light, and they pressed the gas with gusto. The next 50 years witnessed what one scholar called "the rise and rise of the administrative state"— the growth and growth of federal power.[4]

Farmer Filburn naturally assumed he had the freedom to operate as he desired on his own property, but he was mistaken. He was not fundamentally wrong, simply unaware that his rights under the Constitution were restricted. Thousands of other cases

---

[4] Justin Collings, "Opinion: What 'Rights' Do States Really Have under the Constitution?" DeseretNews, September 18, 2021. www.deseret.com/opinion/2021/9/18/22653133/opinion-what-rights-do-the-states-really-have-under-the-constitution/.

have arisen in which a person thought they were free and could pursue happiness, only to be let down.

This text on the National Archives website describes the Bill of Rights as follows:

> The Bill of Rights is the first 10 Amendments to the Constitution. It spells out Americans' rights in relation to their government. It guarantees civil rights and liberties to the individual—like freedom of speech, press, and religion. It sets rules for due process of law and reserves all powers not delegated to the Federal Government to the people or the States.[5]

The above summary sounds great, but it is not realistic or put to practice. Often, there are conflicts between state constitutions and the national government, as explained in the following extract. Notice that according to the description, under Justice Miller's interpretation, Louisiana was not required to protect individual livelihood nor to protect businesses from state corruption.

> In the *Slaughter-House Cases* [April 14, 1873], waste products from slaughterhouses located upstream of New Orleans had caused health problems for years by the time Louisiana decided to consolidate the industries into one slaughterhouse located south of the city. Slaughterhouse owners were incensed; they sued Louisiana and argued that the state-sanctioned monopoly infringed on their newly ratified 13th and 14th Amendment rights. Justice Samuel Miller dismissed the butchers' claims regarding due process and involuntary servitude. He then looked to Article IV, which entitled

---

[5] National Archives, "Bill of Rights Day, December 15." www.archives.gov/news/topics/bill-of-rights.

"the Citizens of each State" to "all Privileges and Immunities of Citizens in the several States" and to the 14th Amendment, which guaranteed the protection of the "Privileges or Immunities of citizens of the United States." Miller reasoned that the two clauses protected different bundles of rights, with Article IV protecting the rights of state citizenship and the 14th Amendment protecting rights of national citizenship. The privileges and immunities of U.S. citizenship were narrow and only those specified in the Constitution, which included the right to freely travel throughout the states. Not included, Miller said, was the right to one's livelihood or be protected against a monopoly.[6]

There must have been a way to solve the health problems while also protecting the rights to livelihood. Yet the state won; personal livelihoods lost. Even when a belief as basic as the freedom to work is assumed, it can be construed differently at local and national levels. For example, New York State has a narrower definition of religious freedom than that enshrined in the federal US Constitution.

The first half of the First Amendment in the Bill of Rights reads:

> Congress shall make no law respecting an establishment of religion, or prohibiting the free exercise thereof.

Here is New York's verbiage in Section 3 of its Constitution:

> [Freedom of worship; religious liberty] §3. The free exercise and enjoyment of

---

[6] NCC staff, "10 Supreme Court Cases about the 14th Amendment," National Constitution Center, July 9, 2020. https://constitutioncenter.org/blog/10-huge-supreme-court-cases-about-the-14th-amendment/.

> religious profession and worship, without discrimination or preference, shall forever be allowed in this state to all humankind; and no person shall be rendered incompetent to be a witness on account of his or her opinions on matters of religious belief; but the liberty of conscience hereby secured shall not be so construed as to excuse acts of licentiousness, or justify practices inconsistent with the peace or safety of this state.[7]

We immediately notice that the federal rights of a citizen are much broader than the rights of a person living in New York State. This state gets to decide how much religious freedom its citizens have depending on the ever-changing interpretation of "peace or safety." We should know who gets to decide what it means. But when a conflict arises between a state and the federal government, who wins? This question has never been properly answered.

> The First Amendment is not absolute and over time, the Supreme Court has determined which speech is protected under it and which is not.[8]

Don't "We the People" have the ultimate power by granting law-making and interpretation powers to public servants? Since our servants and the legal community cannot determine a simple definition of "the People," why can't we dictate to them? Should *We the People* determine the definition, or should public servants do so? The answer is obvious.

---

[7] The Constitution of the State of New York, Article 1, section 3. www.nysenate.gov/sites/default/files/admin/structure/media/manage/filefile/a/2024-02/586_ny_state_constitution_-_generic_version2.pdf.
[8] Historical Society of the New York Courts, "Freedom of Speech." https://history.nycourts.gov/democracy-teacher-toolkit/first-amendment-civil-liberties/free-speech/.

Do employees have the right to define for their employers the meaning of "employer"? This is the part of the book at which you are supposed to laugh. The absurdity of the situation is that if The People have the ultimate power, or any sovereignty, we should not need our public servants to define the control we have. However, having forgotten the source of power – or having gotten lazy – we let them define the terms.

If our administrators fail to define "the People" who pay their salary and grant them power, then how can they interpret more complicated concepts like the *rights* of The People? Not only are both definitions needed, but also how the two definitions interact.

The Rights of the People

Since we have outsourced to representatives from the beginning of the nation, we are left trying to understand the meaning of the phrase, "consent of the governed." What do we allow, and what do we control?

> That to secure these rights, Governments are instituted among Men, deriving their just powers from the **consent of the governed**—That whenever any Form of Government becomes destructive of these ends, it is the Right of the People to alter or to abolish it, and to institute new Government.[9]

We have allowed public servants (aka our employees) to establish oodles of laws over us, and to expand more control over the original freedoms that were laid out at the founding of the USA. We can consider ourselves to now live in an administrative state, under a plutocracy, more than in a republic or democracy, but that is for a separate discussion; for now, we need to identify who really has sovereign rights, and if our consent really matters.

---

[9] US Declaration of Independence, July 4, 1776, (emphasis added). www.archives.gov/founding-docs/declaration-transcript.

At the founding of the USA, since the Divine Right of kings to rule over the people had been rejected, citizens would probably have asked themselves if they possessed sovereign rights. Were *We the People* in supreme control then, or at any time? No. There has always been balance and tension. That's the rub.

> The Founders believed a government could only be legitimate if its authority comes from the people, but they also knew that the desires of **the people should be constrained**. They aimed to create, therefore, a republic—a society in which **the people are sovereign**, but which at the same time limits the power of government in order to protect individual freedoms.[10]

The People are constrained, and The People are sovereign. This seems contradictory at first, yet the logic is understandable after reflection. The governed need to live in balance by agreeing to constrained freedoms, while also knowing there are restrictions upon the government they live under.

Theophilus Parsons, a little-known Founding Father, gave one of the best explanations of this concept. He helped to negotiate the amendments of the Constitution to win over some antifederalists so the nation could be formed. He hit the nail on the head in "The Essex Result," in which he described the difference between limited and fundamental rights, and alienable and unalienable rights. Notice how he explains the nuance of *surrendering control* over our rights, not *parting* with them.

> All men are born equally free. The rights they possess at their births are equal, and of the same kind. Some of those rights are alienable, and may be parted with for an equivalent. Others are unalienable and

---

[10] Bill of Rights Institute, "Essay: Popular Sovereignty and the Consent of the Governed," (emphasis added). www.billofrightsinstitute.org/essays/popular-sovereignty-and-the-consent-of-the-governed.

inherent, and of that importance, that no equivalent can be received in exchange. Sometimes we shall mention the surrendering of a power to control our natural rights, which perhaps is speaking with more precision, than when we use the expression of parting with natural rights—but the same thing is intended ... The alienation of some rights, in themselves alienable, may be also void, if the bargain is of that nature, that no equivalent can be received. Thus, if a man surrender all his alienable rights, without reserving a control over the supreme power, or a right to resume in certain cases, the surrender is void, for he becomes a slave; and a slave can receive no equivalent. Common equity would set aside this bargain.

When men form themselves into society, and erect a body politic or State, they are to be considered as one moral whole, which is in possession of the supreme power of the State. This supreme power is composed of the powers of each individual collected together, and VOLUNTARILY parted with by him. No individual, in this case, parts with his unalienable rights, the supreme power therefore cannot control them. Each individual also surrenders the power of controuling his natural alienable rights, ONLY WHEN THE GOOD OF THE WHOLE REQUIRES it. The supreme power therefore can do nothing but what is for the good of the whole; and when it goes beyond this line, it is a power usurped. If the individual receives an equivalent for the right of control he has parted with, the surrender of that right is valid; if he receives no equivalent, the surrender is void, and the

> supreme power as it respects him is an usurper.
>
> Let it be thus defined; political liberty is the right every man in the state has, to do whatever is not prohibited by laws, TO WHICH HE HAS GIVEN HIS CONSENT. This definition is in unison with the feelings of a free people. But to return—If a fundamental principle on which each individual enters into society is, that he shall be bound by no laws but those to which he has consented, he cannot be considered as consenting to any law enacted by a minority: for he parts with the power of controuling his natural rights, only when the good of the whole requires it; and of this there can be but one absolute judge in the State.
>
> That the legislative power of a state hath no authority to control the natural rights of any of its members, unless the good of the whole requires it.[11]

Since day one in the USA, *We the People* have allowed representatives to establish more laws over the land. This is consent. We have been consenting to more and more laws for about 250 years.

What if we went back to simpler times with fewer laws, or had another constitutional convention to combat the vast administrative state? Things could actually end up worse than they are now. Perhaps it is best to leave the original intent, as it was designed for moral people to begin with.

A reset and a return to the foundational documents would only work in a moral culture. The number and scope of laws increase

---

[11] Theophilus Parsons, "The Essex Result," quoted at Founding.com, https://founding.com/founders-library/american-political-figures/theophilus-parsons/.

as morality decreases. A moral culture knows better how to govern itself and requires fewer restrictions (i.e., a smaller government is required). John Adams knew this.

> Our Constitution was made only for a moral and religious People. It is wholly inadequate to the government of any other.[12]

"Public virtue," wrote John Adams, "cannot exist in a nation without private [virtue], and public virtue is the only foundation of republics."[13]

Perhaps the only remaining option is to get back to the original intent of the Founding Fathers and re-establish our Christian national heritage so we can promote moral virtues. What? We were never founded as a Christian nation? The following statement was unanimously approved, without dissent, by the Senate in 1797.

> [The] government of the United States of America is not in any sense founded on the Christian Religion.[14]

The Founding Documents

Freedom advocates will say our rights are derived from God or natural law. This belief stems from the wording of the US Constitution, with its Bill of Rights, and the Declaration of Independence, but perhaps these documents were written too vaguely. As is clear from the case law we looked at above, the administrative state often interprets rights as being derived from the government.

---

[12] John Adams, letter to Massachusetts Militia, 11 October 1798. https://founders.archives.gov/documents/Adams/99-02-02-3102.
[13] John Adams, letter to Mercy Otis Warren, April 16, 1776. https://founders.archives.gov/documents/Adams/06-04-02-0044.
[14] Treaty of Tripoli, 1797, quoted in Constitution Annotated, "Amdt1.2.2.8 Early Interpretations of the Religion Clauses," note 26. https://constitution.congress.gov/browse/essay/amdt1-2-2-8/ALDE_00013275/#essay-26.

The Constitution states that *We the People* have the right to establish government. In fact, this right may not have been intended for common people, through any directly meaningful or contributive act like voting in a pure democracy, but for the very delegates and wealthy representatives that conceived the original wording. They established a republic, not a democracy. These leaders claimed sovereignty for all, while using language that sounds great but actually made it easy for the Beast to grow. Whatever the original intent, the Beast interprets freedoms for itself and its followers, not for the masses.

Also, there is no mention of divine ordination in the US Constitution. It is a purely secular document. The Founders claimed the power to establish the nation by seemingly lumping themselves together with the common folk to get it off the ground—otherwise, it would have been suspect of a new country ruled by a plutocracy of the elite. The key part they left out is that *We the People* need to continually maintain it.

> **We the People ... do ordain** and establish this Constitution ...

Since the Constitution does not clearly spell out where the authority of The People was derived from, it is helpful to look more closely at the Declaration of Independence.

> ... and to assume, among the **powers of the earth**, the separate and equal station to which the **laws of nature and of nature's God** entitle them, a decent respect to the opinions of mankind requires that they should declare the causes which impel them to the separation.

While the Declaration of Independence is not a legal document, it helps us to understand the root cause of one major assumption we find ourselves making today. Thomas Jefferson writes:

> A free people claim their rights, as derived from the laws of nature, and not as a gift from their chief magistrate.[15]

This sounds very fair for The People as the playing field seems leveled by nature without any special divine rights. It should be noted that the Founders like Jefferson agreed that rights came from nature's God in the form of natural law. This law assumes to provide unalienable rights that were not defined well by Jefferson, but conveys that all people are born with them and they can't be taken away (until the clarification of the 14th amendment that the law is supreme, not The People). Theophilus Parsons does a much better job of clarifying what unalienable means in terms of rights in terms of pragmatic usage.[16]

Let's summarize.

- America is a republic, not a democracy, although it uses a democratic process to elect representatives to make the laws of the republic.
- America was never established as a Christian nation.
- America was established by the leading minds and the elite of the day, not by the common people through a mechanism such as voting.
- The "Creator" was defined as nature's God, enabling the laws of nature.
- Natural law was the basis for the unalienable rights the Founders spoke of.
- Life, Liberty and the Pursuit of Happiness are conditional unalienable rights but not guarantees.
- There was and is a clear separation of Church and State (yet people of faith influence the state).
- The Founding documents were designed for individuals to live under a system of fair laws, not tyrants.

---

[15] Thomas Jefferson, *A Summary View of the Rights of British America* (1774). www.loc.gov/item/08016823/.
[16] Theophilus Parsons, "The Essex Result," quoted at Founding.com, https://founding.com/founders-library/american-political-figures/theophilus-parsons/

- Freedoms are limited within state and federal laws, depending on the jurisdiction.
- There is a tension of being constrained under the law while realizing the remaining balance as freedom.

The laws and regulations that are issued by our consent become the rulers over us. We are bound by the system of state–federal tension we inherited from thousands of mini-tyrants and, perchance, some law-makers with good intentions. We need to be involved in the tug-of-war if we want to keep the system as fair as possible for the majority of citizens. Otherwise, public servants will continue to do what they deem is best, and not what may be in the best public interest.

The system in place within the USA is a complex, interrelated federal–state–individual system. Many legal problems are settled in favor of the power center and against the citizens. Only mass movements of people who are on the same page have had any effect upon government. Perhaps this is why we are constantly bombarded into many factions like the party system. Is this intentional, so that we do not build a mass power center to combat the Beast?

A big question remains: Do we honor the system of tension we find ourselves in?

Do citizens have the power to make a change? Do we even have the will to effect change, or are we frogs boiling slowly in a pot of debt servitude, giving up more of our rights and privileges without notice?

The past offers us some success stories, for example, the civil rights movement and the movement for women's suffrage, but what about revolts, led by common people, when things got out of hand?

Other than a handful of examples, including the Aragonese revolt of 1591 and some other very minor success stories from Europe and China, most rebellions have been crushed. The biggest army always wins. Nonetheless, the biggest gains usually come afterward, like after the Peasants' Revolt of 1381, which helped to squash serfdom for good in England. While serfdom was already on the decline, the mass uprising – although it failed militarily – helped to speed things up.

> The participants of the Peasants' Revolt demanded the following changes:
> - the total abolition of serfdom
> - a repeal of labour laws limiting wage increases brought in after the Black Death
> - free fishing and hunting rights for all
> - more peasant participation in local government
> - the Crown should be the only authority in the counties, not local lords
> - the redistribution of the Church's riches, especially of the great abbeys
>
> These demands were frankly ludicrous for the period but they did at least have some basis in reality.[17]

The American and French Revolutions were not led by common people, and the most successful revolts had a trained army carrying out a military coup d'état. Great victories were usually achieved by powerful individuals – like the Founding Fathers – backed with help from foreign investors who have a common enemy (like France helping the US).

Many of the freedoms we hold dear were first won in England. The English made attempts to transition away from a monarchy well before the US was formed, and a lot of the philosophies that the Founding Fathers built upon were derived from prior English

---

[17] Khalid Elhassan, "When the Lower Class Fights Back: 12 of History's Greatest Peasant Revolts," History Collection, November 24, 2017. https://historycollection.com/lower-class-fights-back-12-historys-greatest-peasant-revolts/.

experiments that allowed more freedoms for the plebs. (See the examples of John Locke and Francis Bacon, who were very influential upon Thomas Jefferson, in Chapter 6.)

The Big Lie

A good citizen is supposed to get involved with government and the community. Inactive citizens don't perform any civic duties or vote, but an intermediate group consists of lukewarm citizens who vote and then think they did some great thing by stamping their civic-duty card. Being a citizen is truly a day-to-day activity; it is not our sole democratic power to vote out the bad guys. Yet many uniformed people don't think they can affect change outside of voting.

The big lie is to distract us, so that the average citizen gives up any power or control they have and awards it to the politicians who enable the ever-increasing administrative state (It is also hard to change the administrative state because they are non-elected). The (false) hope is that we will simply be able to vote them out of office next time. A better approach is to influence them while they are still in office.

The relationship of citizens to government should focus more on holding officials accountable through an on-going process of communication, petitioning, and legal action. However, it is hard for our voices to be heard.

Know Your Rights

> The right to "petition the Government for redress of grievances" is among the oldest in our legal heritage, dating back 800 years to the Magna Carta, and receiving explicit protection in the English Bill of Rights of 1689, long before the American Revolution. Ironically, the modern Supreme Court has all but read the venerable right to petition out of the Bill of Rights, effectively holding that it has been

> rendered obsolete by an expanding Free Speech Clause.
>
> Today, in Congress and in virtually all 50 state legislatures, the right to petition has been reduced to a formality, with petitions routinely entered on the public record absent any obligation to debate the matters raised, or to respond to the petitioners.
>
> The precise role of a robust Petition Clause in our twenty-first century democracy cannot be explored, however, until the Supreme Court frees the Clause from its current subservience to the Free Speech Clause.[18]

What about our Democrat and Republican Parties? This duality seems well designed to separate people and create arguments to distract us from reality, which is that a mass movement of people who agree on common goals can affect change outside the party system.

The USA is a Republic with a democratic process built under it. People tend to forget this, or they choose not to believe in the Constitution. The term "democracy" is used far more than constitutional terms by talking heads, when in fact the USA is not technically a democracy. While the media and some politicians want us to think we live under a people powered democracy in order to distract us, The People's vote is not as significant as they lead us to believe. It is a big lie. The Beast owns the media as we have seen; we can simply look at the names of the shareholders of media corporations.

This distraction puts people into a partisan mindset, promoting the view that "we are not as bad as the other party," or that "our side will win if we get enough partisan votes," instead of

---

[18] National Constitution Center, "Right to Assemble and Petition." https://constitutioncenter.org/the-constitution/amendments/amendment-i/interpretations/267.

enabling the masses to find common ground with likeminded people – who may even be registered with the other party.

This is not a message that your vote does not matter, nor that you should not vote. This book is simply a caution to beware of the money/control system and how to prevent it from growing too large. It is also important for us to focus on building mass movements outside of the well-established power centers of the Beast. Is it more important simply to vote, thus maintaining the system, or, better yet, to improve the system? Sometimes the system needs to be improved upon from the outside if it can't be managed from within.

Conclusion

This book has covered a broad spectrum of interrelated history, philosophy, and politics. Now it is time to wrap it up.

Our freedoms are at war with controls. The truth is that we need both; too much freedom leads to chaos, while an excess of controls leads to resistance.

We find ourselves in a position where controls are increasing over us in the Beast system. As a result of this downward pressure, resistance is building. We have two basic options:

- fight the Beast
- join the Beast

We do not have the option to do nothing at all. Now that we are armed with information about the Beast, doing nothing is to be a willing participant in this system. Doing nothing is the easy path, and it is understandable for those of us who wish to hold onto our job and feed our family. But sometimes, the pressure becomes too great. We can take this build-up and focus this energy on fighting the Beast.

If we choose to fight, we should aim to find a better balance between limits on controls and limits on freedoms.

With knowledge of the past, we can understand our enemy. Our nemesis is the Beast. But instead of setting out on the task of defeating it, we can fight it by trying to keep it from growing too large and trying to keep it in balance.

Who or What Is the Beast?

The Beast is not a person, a group of people, a nation, or a global government system. It is an invisible force that joins people who want to control others.

We may call it an unseen power, a dominating spirit, Beast consciousness, or something else. The main identifier is that it creates a commonality between elites from many disciplines and walks of life, including CEOs, bankers, and politicians. It is not that everyone in these roles is an elitist operating directly for the Beast, but they certainly all agree that they must reign supreme. They may not all believe in ideas that they are superior to others, and that therefore they *must* preside over them. At a minimum, they may believe a tight system of control is required. They might not even be aware that an interconnected system of Beast consciousness is in place. These unknowing participants simply agree with the principles of the Beast system.

These Beast-followers often believe they are doing the right thing – for example, that smart people are required to lead the less intelligent, or some other excuse by which they can justify their positions. Some may indeed think they are superior, and that they are destined to be in control. There are different levels of Beast-followers.

To operate, the Beast utilizes two groups of actors: willing partners and unwitting followers. However, the general public needs to continually protect its interests through freedom advocacy and learn how to balance this through enough consent to allow leaders to govern fairly. We could say that everyone, the public and its leaders, should just follow the laws in place and the Constitution, but that leads to interpretation of the law. We know how that turns out.

The bottom line is that it is still about people interacting with people. We can oversimplify two groups of people for our discussion.

- *Freedom advocates* believe that the laws that grant us our freedoms reign supreme (whether by being naturally born as a free person or because nature's God grants us freedom as part of our human nature). The laws we live under in a state or national government are derived from natural law. Freedom advocates tend to get angry when the administrative state does not respect the higher natural laws and interprets the constitution to restrict the rights of freedom advocates.

- *Controllers* are Beast-followers who believe that they or the state must govern others because the masses cannot govern themselves. By this logic, with nothing to stop it, the administrative state will continually gain more and more control. Its goal is to manage the entire earth, until everything is in order. Remember Edward Bellamy's prediction from the end of Chapter 1? Everything will merge into the "Great Trust." They probably like the quote as if it is a good thing.

Is a bridge possible between these two groups, or is it too late?

I firmly believe that we need to understand the two categories of people and find a balance between them. If I am the biggest freedom advocate in the world, and will fight hard to protect the rights I hold dear, but if I do not know my enemy, I am not prepared for battle.

If I were to put myself in the shoes of a Beast-follower, I would probably not understand why people hold natural law or freedoms in such high regard. Nor would I believe that morality can help The People govern themselves, nor that I could trust others to manage their own affairs without intervention.

Knowing how Beast-followers think allows us to understand their logic, allowing us the opportunity to understand the other side. Yet consider a corporate team-building challenge in which an employee must walk in the shoes of a fellow employee to appreciate them more; the sad truth, based on personal experience, is that neither group even wants to understand the other side.

This brings us to the happily-ever-after. The story is not over, but we can only improve things if we know the other side and how to coordinate effectively. If we do not try, if we do not get involved, then the story's ending is already written for us. The Beast will not be transformed, or even tamed.

Chapter 9: Ideas for the Future

We have examined many statements from the elite of both the past and the present eras, all of whom used diverse tactics to achieve their goals. Use of communism, socialism, or democracy was and is irrelevant to these actors. In the modern era, technology and science have been added to the mix to help speed up the plans through technocracy.

Predetermined Free Will

A hybrid model for the civic life of the masses involves both free will and predetermination. This is a paradox. We need to think of something quick this dilemma, or our freedoms will continually erode – faster than AI learning how to program itself.

The paradox correlates to our individual human nature in conjunction with a higher nature. Let's say that human nature is our individual free will, and a higher nature is our collective, aligned will of multiple individuals (it is not aligned with the will of Beast-lovers, though – that's where we draw the line). Please be patient with this section of the book. It takes a while to figure out a paradox puzzle.

We can "choose" to follow a "predetermined plan." This is a hybrid solution. What comes first, free will or the plan? Perhaps this is the oldest paradox on the planet, a mix of our will with another's. What if we decide to follow a plan that someone else has laid out for us?

A plan is no good without people to follow it, and we can't develop a plan using the individual free will of each of us, because there will be too many viewpoints. Looks like we are still stuck.

Can we follow someone else's plan, or do we still want to do things our own way? How has that worked so far?

Let's come at this from a different angle, with the "common-enemy plan." It is someone else's idea, so we can borrow it; the patent has expired. We just need to use our ability to choose, and agree that it is the best option. The plan will rally a bunch of like-minded people, in agreement that there is a common enemy in the Beast.

Would you rather watch someone destroy the Beast on TV, or be an active contributor who helps your tribe do it?

We don't need to develop a complex plan like the technocrats. We can simply agree to rebel against them and their Beast-loving cousins. How about we all simply agree to fight the Beast? This is the answer to the paradox. We all individually agree to follow a predetermined common enemy plan.

We do not need to agree that a demon or an alien controls the Beast. It doesn't really matter. What matters is that the Beast and its elite followers must be halted before things get worse. I have listened to enough of their nonsense to get motivated to write this book, and I have joined with some local people in this common mission. More people need to get involved with a common agenda, so let's develop some action items and implement what we already know can work from past experiences.

What Options Do We Have?

What have we done so far? We've followed the journey of this book, and maybe we've watched a video about Elon Musk's technocrat grandfather. Big deal. Zero points will be stamped on our Beast-battler cards.

We need to take extra steps beyond watching videos or listening to podcasts about how bad things are getting. I have taken a few small steps in the past few years. I am involved in gold-processing for backing currency, I support local organic farmers, and I have joined a Beast-battler club, where about twenty of us find tasks we can do locally. Now it's your turn to find similar outlets and networks.

Beast-followers may tell us that some freedoms we hold dear are bad for us and everyone else. They will say we are creating problems on the earth that need to be stopped, so we need to give up some of our freedoms. However, their solutions are worse than ours, the few of us shouting from the mountaintops.

People rally against a common enemy. The problem we face is that the Beast hides in the open. It is all around us, but not enough witnesses have testified about its deceptions. People who are open to the truth will come to realize it exists if they are educated; our job is to show them this different view, not to hit them over the head with our truth-hammer. Unfortunately, the many who already believe in the lies of the Beast may not be able to see the false premise of the control scheme.

The Beast has divided us into factions so that we do not unite against it. The Beast's strategy is to separate people so it can remain in power.

While it is difficult to unite diverse people, by finding tasks we can all agree upon we can focus on creating healthier communities.

It is interesting to consider that collectivism can be both a good and a bad thing. We want individual freedom, but we need collectivism to obtain it or protect it. Collectivists give up individual freedom to strengthen the collective. Collectivism such as under communist rule or rule by technocrats is a wrong type of collective that gives up freedoms to the elite.

Simple Steps

We need motivation to take action. I might not be able to motivate you, and you might be too set in your ways to listen to a motivational speaker. You can motivate yourself if you can visualize a cause, something to grasp onto. Why not use your grandchildren, or some important person in your life, to get you off the easy chair?

Picture those special people as prisoners in the Global World Order, being slowly brainwashed and following the Beast into losing more freedom. Imagine an ID card with which they can only travel x amount of "freedom travel" per week to save the planet, or that they're limited to only eat y amount of meat. Perhaps they'll give up their freedoms to save the planet, or they'll do it grudgingly to maintain their social status.

A police state that forces people into a box will often see people rebelling against this oppression; instead, the Beast finds brainwashing to be more effective. A loved one might think that they are doing the right thing for the world, and no matter what we do, we might not be able to convince them to snap out of the trance.

Many other motivations can be visualized; just pick something powerful that you do not want to see happen to anyone you know. Think of your grandkid twenty years from now saying, "I wish that grandma and her generation had done something to prevent me from being connected to AI." Perhaps even this scenario is unrealistic, with our grandkids being brainwashed enough to not even notice—or even thinking how ridiculous grandma was for not having loved AI.

We can make various priorities, and while they might not be the most impactful things we can do, they will allow the more important steps that follow.

- Stop watching TV and mindless videos and listening to people yap on podcasts. Unless you're searching for real educational resources, these can be a waste of time if you just want to be "entertained." Free up your time. Stop anything that distracts you from accomplishing the plan at hand of becoming a superhero and helping destroy the Beast.

- Stop hating Beast-lovers. Having an enemy makes us feel better, allowing us to pat ourselves on the back and tell ourselves that we are not as bad as "those guys." Our enemy should be the Beast itself, not the misguided. I am not sure how I would react if I met Elon Musk. Would I yell at him, or hug him? I think I would yell at him, and that means I need to change my attitude. The genuine issue is the Beast system itself, not someone like him. We can show sympathy for the followers who may have been brainwashed. Hatred is a distraction. It wastes time and energy for greater work that needs to be done. Remember, attack the heart of the dragon, not its members.

- Strengthen the local community. Volunteer. Network with people to fight the Beast—anything to help people stop signing up for Beast programs.

- Support local businesses. Stop buying from big-box stores or online megastores. Small businesses have difficulties staying open in this climate. They need your help and support. Use local credit unions. Hit the Beast where it hurts. Limit its funding so it can't expand its programs.

- Support local farmers. Start food-buying clubs or co-ops to save cash on high-quality, fresh meat, cheese, eggs, herbs, and vegetables. Approach the farm directly in a group of five, ten, or twenty people and buy in bulk, bypassing the middleman. In effect, this is investing in a farm. Join a community-supported agriculture (CSA) program. They are great.

- Use cash, and start learning how to trade. If cash gets programmed and controlled, you will really need to know how to barter services, precious metals, resource-backed blockchain currency, and other methods.

- Set up private membership associations (PMAs). This legal mechanism is a great way to self-regulate your group without needing to follow more restrictive public organization laws. Your food-buying club, religious group, local trade network, or other group can benefit from being private and not public. Anyone invited to join from outside needs simply to become a member and to follow the association's rules.

- Become a community prepper. Traditional "prepping" often ends up as a bunch of individuals living on food- and weapons-islands, and while prepping individually may be necessary in extreme times, I like group-prepping better. Set up a canning club and meet to share ideas with each other. Prevent farmers from throwing out food and store it when it becomes available.

- Network your local group with regional and national groups like the Freedom Grid and Freedom Cells.[1] You can set up local chapters easily on their websites. Meet new people who are like-minded.

- Develop new means of communication outside of the traced networks. Stop using popular social media for communicating with your Beast-battler networks. Get a knowledgeable friend to hook you up with platforms like Bastyon[2] to connect with others.

- Fight battles at the local level initially. Start by worrying less about national or state problems and more about what you can do to influence your own neighborhood. Learn about how to get on school boards, local councils, and election committees. Become a local leader of battling the Beast. Go to local meetings and get involved.

- Stop believing in the current electoral democracy as a solution to these problems. How has it worked in the past? We need to take back power little by little on the grass roots level. It has taken decades of decline to get into the mess we are now in. There is no superhero politician coming to save us. We are the ones who need to do the work. It is a lot of work. It cannot be outsourced. That is why we got to this place by believing our representatives can really make a change when it comes to the banking system, globalism, retirement accounts feeding the Beast, and everything else we discussed.

A final remark from Carroll Quigley brings this home.

---

[1] The Freedom Cell Network, https://freedomcells.org/; Freedom Grid, https://freedomgrid.org/.
[2] Bastyon, https://bastyon.com/index.

> The argument that the two parties should represent opposed ideals and policies, one, perhaps, of the Right and the other of the Left, is a foolish idea acceptable only to doctrinaire and academic thinkers. Instead, the two parties should be almost identical, so that the American people can "throw the rascals out" at any election without leading to any profound or extensive shifts in policy.[3]

There is only one group to consider above partisan lines, The People. *We the People* have forgotten about what unites us at the core level and have let the Beast distract us while we argue amongst ourselves, or blame someone else for the problems in the world. The real problem is that we need to look in the mirror and *share* some responsibilities as citizens. Left unchecked, the Beast will only grow in its unseen lair until it knows it is too big for anyone to stop it from coming out into the open.

---

[3] Quigley, *Tragedy and Hope*, p. 1247.

About the Author

Steve is a manufacturing specialist / entrepreneur with 40 years of experience in manufacturing. He gained knowledge in designing many custom electro-mechanical systems and processes that have continually honed his skills throughout his career. This eventually allowed Steve to be able to analyze and simplify complex technologies then integrate them into more efficient production solutions.

His only hobby that lasted throughout the years is studying history. This has led him to take notes about some interesting findings he came across and assemble them into this book. Since Steve has integration experience through his work career, he was able to coordinate his findings into a common thread that eventually became noticeable after years of research.

Steve also enjoys hanging out with farmers and local business owners in the Niagara Falls and Buffalo, NY area.

If you want to join Steve's email list, please submit your address via the Freedom Grid contact form at www.FreedomGrid.org, or email Steve directly: steve@freedomgrid.org.

Please leave a review of this book with the online bookstore that you purchased it from to help spread the word. Thank you.

www.ingramcontent.com/pod-product-compliance
Lightning Source LLC
Chambersburg PA
CBHW020532030426
42337CB00013B/821